Advance comments on *The People's Catechism* . . .

"*The People's Catechism* is just that: for the people, drawn from human experience, revealing grace all along the human journey. Easy to read and identify with, written in modern idiom for real people, this book will be a gift to seekers and searchers and to those who wish to appreciate better the ancient truths in an engaging, readable style. A truly contemporary catechism worth the attention of catechists, pastors, and RCIA teams."

— WILLIAM J. BAUSCH, parish priest
and author of *The Total Parish Manual*

"A wonder-ful, prayer-ful book! Appealing to both head and heart, just as Jesus did, it ties together belief and worship and human life. You will think about this book, relish it, and talk it over with friends."

— FRANCIS J. BUCKLEY, S.J., Professor of Systematic and
Pastoral Theology, University of San Francisco

"This is exactly what we need as an adult follow-up to the new *Catechism of the Catholic Church*. Authored by a talented group of religious educators, directed to mature Catholics who are serious about their Christian faith and life, structured for individual reflection and for group discussions, this volume is both understandable and stimulating, a catechism worthy of the people of God."

— BERNARD COOKE, Loyola Professor of Theology, Emeritus,
College of the Holy Cross

"An in-depth presentation of the Creed, the Sacraments, Morality, and Prayer, easy to read and up-lifting — *The People's Catechism* will lead you in a compelling way to enrich your mind with truth, live your faith in action, and relish the encounter with God in the liturgy and prayer."

— SISTER MARIA DE LA CRUZ AYMES, S.H., Society of Helpers

"*The People's Catechism* is true to its title! It is indeed 'a clear exposition of the essential contents of faith and morality' (John Paul II's definition), but with an engaging style and very readable prose, it presents Catholicism as the living faith of a people. Its stories, examples, reflective questions, prayer moments, and invitations to decision, as well as its very faithful theological content, make it an ideal resource for people sharing faith together. Imagine — a Catechism that is a delight? Here it is!"

— THOMAS H. GROOME, Professor of Theology and
Religious Education, Boston College

The PEOPLE'S CATECHISM

William J. O'Malley, S.J.
Mitch & Kathy Finley
Kathleen Hughes, R.S.C.J. & Barbara Quinn, R.S.C.J.
Timothy E. O'Connell

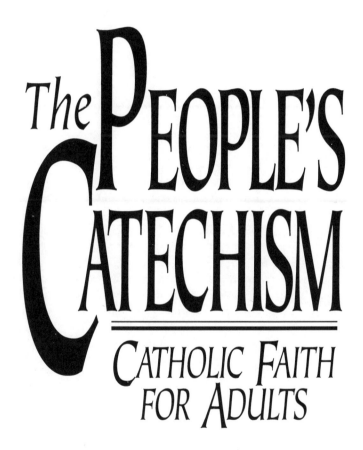

The PEOPLE'S
CATECHISM

CATHOLIC FAITH
FOR ADULTS

Edited by Raymond A. Lucker,
Patrick J. Brennan & Michael Leach

CROSSROAD • NEW YORK

Scripture quotations are from the New Revised Standard Version of the
Bible, copyright © 1989 by the Division of Christian Education of the
National Council of Churches of Christ in the U.S.A.

Quotations from the Second Vatican Council are from Norman P. Tanner,
S.J., ed., *Decrees of the Ecumenical Councils,* 2 vols. (London: Sheed &
Ward, and Washington, D.C.: Georgetown University Press, 1990).

This printing: 2000

The Crossroad Publishing Company
370 Lexington Avenue, New York, NY 10017

Copyright © 1995 by The Crossroad Publishing Company

Printed in the United States of America

Library of Congress Cataloging-in-Publication Data

The people's catechism: Catholic faith for adults / edited by Raymond
A. Lucker, Patrick J. Brennan & Michael Leach.
    p. cm.
    Includes index.
    ISBN: 0-8245-1466-1 (pbk.)
    1. Catholic Church—Doctrines. 2. Catholic Church—Catechisms—
English. I. Lucker, Raymond A. II. Brennan, Patrick J.
III. Leach, Michael.
BX1751.P39 1995
238'.2—dc20   95-13771
                                                CIP

Contents

Part Three
CELEBRATING THE FAITH: THE SACRAMENTS
Kathleen Hughes, R.S.C.J., and Barbara Quinn, R.S.C.J.

Part Four
THE MORAL LIFE
Timothy E. O'Connell

Introduction

John Paul II has called the Roman Catholic Church to a "new evangelization." That term speaks of new, creative efforts to bring Jesus Christ and his message to those who have not yet encountered him and to elicit from them a response in faith. Evangelization means entering into a personal relationship with God, who has first loved us. The new evangelization also refers to renewed efforts at re-evangelizing those already initiated into the Church. *The Catechism of the Catholic Church,* which the Pope ordered published on October 11, 1992, is a gift to the Church adding foundational clarity to the essence of the Catholic expression of Christianity, thus facilitating this mission of "new evangelization."

The People's Catechism is yet another tool to assist in the Church's evangelical-catechetical mission. The categories used in *The Catechism of the Catholic Church* — the Profession of Faith, the Celebration of the Christian Mystery, Life in Christ, and Christian Prayer — have parallels in *The People's Catechism* titles: The Foundations of Faith, The Message, Celebrating the Faith, and The Moral Life.

The People's Catechism attempts to bring life and a fresh understanding of the truths of faith contained in *The Catechism of the Catholic Church.* A catechetical methodology is followed in each chapter, with relevant passages from Scripture; stories from contemporary human experience; the teachings of the Church presented in popularized, understandable, existential language; questions for discussion and faith sharing; suggestions for putting faith into action; and shared prayer. In *The People's Catechism,* the truths of faith are presented in a style and format that makes it a useable tool in adult faith formation sessions, small groups or Christian communities, ministry training programs, and personal enrichment or study.

The People's Catechism is designed to be of service to the ongoing growth in faith of Catholic adults. We especially hope that it will be used for enrichment and for sharing faith at the beginning of parish council meetings and parish committee meetings. It may be used for small faith-sharing groups or for those who have experienced a remarkable conversion as part of RENEW, the Cursillo movement, Marriage Encounter, or other renewal programs. Catechesis is a lifelong process involving especially adults living in a community of believers.

Appropriating the rich tradition of the Church is not just a cerebral undertaking. Faith is a total human response to the living word of God. Wholistic faith must include a relational component in which we find ourselves in communion or relationship with God and the body of Christ, the Christian community. Wholistic faith indeed must have an intellectual component — we need to know the historical evolution of who we have been, and who we are. Wholistic faith demands a personal relationship in love and trust in the God who first loved us. There must also be a behavioral, lived component to our faith lives. *The People's Catechism* challenges its readers not simply to know about God and the Church passively, but rather to live in God, live for God, and live proactively as intentional members of the body of Christ.

The publication of this catechism is an opportunity for Christians who have allowed themselves to become perhaps too rote in their faith style or too non-reflective about matters of spirituality to bear down on the core mysteries of faith. In so doing, readers can experience what Paul VI referred to in *Evangelii Nuntiandi,* that the good news need not lose its power. It is ever good, ever fresh, ever exciting news. But the message of Christ and the tradition of the Church must always be enculturated, planted in a culture so that they might develop into a new, exciting expression of Christianity that has never been experienced before. *The People's Catechism* attempts to present Jesus and the Tradition as life-giving, life-changing experiences.

All of our writers are seasoned catechists, educators, and pastoral workers. Their writing and methodology are committed to the generation of a living faith. While their voices are as varied as their experiences, the form and content of the faith presented join together as one. We are grateful to them for their excellent contributions and for their persistence in the long process of editing and synthesizing material.

According to Pope John Paul II, echoing a long tradition in the Church, a catechism is "a concise and clear exposition of the essential and fundamental contents of the faith and of Christian morality." *The Catechism of the Catholic Church* was published as a compendium of the faith of the Church. It is to be used as a guide in the development of other catechisms. There will never be a definitive catechism since every age needs a fresh expression of the faith and application of the Christian message to new circumstances. Unity is enhanced by a pluralism of expressions. As the old adage has it, there is one faith and many theologies, many ways of expressing that faith. Essential doctrine does not change — the expression of those doctrines does change.

No one group in the Church of Jesus has a corner on truth. Rather truth and our ever-deepening understanding of revelation emerge from the entire people of God in dialogue and communion with each other and with those who have the responsibility for safeguarding the truths of faith. This catechism was written by representatives of the diverse People of God for the diverse People of God — from people, for and to people. The contributors include laity, women religious, and clergy. We believe that such collaboration of diverse types in the Church — which occurred in the production of this catechism and, we hope, will occur in the use of this catechism — is the route that the Church has to travel if it is to remain at one with the vision of the kingdom and the lifestyle of Jesus Christ.

RAYMOND A. LUCKER
PATRICK J. BRENNAN
MICHAEL LEACH

March 1995

Part One

The Foundations of Faith

William J. O'Malley, S.J.

The Meaning of Faith

"I believe. Help my unbelief!" (MARK 9:24)

Faith is not a blind leap in the dark. Faith is Annie Sullivan and Helen Keller. There was no certitude between them, only a tentative, slowly deepening trust. Annie was half-blind herself, but she had faith in the human spirit she knew lurked within that blind, deaf, utterly lonely child. She trusted that somehow, somewhere, Helen would bump into that pump — or something, and suddenly realize, "My God! I'm not *alone!*"

How many hours did Annie draw signs in Helen's uncomprehending, angry hands? How many hours did Helen endure that silly game? Any teacher or parent can empathize with Annie; any child can empathize with Helen. Like Annie, God draws signs in our hands every moment of every day, patiently, aware that — at least for now — the signs are unheeded, meaningless. But God has never grown old or disillusioned. God has infinite patience.

Faith is trust that the God-given human mind — and human soul — can discover that self-indulgence and materialism and utilitarianism just aren't *enough;* like communism, they will collapse of their own untruth. Sooner or later, the good-souled must ask, "Is that all there is?" No. There is far more.

Faith is not a blind leap in the dark. Like a marriage, faith is a *calculated* risk. Part One of this book is about the calculation we believe justifies that risk. It attempts to lead the reader to say, perhaps breathlessly, "My God! I'm not *alone!*"

It is amazing how many times a day we place faith in people we do not know. We trust there is not a murderer on the bus, that what teachers, newscasters, and magazines tell us is basically the truth, that the food we buy is not contaminated. We trust that most checks will not bounce, that someone is actually listening, that friends will not betray our secrets. Without any background check into their grades, we trust that our doctors did not graduate last in their medical school classes.

But what is faith? Not just faith in God. Any faith.

There are two kinds: childlike faith based on the fact that, in the past, most people have proven themselves trustworthy, and reasoned faith based on solid (but rarely certain) evidence.

Children have faith in adults; little choice, since they cannot yet figure things out for themselves. An adult says the moon is Roquefort cheese; so it is. Even adults have childlike faith more often than we realize: Some of us never went to China nor to the moon, but we trust China is not a conspiracy of cartographers and there are footprints in the moon dust. No one ever saw an atom; our eyes are not quick enough, yet we deny the evidence of our senses and accept that the chairs we sit on are not really solid but a galaxy of fiercely whizzing particles. The knowledgeable people who testify to those things seem to have no reason to deceive us nor do they profit from our gullibility.

But as we age, we learn people sometimes do have motives to deceive. Or they are just unwittingly dead wrong: the earth is not flat; tomatoes are not poison; Jews are not Christ-killers. One cannot trivialize the trauma of children who find parents have been (for reasons they cannot yet fathom) "lying" to them about Santa Claus. Parents worry that their children will be too credulous and accept rides from strangers. People offer you seeming bargains, sight unseen. Prudent skepticism is an adult's insurance against hoaxes. According to psychologists the function of adolescence is to *critique* certitudes uncritically "taped" from parents, teachers, peers, and the media, to find which square with objective reality and which do not. Ideally, if we continue to evolve as humans, that process never ends. Even the best-tested certitudes can be fine-tuned.

Then who is to say there is a God? Who is to say God is not a fabrication — like Santa Claus or the bogey man — to keep us in line? "Makin' a list, checkin' it twice...." If there is no God, read no further. All Scriptures of all religions are so much self-delusive trash. Obviously, the authors feel they have strong evidence God does exist. Or we would not have done all this typing. And we have no reason to deceive.

Adult faith is a calculated risk based on reasoning about objective facts, a conclusion convincing, but not certain enough to compel assent. If it were certain, assent would not be based on believing but on knowing. You do not believe you are sitting reading this page; it is self-evident; you know it. In contrast, you do not know your friends love you or that you should continue at your present job or that this stock is a sure-fire investment. But you have come to reasoned conclusions based on objective facts, and there seems no serious reason to doubt them. Like any good jury, you are sure beyond any *reasonable* doubt. But there is always a possibility you are wrong. Even physics, the "hardest" of the hard sciences, can offer no better than a high degree of probability. Theology can do no better.

Reason starts with facts that are certain and argues to conclusions that are *probable*. Whether we are deciding to put faith in a career or a spouse or a God, that is the best we can hope for: probability. The more calculation, the less risk.

So let us start with a fact: our intelligence. No doubt we have it: the one thing that separates our species from all others. Unlike rocks or rutabagas or orangutans, we can anticipate the not-yet-real, fathom the nuances of *Hamlet,* at least begin to understand the purposes of things around us. No sow snoring in her ring of piglets has her dreams disturbed by the fact that one day they will all die. Human beings can know that and, to a degree, try to understand it.

And that intelligence tells us no effect can be greater than its causes. If, for instance, a pumpkin began belting "Hey, Big Spender," we would have to conclude there was a speaker inside. A pumpkin, all by itself, cannot produce that effect.

Apply that principle — no effect greater than its causes — to intelligence itself, to the universe, to evolution.

INTELLIGENCE. There is power in the inanimate elements around us: hurricanes, avalanches, atomic energy, but those forces at least do not seem able to "change their minds." We do not expect water to get bored flowing downhill and reverse direction or rocks to fly about on a whim. They work dumbly according to their inner programming (the laws of physics) and outside forces beyond their control. But humans have the freedom to alter their given lot. We are not slaves of DNA: if nature did not give us wings, we can make them and fly. If a new ice age dawns, we need not just sit and be engulfed like boulders; we can run, find shelter, make fire. Where did that freedom come from? What caused it?

There is adaptability in plants and vegetables, but they at least don't seem to have the power freely to *change* their ways, independently of outer and inner factors *forcing* them to change or perish. They work dumbly according to their inner programming (the laws of chemistry) and external forces beyond their control. But unlike lower species, humans can go on hunger strikes, take vows of celibacy, surrender their lives even for enemies, commit suicide. Where did that freedom come from? What caused it?

There is a kind of "intelligence" in other animals, a canny shrewdness in detecting unusual changes around them, a trainability, even an ability to communicate. But the cleverest animals, like dolphins or dogs, at least give no indication they have the ability to *understand,* to ask *why.* Where did that freedom come from? What caused it?

How did intelligence emerge from something not itself intelligent? It had to come from some higher intelligence. Perhaps some race of extraterrestrial aliens came and triggered intelligence in a promising tribe of apes. But we certainly did not get our potential to reason and understand from King Kong.

It is beginning to seem there had to be a Mind behind it.

THE UNIVERSE. Consider the universe: every object out there is doing exactly the same thing: turning on an axis. That seems pretty coincidental. Beyond that, each of them slowly moves around another, and that pair moves around another, and systems moves around systems. An enormous dance! And no Choreographer?

We do not *impose* inexorable laws of physics on the universe. We *discover* them; they are already there. The mind-boggling, meticulous order of the periodic table is written right into the nature of things. If there is no God, the universe came about just as a series of accidents, without intention or purpose. You could get *variety* out of accident but not order, not the laws of physics, not the periodic table, not predictability. How do you get law out of luck, or predictability out of an accident?

If you were to accept the premise that the dance of the universe came about by accident, you would have to be at least open to the possibility that, if you dropped an atomic bomb on Mount Everest, the pieces might come down as a working Disneyland. Or that if you threw the parts of a computer into the air, even an infinite number of times, sooner or later Part A would correctly attach itself to Part B, and (without coming apart) A-B would sooner or later attach correctly to Part C, etc., until you finally had a working computer.

It is beginning to seem there had to be a Mind behind it.

EVOLUTION. Evolution also at least seems to be a slowly realized *plan.* But atheists claim it occurred, again, simply through an almost endless series of accidents. If that is true, as Carl Sagan admits, a nearly infinite series of cogs had to fall into place in "the cosmic slot machine" for even vegetative life to occur on earth — much less sensate life, much less intelligence.

If the subcontinent of India had not shouldered up into Asia and created the Himalayas, the whole climatic pattern of the earth would be different. Is that luck? The earth rotates at 1,000 miles per hour at the equator; if it were any different, we would long since have frozen or fried. Is that luck? The earth tilts at 23 degrees; if it did not, we would have no seasons. Is that luck? If the crust of the earth were ten feet thicker, there would be no oxygen, and if the oceans were a few feet deeper, carbon dioxide and oxygen would have been absorbed and no vegetable life could exist. Lucky?

The possibility that all those factors — and countless others — just fell into place by chance flies in the face of probability. If for instance you shuffled ten cards, ace through ten, the chance of your drawing all ten in sequence would be one in 3.6 million. A pitifully simple sequence compared to the number of factors on which life on earth depended. Not to mention minds.

In order to get rid of the need for a God, non-believers are forced to "bestow" intelligence on agents of evolution that do not in fact have it. In his book *Cosmos,* for instance, Carl Sagan says, "One day, quite by accident, a molecule arose that was able to make crude copies of itself." That was one bloody clever molecule! Later he writes that trilobites "stored crystals in their eyes to detect polarized light." How did those dumb trilobites "know" there was light if they had no eyes? Or rational minds? Any teacher would find it handy to have an extra eye in the back of her head, but try as she might, she cannot figure out how to do what some mindless trilobite did.

The human eye alone is enough to convince many people there must be a Mind behind evolution. Even Darwin puzzled to explain how such an intricate system — which no human could duplicate — came about by sheer chance. We have two blobs of jelly in the front of our faces (so we can see in three dimensions), with a self-adjusting diaphragm and lens that work automatically, even in impaired children. They take color pictures eighteen hours a day, and you never have to change the film or send it out to be developed. And those pictures turn into abstract ideas!

It is beginning to seem there had to be a Mind behind it.

We don't *know* there is a God, but we *believe* it is more likely than that there is not. That's faith.

At least the beginning. There is a lot more to come.

Real faith — living faith — is not just about truths or doctrines or "proofs." Of course we have to explain (first to ourselves) what we believe and on what objective grounds we believe it. But Jesus did not go for the head; he was going for the heart. He did not aim for logical completeness but for a change of values, priorities, attitudes: conversion — a complete turnabout in the direction of one's living.

Voltaire knew immeasurably more about theology and Christianity than Joan of Arc. But the unschooled Maid of Orleans knew God far better than the great Enlightenment satirist ever would. His head got in the way of his heart.

That is the ultimate purpose of Christianity, not to know more about God but to know *God* better. The word "religion" means "to fasten." It is about a *relationship*, back and forth, between oneself and God, between oneself and one's fellow believers.

When two people marry, they are making an act of faith. But the wedding itself is really only one brief part of a marriage — which is not so much a single act of faith as it is a *process* of faith in three stages of "becoming" married. First, of course (if they have any sense at all) they genuinely analyze the relationship rationally, to be sure this is the right person to take responsibility for "till death do us part." That is the "calculation" part. Then — no matter how nervous they are — they make the official act of joining their lives, most often in front of an intimidating assemblage of witnesses. That is the second stage, the "risk" part. But finally comes the third stage of becoming married: the rest of their lives. Provided the two continue to be creatively interested in one another, and given the way life has of surprising us with unexpected detours, they will find themselves becoming *more* married every year of their lives together, surely more married than the day they took their vows to one another.

The same is true of our relationship with God. Real faith can never be merely a relationship with book-learning, and surely not with an "idea" like The Uncaused First Cause. It is a relationship with God, person-to-Person(s). Like any friendship (which is also a process of faith), it must grow, deepen, become richer in communication and sharing — just as in a marriage. Jesus said, "I have come that you may have life, and have it more abundantly." That is what living faith is: living a more abundant life than one had planned on.

When Claire Booth Luce was considering conversion to Catholicism, she said she found herself looking at Catholics and saying to herself, "You say you have the truth. Well, the truth should set you free, give you joy. Can I *see* your freedom? Can I *feel* your joy?"

Fine questions, Mrs. Luce.

Questions for Reflection and Discussion

1. Brainstorm all the people in whom we routinely place childlike faith: doctors, airline pilots, chefs, people we pass in the street.

What is it in those complete strangers that grounds a legitimate expectation they will not betray our trust (and it usually does pay off)? On the other hand, who are the people you have known for a lifetime in whom you are still reluctant to place trust? Why?

2. When two people stand before an intimidating assemblage in church and vow to take responsibility for one another "till death do us part," that's an act of faith. When you entrust a secret to a friend, settle on a college or career, choose a stock, those are acts of faith, too: commitments without certitude they will work out. In each of those cases, for you personally, how much was calculation and how much was risk?

3. Along the way, doubts inevitably arose as to the wisdom of each of those commitments. When they did, how did you resolve them?

4. What hard evidence do you personally have that your idea of God is not a deception, that there really is an Entity outside your mind who validates that idea? Don't settle for "they say" or "everybody believes...," or even that "Scriptures say..." or "the Church says...." What external evidence do you have to ground your trust in Scripture and tradition?

5. Along the way, doubts inevitably arise as to the wisdom of that commitment to a belief in God. When they do, how do you resolve them?

Faith in Action

As you walk through the corridors where you work or around your neighborhood, focus on each of the faces you pass. Of how many can you say, "Why I've *never* seen her before"? Why do we "filter" out people if not to defend ourselves from their intrusions? What do psychologists call people who suspect everyone is out to get them? Why do we impoverish ourselves like that?

Prayer

Silent God,
help me let go awhile of my critical mind,
the skeptic in me, the one whose guard is always up,
who senses a hoax round every turn.
Help me be humble before you,
childlike, willing to be taken in. Amen.

2

Clues to the Mind of God
from Other Religions

From one ancestor [God] made all nations to inhabit the whole earth, and he allotted the times of their existence and the boundaries of the places where they would live, so that they would search for God and perhaps grope for him and find him — though indeed he is not far from each of us. (ACTS 17:26–27)

A lone mountain climber was approaching the crest of a craggy peak when he lost his footing, careening down through the loose rock, scrabbling out for anything that might give him a handhold. Just as he was about to slip over the edge of an outcrop to plummet hundreds of feet to the floor of the canyon, he grasped a tough-rooted bush. He laid hold of it with both hands, gasping for breath and sweating from terror and exertion, his legs hanging helplessly in midair.

"Help!" he cried. "Is there anybody up there? Help!"

Suddenly, from nowhere came a booming voice: "This is God! Let go! I'll catch you."

The climber rested his head against his straining arms. And he cried out, "Is there anybody *else* up there?"

No one really sees you. All they see is your *body*. The real "you" is invisible. They may take a look at the way you use your body, the words you use, the subjects you seem interested in, and then make *educated guesses* about what the real "you" is really like. It is the same with atoms, with trustworthiness, with a great many realities we depend on every day. Educated guesses have a lot to do with what we know about God, too.

For those who have more or less "settled" the question of the existence of a Mind behind human intelligence, the universe, and evolution, the next question becomes: What is this Mind like? Equally important, what does understanding that Mind tell us of our specific purpose as human beings? What does this Purpose-Giver want of me?

We can learn a great deal about the nature and personality of the Creator without recourse to any religion whatever, just from looking at the Creator's work, as we can tell a great deal about the personality behind the work from any artist's productions. Their paintings show Picasso's and Dali's minds quite different from Rembrandt's and Michelangelo's — and from one another's. From the way God made the universe, we have already seen God is "into" order: the laws of physics, the dance of the universe, the predictability of nature. Yet at the same time, God is "into" surprise: every snowflake in Antarctica is exactly the same basic pattern, yet no two were ever identical; every planet follows exactly the same laws, yet some are dust, others fire, still others ice; the four seasons follow one another with rhythmic predictability, yet no two years are the same. Carl Sagan sneers that the species that arose and died out in the course of evolution do not argue to a very efficient Designer. Of course not, simply because efficiency is not as high among the Designer's priorities as it is among Carl Sagan's. There is something whimsical about a God who invented the giraffe and the rhino and the hairy-nosed wombat. Not to mention sex.

Evolution shows God also wants growth to keep happening. The Creator does not seem to want things to be fallow for long, yet on the other hand God is not in too much of a hurry. But growth is written, sometimes painfully, into the evolving history of the earth and into the lives of each human being. For nine months in the womb, we are as close to paradise as we will ever be in this life: fed, warm, floating, serene, without any worries because we cannot think. Then we are painfully ejected out into the cold and noise — so we can grow. Each disorienting crisis after that is an invitation to grow even further: weaning, being shoved out to play with other children, the awful betrayal at the kindergarten door, the disorienting challenge of adolescence, courting, marriage, children — all inviting us to live larger lives than we had planned. But each is an invitation we can refuse or finesse.

That is something else God is "into": freedom. Of all the species we know, ours is the only one free *not* to live up to its specifically different programming. No rock can refuse to be stony; no carrot can refuse to vegetate; no lion can refuse to be leonine. But the daily papers are packed with evidence humans can refuse to act human. We can degrade ourselves and others to stepping stones; we can treat them as callously as week-old bread; we can herd them like dumb beasts — and thus become little better than vicious beasts ourselves. But apparently God thought it worth the risk because, according to wise folk, God is also into loving — which is impossible unless there is freedom not to love.

The Creator also made up "the rules of the Game" and wrote them right into the natures of everything created. We can tell how God intended things to be legitimately used simply by the way God made them. But again we — and we alone — are free not to use them as God intended, though sooner or later the natures of things are going to rise up and take their revenge. You are free, for instance, to treat gin like ginger ale, but sooner or later the natures of gin and the human liver are going to prove you are wrong. You are free to treat human sex as if it were no more than a physical act, like animal sex, but sooner or later it is going to become for you no more meaningful than animal sex.

That is perhaps the major reason non-believers balk at belief in God: it means someone else directs the play and they do not. We are free, but only within limits. Someone Else is in charge. Further, bowing to the fact of God automatically admits we are indebted: we did not create ourselves; we *were* conceived, carried, born — without any cooperation or deserving on our part. Many people do not enjoy being the subject of passive verbs and even fewer enjoy being indebted. Most of us do not seek the company of our loan managers or bookies. But if God created us, we are indebted — like it or not — for everything.

There is an old story about a group of blind men in a park in Calcutta whose guide keeled over dead. There they were, pawing helplessly around, when suddenly one held up his hands against a rough obstacle and cried, "I've found a wall; maybe there's a gate nearby." Another one scoffed, "No, no. We're still in the woods; I can feel the tree stumps." Still another sighed, "You're right. I can feel the palm leaves." And then he yowled, "Ahh! There's a fat snake in the tree!" "Ooh," cried yet another, "it's a spear. Are you a guard? Can you help us?"

Of course what they had stumbled on was an elephant, and although each one's perception of what they had found was pitifully inadequate to the reality, had they just paused a moment and tried to put them all together, they might have come to a more enlightened conclusion. The same is true with God. It is the same God, filtered through the preconceptions, cultural differences, and life experiences of a particular place, time, and people. Nor does any religion have a monopoly on God — not even Christianity or Catholicism. In fact, like the blind men groping around a reality that is definitely there but that none of us can see, we can each enrich — and balance — our parochially limited understanding by listening to one another's different insights into the same Reality. Then, like Goldilocks, we can try them all and find which ones are "too hard," which ones "too soft," which one "just right" — even if it might not be perfect.

At this point, however, we have to admit our own judgments about other religions are colored by our own experiences of God. Many (especially males) find that, if God is a woman, she is certainly no softie: often distant, capricious, and hatefully silent for very long times! On the other hand, many of us experience God at times closer to us than our own skin, flooding us with a joy we could never have imagined. And again it is the *same* God. Thus a religion one can find acceptable has to accommodate *both* aspects and also be an honest balance of the two.

Overly *immanent* religions (that is, "locked within" the physical universe: pantheism, polytheism, paganism, even black magic) seem to imprison God too tightly within creation. For them, the god is in the waterfall, the thunder, the stream, and sacred amulets and totems seem to "contain" the power to manipulate the god with mystic incantations. The gods of Greece and Rome, for instance, were no "higher" above the people than the crest of Mount Olympus, nor did they seem any purer than their human counterparts: arbitrary, grudge-bearing, playing favorites.

Such an approach makes God more than a bit too "chummy," as with the cowboy songs that make God just another "good ol' Buddy." We also experience the distant, silent, inscrutable God who belies that too-simplistic picture. As Job — or anyone else who has faced unmerited suffering — inevitably discovers, the most difficult aspect of accepting a loving God is that God is definitely not answerable to us. God's reasons are far beyond the limits of my earthbound mind.

At the other extreme, overly *transcendent* religions (that is, "beyond" the physical universe: deism, platonism) seem to make God much too distant, cold, and unreachable. Deists realize the order and design of the universe demand a Mind, but in their view God was the original architect of the universe yet far too pure and "other" to sully his hands with the perverse likes of us. God merely tinkered around with the spinning tops of the universe and then withdrew to contemplate more important matters. Thus, deists do not pray, since the Architect is neither listening nor interested. For platonism, God is the necessary Uncaused First Cause, as far removed from what we believe to be reality as solid objects are more real than their shadows.

Such an approach makes God too distant and chilly, and it belies our experience of God as undeniably "present," here and now, within our hearts and souls. It denies those numinous moments we have all experienced when we feel our breath taken away by the mountain at dawn or the infant or the painting. Even more, it denies the moments when the breath is knocked out of us by a near accident or the death of a loved one. God is *there*.

The immanent views of God make divinity "too soft," and the transcendent views make divinity "too hard." And yet what seem overly immanent views of God can act as a very salutary corrective when we get too cerebral and heady, theologizing about the Prime Mover. God is right here at our elbows; God is in our hearts. And overly transcendent views of God can balance our views when we become too comfy with the Good Shepherd of so many sick-sweet hymns who pats our wooly heads and makes everything nice. No matter our warm and affirming experiences of God, we have also encountered a God whose will is as unyielding as steel. It has to be both.

The Hebrews experienced God as both immanent and transcendent; on the one hand holy bushes burst into flame in God's presence, and God's name ("I am") was so holy that uttering it was blasphemy; on the other, Yahweh's home was right in the middle of their city, and the glowing divine presence hovered within the Holy of Holies.

Yahweh's nature is most clearly evident for the Hebrews in Moses' encounter with God on Mount Horeb. When Moses asked who Yahweh was, the enigmatic answer was: *"ehyeh asher ehyeh,* I am who am."* Now for a Jew, as for anyone in medieval Europe, your name was not only a personal label but also a job description. If your name was Carpenter or Smith or Harper, that is what you did for the community. To the Hebrews, "to be" in isolation had no meaning; one had reality only in relation to the whole community of Israel. Therefore, Yahweh is saying, "I am with you; here I am." But God is also saying, "I am existence; I am the pool of being out of which everything-that-is takes its 'is.' "

It is interesting to align that Hebrew insight with the insights of modern science into reality. Science says there can be no reality faster than physical light. Yet science delights in playing "what if." What if there *were* a reality faster than light? It would be moving so fast it would be everywhere at once. Like God. It would be so hyper-energized it would be at rest. Like God. And scientists now say that, when they crack open the final building block of the atom, what they find will quite likely be non-extended energy. Like God.

Unfortunately, most of us get our ideas of what the Hebrews thought of Yahweh not from a thorough reading of the Old Testament but from biblical movies and almost uniformly poor church art. The Hebrew God is someone bearded and grumpy, like Charlton Heston. On the contrary, there are many "faces" of God in the Hebrew Scriptures: wrathful, fond, promising, wooing, even whistling! Leviticus, Deuteronomy, and some of the more hot-tempered prophets emphasize the lawgiver and judge; Hosea, the Canticle of Canticles, and Isaiah emphasize the lover and savior — transcendent and immanent.

Unlike Christians, whose initial — and formative — idea of Yahweh comes from the Book of Genesis (because it is first), the Jew's idea of Yahweh comes from the more focal Book of Exodus, when Yahweh made an unbreakable *Covenant* with the people of Israel: "I will be your God, and you will be my people." It was a marriage, a union of the Transcendent with the immanent even more intense than the presence of Yahweh in nature.

But throughout their centuries-long relationship, most often Yahweh is cuckolded by his false-hearted wife, Israel, who at every turn runs faithlessly after the fertility gods of Canaan. Their love in good times is captured in the Canticle of Canticles (which is rarely read in church because it's rather steamy): "Sustain me with raisins, refresh me with apples; for I am faint with love.... Your two breasts are like two fawns, twins of a gazelle, that feed among the lilies.... Your lips distil nectar, my bride; honey and milk are under your tongue" (2:5; 4:5, 11). More frequently, Israel had run away from her Spouse, who had never been unfaithful to her, and always Yahweh goes looking for her:

> But you trusted in your beauty, and played the whore because of your fame, and lavished your whorings on any passerby.... You took your sons and your daughters, whom you had borne to me, and these you sacrificed to them to be devoured. As if your whorings were not enough!... So you were different from other women in your whorings: no one solicited you to play the whore; and you gave payment, while no payment was given to you; you were different. (Ezek. 16:15, 20–21, 34)

But invariably in the Hebrew Scriptures, Yahweh cannot be content with wrath; it is against God's nature and their Covenant. The agreement was not *if* you will be my people, I will be your God. No matter how unfaithful Israel was, Yahweh could not be:

Then she will say, "I will go and return to my first husband —
for it was better for me then than now.... " Therefore, I will now
allure her and bring her into the wilderness, and speak tenderly
to her. (Hos. 2:7, 14)

There is also a remarkable insight into the Hebrew experience of
God in the people Yahweh chose to carry out his wishes, people who
prove conclusively the old cliché that "God's ways are not our ways."
When the Eden experiment had failed, would most of us have started
over again — with the *same* two fumblers who missed the whole point
in the first place? If we had decided to flood the world and start over
(yet again), would any of us have thought twice about Noah, who had
fathered a quite eccentric family? If we set out to find a couple to start
a great race called Israel, which of us would have given two thoughts
to Abraham and Sarah, both in their nineties and barren as brick? If
we wanted to lead the Hebrews out of slavery in Egypt, who would
consider Moses, who (quite unlike chesty Chuck Heston and more like
Don Knotts) stammered and tried for four long pages to weasel out of
the job? If we had to bring down a giant like Goliath, would any of us
pick a spindly kid with a slingshot?

That pattern of God's personality continues consistently into the
New Testament: If we wanted the mother of the messiah, surely we
would go to Rome or Athens or Alexandria, not to a no-name village
in a nothing province to find a hill girl and then ask her *permission*.
If we wanted to start a worldwide crusade, would any of us choose as
the leader a friend who had denied any knowledge of us, with oaths,
not once but three times — and not to a soldier with a knife at his
throat, but to a waitress!

This is the same side of God we saw when we considered evolution,
a God who had the patience to dally with trilobites for millions of
years, a God who surely will show patience with us. That is the God
of both the Old and New Testaments: the God who never gives up on
us, the God who always wants to start over.

Questions for Reflection and Discussion

1. In your experience, is God distant, silent, "other" or close, reassur-
   ing, a friend? On the other hand, is *your* posture before God that
   of the inquirer — trying to understand, comprehend, perhaps even
   dominate God, or is it more submissive, accepting, biddable? In
   what fashion could you "get out of God's way" more?

2. A covenant is not a contract; it goes deeper than that. A contract is executed by two parties *depending* on specific conditions being fulfilled. "If you don't do this, you've violated our agreement, and I am released from my reciprocal obligations." At Baptism and Confirmation, you make a mutual covenant with God. Do you ever deal with God as if that were a contract?

3. Carl Jung stressed the difference between sex and gender. Sex — male/female — is a matter of objective physical fact; gender — masculine/feminine — is more of a judgment call. Ernest Hemingway and Robert Browning, for instance, were both objectively male, but Hemingway's sensibilities seemed much more "masculine" and Browning's more "feminine." A well-balanced soul of whichever sex, Jung maintained, should be androgynous — a blend of both "masculine" and "feminine." A healthy female soul should cultivate her decisive, analytic, aggressive side, and a healthy male soul should be yielding, inclusive, vulnerable.

In recent years, there has been much discussion about the strictly patriarchal, "masculine" image of God — through all the pages of the Bible and through the consistent tradition of the Church. God is assuredly neither female nor male, yet we have no pronouns to characterize such an entity. Pool the ideas of the group about God's "personality" from each person's unique experience of God. The discussion is not to solve "the pronoun problem" but to better understand the God we share.

Faith in Action

Sit quietly outside, in a park or a field or a yard (or in your imagination if it is raining) and focus slowly, one after another, on all you see — the trees, the clouds, the brook, the weeds, the earth, and ask each one: "Tell me about God."

No rush. Don't cut anyone off in mid-conversation.

Prayer

Mysterious and elusive Friend,
my mind is far too small to snare You in a web of words.
Help me, instead, to hear you in my heart
where, like a silent Lover,
you can conceive your Son in me. Amen.

3

Jesus: The Embodiment of God

Long ago God spoke to our ancestors in many and various ways by the prophets, but in these last days he has spoken to us by a Son. (Hebrews 1:1–2)

But while the boy was still far off, his father saw him and was filled with compassion; he ran and put his arms around him and kissed him. Then the son said to him, "Father, I have sinned against heaven and before you; I am no longer worthy to be called your son." But the father said to his slaves, "Quickly, bring out a robe — the best one — and put it on him; put a ring on his finger and sandals on his feet. And get the fatted calf and kill it, and let us eat and celebrate; for this son of mine was dead and is alive again; he was lost and is found!" (Luke 15:20–24)

Note the details in the story. The father sees the boy while he was "still far off" — which shows the father has been watching and hoping every day. The father runs to the boy, not the other way round. What does that tell of him? The father embraces the boy and kisses him *before* the boy has a chance to apologize. What does that reveal of the father? The father does not say, "I want an account of how you spent every shekel of my money before you get back into this house." He requires no list of specific sins. He gives no penance for atonement; instead, he gives the boy a party!

What is Jesus telling us here about God's "personality"?

All other religions, even Judaism, come to understand the personality of God — God's likes and dislikes, purposes and plans — through agents, prophets, interpreters of God's will. But Christianity claims that at one time God, from beyond space and time, focused divinity into the man, Jesus Christ, a Jewish carpenter who lived, preached, healed, suffered an ignoble death reserved for traitors and runaway slaves, and returned from death to validate his claim that he was the embodiment of God. Yahweh had made a marriage with Israel; in

Jesus, God became one with all humanity and invited us to be divinized in his continued physical embodiment: the Church. If his claims were true, there is no better way to begin to understand the personality of God.

No one can claim Jesus was merely a fine moral teacher. It is beyond dispute he claimed to be the Son of God. On Palm Sunday, the crowds hailed him as the Son of David; the following Friday they screamed for his execution. There is only one reason for that total turnabout: when the high priest asked him, "Are you the Christ, the Son of the Blessed?" Jesus answered the unspeakable for any Jew: "I am." He had blasphemed, and the people who had hailed him on Sunday now called for his blood.

Thus, he either was who he claimed to be, or else he was a lunatic or a charlatan. But nothing he said or did supports those negative appraisals. He earned nothing but his daily bread from his work; he had no home, nothing to bequeath but his one tunic. And everything he said and did was trying to heal, to enliven, to bring people out of their self-protective cocoons. Gandhi was once asked what he thought of Christianity, and he said, "It's perfectly marvelous. I just wish someone would try it."

The whole question of the importance of Jesus to human history pivots on the resurrection. No one claimed to have witnessed it, which bolsters the credibility of the Gospels. It would have been child's play to have written a real Spielberg scene with rocks cracking, thunder, flashes of unworldly light. But the Gospel writers did not. There are several other persuasive facts that argue to the truth of what the disciples claimed, however. First, Holy Thursday night when Jesus was arrested, they all abandoned him, and for the next three days they cowered in the room of the Last Supper, craven cowards. The only ones with the courage to witness Jesus' burial and the empty tomb (which the Gospel writers do not hesitate to admit) were three women whose news the men initially scoffed at as mere women's prattle. And yet, within little more than a month, they were out in the streets preaching their heads off, unafraid, even when they were forbidden to preach at the Temple, imprisoned, whipped. Within such a short time they went from being arrant turncoats to being fearless preachers! They said what had changed them was experiencing the risen Jesus. And most persuasive of all, they went to horrifying deaths rather than deny it. Deathbed confessions carry a great deal of weight.

As with the very existence of God — or any other act of faith — there is always a chance one is wrong. Still, to anyone with a fair mind, the evidence shows a high degree of probability that Jesus was neither madman nor charlatan but in fact what he indisputably claimed to be, and the testimony of his disciples' later lives and deaths is strong evidence to validate their claim to having experienced Jesus again after he had clearly died.

It might seem an unnecessary diversion to speak of Jesus' appearance, and yet what we *think* Jesus looked like has a strong negative effect on our willingness even to sit down and listen to what Jesus says, much less giving it an honest hearing. Even in our best moments, no matter what our resolutions, we cannot help in fact "judging a book by its cover."

There is no physical description of Jesus anywhere in the New Testament. Then where do we get our image of him? From the same place we get our image of Yahweh: from biblical movies more interested in bucks than in the Bible and from second-rate religious art. Even the best of films, like Zefferelli's *Jesus of Nazareth,* and the greatest of Renaissance art make Jesus look like a delicate, very pale, blue-eyed European — the way God would have fashioned a Messiah had God understood the wider audience better. Jesus seems somehow aloof and disconnected, even slightly embarrassed to be slumming with these smelly workmen. Such works overemphasize the transcendence of Jesus, his other-worldliness, over his humanity.

More recent films like *Jesus Christ, Superstar* and *The Last Temptation of Christ* have gone the other direction and overemphasized Jesus' humanity to such a degree that Jesus is easily accessible — but just as dismissable as the aloof, other-worldly Jesus. The Jesus of *Superstar* does nothing but whine all the time, and, as Magdalene sings, "He's just a man." It is interesting that in the script the actor playing Jesus makes no curtain call, which makes a point. In *Last Temptation,* Jesus is so spineless he can scarcely accomplish the ordinary tasks of daily life and spends most of his time dithering.

Both those extreme images and the resultant ideas we have of Jesus' personality are false. In the first place, the real flesh-and-blood Jesus *could not* have looked like the holy-card Jesus. He was a Jew. Look at pictures of Israelis or Arabs who work out in the sun all the time. Their skin is dark; few have blue eyes. And Jesus was a carpenter for twenty years; no carpenter has the tapering pianist's fingers of church art or biblical movies. It is difficult to imagine the holy-card Jesus enduring a scourging with leaded whips, the humiliating trek to Calvary, the spikes in his wrists and ankles, and then hanging on for three more hours.

What such limited artists need to do is look at real-life people who have the Jesus qualities, like Mother Teresa, whose face radiates an almost other-worldly serenity and yet is as unstoppable as a runaway train.

To do justice to the people who hanged Christ, they did not eliminate a gentle preacher who just wanted everyone to be nice. Even Hitler would not have executed such an irrelevance. Jesus' executioners found him too dynamic to have around. He thrashed the moneychangers from the Temple with nothing more than a handful of rope and his own towering rage. He showed no proper deference to those of pedigree and high station. In fact he said to the Temple priests (the equivalent of a diocesan priests' council, with the bishop present): "But woe to you, scribes and pharisees, hypocrites! For you lock people out of the kingdom of heaven. For you do not go in yourselves, and when others are going in, you stop them" (Matt. 23:13). He goes on to call them such other uncomplimentary names as: "Blind fools...false witnesses...whitewashed tombs full of bones and all kinds of filth...brood of vipers...murderers of prophets." He called King Herod "that fox"; he thought nothing of upbraiding his wealthy host at dinner for discourtesy, yet praising a sinner who had crashed the party. In fact, other than evil spirits and the storm at sea, the *only* humans Jesus upbraided were churchmen — Temple officials and his own obtuse apostles.

Jesus' love — like all love — shows itself in tenderness, but not only in tenderness. More than a few times the real Jesus proved in word and action that his sole doctrine was not the "turn the other cheek" of the meek and mild holy-card Jesus.

Oh, Jesus mentions sins aplenty: "fornication, theft, murder, adultery, avarice, wickedness, deceit, licentiousness, envy, slander, pride, an obtuse spirit" (Mark 7:21–22, NAB). He was not as blasé about sin as many nominal Christians like to believe he was. But perhaps the root sin is the last in his list: "an obtuse spirit," the narcissism that refuses to admit one did wrong and the inertia that finds it too much effort and embarrassment to go back to the first wrong turn and start over.

But Jesus also offered forgiveness aplenty. When Peter asked how many times we must forgive, Jesus told him "seventy times seven times," and if God expects as much of us, we can expect as much of God. Though sinless himself, Jesus had a remarkable empathy for weakness. Quoting Isaiah, he said, "He will not break a bruised reed or quench a smoldering wick" (Matt. 12:20). "Truly I tell you, people will be forgiven for their sins and whatever blasphemies they utter, but

whoever blasphemes against the Holy Spirit can never have forgiveness" (Mark 3:28–29). Perhaps that enigmatic, sole unforgivable sin is
despair, but a case could also be made for its being "an obtuse spirit,"
impregnable even to the Spirit's movement suggesting something is
amiss and needs forgiving.

Unconditional love and forgiveness of debts are difficult for us to
comprehend. Even catechesis (still) opts for the economic metaphor:
a God so ego-bruised by Adam and Eve that there could be no love
from God till every shekel of ransom was paid in the blood of Jesus.
However well-intentioned, this is blasphemous, making God into a
"Banker" who bore a grudge from the time of Adam and Eve till the
time of the crucifixion — despite the fact that God, through Jesus, has
shown us that no one should keep a grudge even overnight (Matt.
5:23–24).

God loves us as helplessly as a mother loves her child on death row.
Our sins do nothing to God; their effects are in us, even though we
self-servingly refuse to see them.

The key — as so many Gospel episodes show — is opening the eyes,
submitting to the cure of our blindness. Jesus did not come to hawk
guilt; he came to offer a way to freedom from guilt. As he said in his
inauguration "platform" in the Nazareth synagogue, he was sent to
declare the Year of God (Luke 4:16–19): unconditional amnesty for
those willing to avail themselves of it.

Consider three episodes of the Gospel where Jesus deals one-on-one
with a sinner: the known sinner who breaks into the banquet of Simon the Pharisee (Luke 7:36–50), the adulterous woman about to be
stoned (John 8:1–11), and the Samaritan woman at the well (John 4:4–
40). Read each carefully. In no single case was there need to crawl, to
vacuum the soul of every peccadillo, to submit to a retaliatory penance *after* an all-merciful God has forgiven. Unconditional amnesty.
The *only* requisite — in the moral practice of Jesus — was to admit
one's need and ask forgiveness.

Jesus does talk of punishment. The God he pictured and embodied
is not a Cosmic Patsy who forgives anything, even when we have no
inclination to apologize. The key to Jesus' moral practice — in every
case, without exception — does involve the humility to admit one has
wandered and the humility to come home.

Of the nearly four thousand verses in the Gospels, Jesus speaks of
hell in Mark only once, in Luke three times, in Matthew six times, in
John not at all. He speaks of judgment in Mark only once, in Luke
twice, in Matthew and John six times each. In his lengthiest consid-

eration of judgment (Matt. 25:31–46), the crucial question pivots on none of the sins Jesus mentioned ("fornication, theft, murder, adultery," etc.) but on the sole issue of one's sensitivity or obtuseness to the suffering of Jesus in the hungry, the thirsty, the imprisoned.

Contrast the relative rareness of instances when Jesus spoke about hell or judgment with the profusion of times in the Gospels that he both spoke and acted as one come to heal and to forgive, and you come away with a picture of Christian moral practice that is far different from what many Christians have come to expect.

No doubt we sin. No doubt we too often blithely slither off the hook and become amnesiac about our faults. But there is also no doubt that, according to Jesus, being forgiven ought to be a great deal easier than we fear.

Still another aspect of Jesus given short shrift by the holy-card/film Jesus is the serenity of his fearlessness. No trace of hesitancy or of planning, no cautious hedging of bets, no diffidence. And he seemed to want that quality to differentiate those who claim his name: "You are the light of the world.... Let your light *shine* before others, so that they may see your good works and give glory to your Father in heaven" (Matt. 5:14, 16).

Always he kept telling them to stop worrying. Could anyone add a foot to one's height by gritting teeth? Do ravens and wildflowers fuss and fret over appearances? Yet Jesus was not set against material things. Some of his closest friends, like Lazarus and his family and Joseph of Arimathea, were well-to-do. Jesus was not a monk; he did not live the life of John the Baptizer. On the contrary, he was accused of enjoying food and drink too much and consorting with known sinners. He traveled some distance to attend a wedding party at Cana and performed his first miracle just to keep the party going. So easy to stereotype Jesus as a puritan; so easy to stereotype Jesus as a liberal. Only one problem: if you read the Gospels, Jesus is both: the rigor is softened by compassion, and the compassion is given spine by the rigor.

You can understand the personality of Jesus — and therefore of God — by the way people reacted to him. A case-hardened grafter like Zaccheus promised on the spot to give away half what he owned to the poor and repay quadruple to anyone he had cheated. Prostitutes thought nothing of silently begging his forgiveness. Children seemed to flock to him; Samaritans begged him to stay with them. And always the poor and sick and sinful felt welcome. Even his opponents kept coming back, fascinated. He just could not be what he seemed. He had come to cast fire on the earth. He was somehow intriguingly dangerous.

— ❖ —

When you ask baptized, educated Catholics what they believe are the rock-bottom, non-negotiable beliefs of Christian doctrine, almost without exception, the answer is "to be good, neighborly, moral: to keep the Ten Commandments." But the Ten Commandments are Jewish, not Christian, and you will find them espoused by nearly every religion on earth. And if the desire to be good, neighborly, and moral made one a Christian, every moral Jew, Muslim, and atheist would be Christian. To be moral means to act humanly; by our mere humanity we are enjoined to be moral.

Christianity *presumes* morality. And then it goes much further. Morality — justice — demands that, once the malefactor has made amends, he or she be released. Christianity asks much more: even *before* the sinner makes amends, he or she must be forgiven. Not the sin, but the sinner. If sinners make amends, it is to assuage their own guilt, not to satisfy our need for vengeance. When Pope John Paul II went to the Roman prison to forgive his attempted assassin, that was love, not justice. Christianity, not morality.

Catholic religious education often tries to make converts Catholics before they are Christian, belaboring them with all the doctrines that separate us from other sincere Christians, elements of the Apostles' Creed that the apostles themselves would be hard put to explain or even comprehend. Far better for the beginner to begin with the non-negotiables all Christians hold and leave the finer points till later. If at all.

At risk of presumption, we can isolate only four rock-bottom, non-negotiable Christian doctrines any Christian would hold to:

1. Jesus is the embodiment of God, God-made-flesh.

2. Jesus-God died in order to *rise* and share with us liberation from the fear of death and to offer us a share in the aliveness of God right now.

3. To engraft oneself into Jesus-God, one must give up the values of what St. Paul called "the world" ("Me first!") and take on the values of what Jesus called "the kingdom" ("Them first — God and the neighbor").

4. We celebrate our oneness with Jesus-God in a community of service and in a weekly public meal.

   1. *Jesus is the embodiment of God.* Somehow (don't ask how until you go for a doctorate in theology, and even then you won't know)

almighty God, from beyond time and space, focused himself into the man Jesus Christ and became one of us. Thus, whatever came from the mouth of Jesus about the purposes of human living can be taken as coming from the very mouth of God. Jesus Christ is the final step in human evolution — from inanimate to animate to animal to human and now into the life of the divinity. "The Father and I are one" (John 10:30). You may be a saint, as Gandhi probably was, but if you don't accept that, you are not a Christian.

2. *Jesus-God rose from the dead.* As St. Paul says, if Jesus did not, then our faith is vain. As we saw before, it all pivots on the credibility of the disciples' testimony to seeing Jesus alive after he had clearly died. And they continued to give that testimony even at the cost of their lives. As a result of that belief, a Christian need never fear death. It is merely a comma, not a period. What's more, the Christian believes, through the sacraments, especially the Eucharist, that we amplify our lives with the transcendent aliveness of God. As God focused divinity from beyond time and space into the man Jesus, in the Eucharist Jesus focuses himself from behind time and space into bread and wine — and thence into us. Our souls — the undying transcendence in us — are energized with the life of God. You might be a fine person, but if you do not accept that, you are not a Christian.

3. *The kingdom's ways are not the world's ways.* The Sermon on the Mount is testimony enough to that. The world deals with image, surfaces, personality; the kingdom deals with substance, character, the soul.

Jesus expressed the radical difference when he said, "Whoever wants to be first must be the last of all" (Mark 9:35). But how can you be first and last — unless of course you're the only one in the race? Simple: there are two races, heading in exactly the opposite directions from one another. The goal of the world's race is dominance: money, fame, sex, and power — all that the media teach us to crave; the goal of the kingdom is service: healing, forgiveness, being useful — and in order to be useful, one must be used. That is exactly what a radical Christian conversion means: a complete turnabout in one's most profound values, a reversal of direction in the trajectory of one's life.

The world still clings to the *lex talionis:* "An eye for an eye; a tooth for a tooth"; the kingdom clings to forgiveness of debts, even to the undeserving.

If the world hates you, be aware that it hated me before it hated you. If you belonged to the world, the world would love you as its own. But I have chosen you out of the world, therefore the world hates you. (John 15:18–19)

That implies that those most successful at being Christian will appear to worldly folk, if not as dangerous subversives, then at least as pitiful fools.

4. *We embody our belief in a community of service and in a meal.* The solitary Christian is a contradiction. Truly good people pray to God in all sincerity in quiet rooms, on hillsides, on beaches, but if they do so exclusively alone — though they are laudable and holy folk — they are not Christian. The first Christian Church gathered to learn from and be fed by Jesus and then were sent out, two by two, to spread the liberating good news. A Christian is, by definition, an apostle and healer, as Jesus was. And at the Last Supper, Jesus said, "Do *this* in memory of me." Anyone may refuse to do that and "get into heaven," but he or she will not enter as a Christian.

There they are: the four non-negotiables. Beyond that, there are doctrines over which Catholics differ with Anglicans or Protestants or Orthodox, but many are — in varying degrees — negotiable. What unites us is far more focal than what divides us. The rest you can leave to graduate school.

Questions for Reflection and Discussion

1. Your image of Jesus is possibly more effective in your understanding of Christianity than your *idea* of Jesus' doctrine. In what ways has church art and practice "softened" Jesus so only one side — gentleness, yielding, obedience — nearly eclipsed the other side — forthrightness, drive, challenge? Is Christianity only a source of consolation or also a chance for commitment?

2. Two Christian beliefs that the chapter claims are non-negotiable are the divinity of Jesus and his resurrection. If a non-believer challenged your belief in either of those doctrines, what evidence and arguments would you use to substantiate your beliefs?

3. Another critical Christian belief is the anti-materialist stance of the Gospel, expressed clearly in the Sermon on the Mount. Brainstorm the ways (and means) by which the world's materialism seeps into the lives of even the most dedicated of us. Then brainstorm ways to combat those influences, not only in ourselves and crucially in our children, but also in the society we share.

Faith in Action

One of the last acts Jesus performed before his arrest was to wash the disciples' feet at the Last Supper. Find a place where you can be alone to reflect, and try to conjure up that scene in your imagination. But when you've captured the scene as an observer, move into the scene yourself — as Jesus. And populate the table with the people with whom you have most contact during the week. On your knees, go from one to the next — slowly — and look at each face looking down at you. There will be some, most likely, about whom you'll say, "Of course. It's an honor to wash your feet." But there will be others who will cause your fillings to fuse.

How will your behavior to those latter people be different next week? Jesus never asked us to like anybody. Just love them.

Prayer

Divine Brother,
your Mother — our Mother — taught me to pray
when she said merely, "They have no wine,"
and left what you would do to you.
Well, then,
I lack your confidence, your conviction;
I lack your profound trust in God;
I lack your nearly tireless stamina;
I lack your patience, your ready forgiveness.
As you can see, Divine Brother, I am in need. Amen.

4

Our Relationship with God

For you did not receive a spirit of slavery to fall back into fear, but you have received a spirit of adoption. When we cry, "Abba! Father!" it is that very Spirit, bearing witness with our spirit that we are children of God. (ROMANS 8:15–16)

— ❖ —

He had the improbable name Bill Fold. A former merchant marine and a patient in the terminal cancer ward of a Navy hospital, he had had his larynx removed and thus could communicate only through a pad and pencil. To make matters worse, he had also contracted tuberculosis and was in isolation.

One Saturday, the priest who visited him every week said, "Bill, it must get very lonely for you."

And Bill wrote on his pad, "Yes. But isn't it wonderful God trusts me enough to give all this to me?"

These pages have claimed that Catholic pedagogy has too often flown directly in the face of the psychology of conversion: trying to make people Roman Catholics before they have internalized the message of Christianity, Christians before they are even sure of the existence of God, and theists before they have even understood the invitation of their humanity. Like starting a pyramid from the top. Or planting before we plow. Or offering a product before the potential buyer feels any need for it.

Therefore, before moving on directly to Scripture (as most such texts do), let us pause to set things in their proper order: First, we discover God and God's importance; then we enter into a personal relationship with God — without which any further study seems merely academic. Only then can we profitably push onward into the revelations of and about that God that we discover through Scripture. Bible study becomes worth the effort only when God has assumed a genuinely important place in our lives. When Jesus preached, he did not speak as a speculative theologian; he did not go for the head but for the heart.

What separates humans from other animals is not the body or the brain (which they share), but the soul. It is the place in us where all the nebulous, non-quantifiable aspects of our selves reside: honor, awe, genuine sentiment, loyalty, remorse, faith, hope, love. Just as our hunger for food is in our bellies, and our hunger for answers is in our minds, our hunger to make sense of life in the face of suffering and death lives in our souls. Your human soul is your *self*: your who-I-am, your character, your conscience. Your soul is the string that holds all the disparate beads of your life together in one coherent whole. Without a personally validated self, your life is just "ODTAA" (One Damn Thing After Another).

All the scholastic philosophers to the contrary notwithstanding, human beings are definitely not just "rational animals." If that were the limit of our being, we would be little more than apes with computers implanted — which is merely a variant of reductionist Scientism. "A sound mind in a sound body" has long been a motto of schools, which might account for their producing so many worthy job candidates and so few fulfilled human beings.

Reductionists fail to account for the difference between knowledge and understanding, between rational causes and meaningful reasons, and between affection and love, which is not a mere feeling but an act of the will when the feelings fail. Perhaps the reason is that they have been educated to know and not to understand, that they have settled for skills rather than wisdom, and they have felt only loyalty but never self-sacrificial love.

A human infant is to an animal cub as an acorn is to a marble. Plant the acorn and marble, and the marble just lies there; it lacks the potential to be anything more than what it is. But the acorn has the potential to be hugely more than what it is: an enormous oak, unrecognizably different from itself. But that potential *need not* be actualized. The acorn could fall into water and rot, onto stone, among thorns like the seed in the Gospel. In the same way, for the first year or so the infant and cub look pretty much alike: eating, sleeping, pooping, watching, and in general just "doin' what comes natcherly." But the infant has the potential to be far more than just a healthy little animal. She begins to ask the human question that, as far as we know, no animal asks: why? And she also has the potential to begin to find at least temporarily satisfying answers.

Furthermore, she has the potential — the human soul — to revel in sunsets, stand in awe at birth, create art to inspire the souls of others. She has the potential to make sense out of life, to forge a personal philosophy about what it is for. She has the potential to evolve an adult conscience, based not on what "everybody says" but on what she knows to be true. She has the potential to reach beyond this life and commune with God.

As with the acorn, that potential need not be activated. She can grow in a cramping environment, beset by filth, hopelessness, and incuriosity, surrounded by humans who never activated their own human potential. There is hope for her, but little.

Thus the word "humanity" covers a whole spectrum of people, from pushers and hitmen and terrorists on one end, to those of us along the spectrum who try our best yet sell ourselves short, all the way to such truly noble human souls as Dorothy Day and Terry Anderson. Some accept the human invitation and carry it down the road like a hurricane; others "sort of" understand but are too afraid; some simply do not even know they have that potential: "Live fast, die young, have a pretty corpse."

Again, not to lead off with the caboose, the first step to conversion is not a study of the Trinity. Rather it is to own the fact that you even have a soul, that you are not just a mere high-level animal, that you have a potential for greatness. The next step is to realize that the human potential will not "turn on" automatically, like a thermostat. It takes effort. You have to *want* something more than mere survival to evolve a soul.

The next step — and probably the most painful — is to accept the fact that God is God and we are not. Because we are smart (but not as smart as God), that takes some yielding. In the myths, Lucifer, Adam, Oedipus, Job, Faust, found that an impossible surrender. "Better to reign in hell than serve in heaven." We want to be "masculine" — in psychologist Carl Jung's sense of that term: dominating, *mastering* the evidence. But if God is God, we are all — males and females — "feminine" before God: receptive, fertile, freely serving. God is not answerable to us.

We are not God's slaves; through Jesus Christ, God has made us Peers of the Realm. But we are not in charge. Rather — if we do acknowledge that we owe everything to the One who invited us into life — we accept a free servitude to God.

The prototype for the Christian before God is Our Lady, when she was asked to do the impossible: to be the Mother of God. She did not understand at all. But she said, "Be it done unto me according to your word." If that is what God wants, that is what I want. Or as John Donne put it more boldly: "For I, except you enthrall me, never shall be free, nor ever chaste, except you ravish me." And any crucifix tells us the will of God: we conquer by surrendering to the will of God, manifest in "the things that cannot be changed."

Here are four rather blurry "stages" by which a good-souled man or woman might stumble blissfully toward a relationship with God. Grace builds on nature — or not at all. Before we leap into the transports of disembodied union with God (much less into the doctrines of the Roman Catholic Church), we have to begin to put some distance between our selves (our souls) and the undeniable animal in us.

1. To develop a this-world sense of the numinous, a sensitivity to an other-worldly presence in nature and in other people and in art.

2. To activate a this-world urge to make sense of it all, to find a pre-religious philosophy of life.

3. To acknowledge a this-world need to live a life of integrity, a life that separates us from mere animal motivation in our choices: a conscience.

4. To realize a hunger not-of-this-world that tries to reach beyond what appears to us to be reality into the transcendent life of God.

1. *The Numinous.* In our cities we are walled off from the earth, imprisoned in canyons of antiseptic steel and glass, smothering in smog. But as Hopkins wrote, "The world is charged with the grandeur of God." Even non-believers feel it, though they cannot acknowledge its source, when they slip away from what appears to be the important everyday rat race and allow themselves to be ambushed by the poetry lurking in the heart of prosaic lives: the silvery arms of trees sheathed in ice, dust devils whirling across the desert, waves harrumphing onto a beach. Something no animal could feel or comprehend stirs in the human soul: wonder, awe, a sense of quest. Tennyson's Ulysses felt it:

> All experience is an arch wherethrough
> Gleams an untraveled world, whose margin fades
> Forever and forever when I move.
> How dull it is to pause, to make an end,
> To rust unburnished, not to shine in use!
> As though to breathe were life!

Awe at the numinous lurking under the skins of everything around us is an act of praise to the Great Surpriser who made the trilobite and the giraffe and the hairy-nosed wombat, in defiance of reason and efficiency.

2. *A Philosophy.* Theology will never make any sense until one pauses to wonder "what's it all about?" The Church recognized that for centuries, having priest candidates study philosophy for three years before going on to four years of speculative theology. Too often, catechesis can ignore that lesson.

Don Quixote felt it. Why do we settle for "the way things are" rather than asking how things *ought* to be? Most people knuckle under to an unintelligible life-sentence, enduring years of schooling in order to make a living, without ever asking what the hell living is for? Without ever asking the uniquely human question: why? What is it in human beings that makes us the only species we know that resists its inner programming to evolve as human? How *should* things be, and what can one do to make the realization of that ideal at least less unlikely? What does "success" really mean? It cannot be what the media claim: money, fame, sex, power; Elvis Presley, Marilyn Monroe, John Belushi, James Dean, Janis Joplin, Jim Morrison, and a host of others had all those things in spades, and yet they killed themselves. Each of us has only one life; how can we get the most out of it?

Every moment in a library is a "prayer" to the Truth.

3. *Conscience.* As far as we know, no tiger goes into a village, gobbles a baby, and lurches back into the forest moaning, "My God! I did it *again!* I have to get counselling!" Humans do. At least good humans do. Bad humans do not. That is one essential factor reductionists ignore when they say humans are no more than high-level animals. Sharks ravage and move on. For those who have even in some minimal way activated their human potential, that is less easy. But those who completely suppress the human invitation settle for acting like tigers and sharks. In fact, they name their gangs after them.

A formed conscience is not inborn. If it were, we would never have had Hitler or Saddam Hussein. The *potential* for conscience is inborn, but — like the soul of which it is a part — it need not be actualized. When people say, "I was stopped by 'a little voice in my head,'" they do not mean their reasoned ethic; they mean the memory of their mothers saying, "No, no!"

When we are born, we are healthy little animals, "doin' what comes natcherly": what Freud called the Id. For the first year or two, if we made a mess, our parents dutifully cleaned it up, since we had no control. But then when we began to develop muscle control and could start "getting into things," we began to hear — for the first time ever — two words we would be hearing in various forms for the rest of our lives: "Good" and "Bad." Our parents "taped" on our minds an unintelligible catechism of do's and don'ts as a sort of survival manual until we could fabricate one of our own: what Freud called the Superego. In our day, that "taping" process is far more complex, since a great deal (perhaps most) of what we "know" to be good and bad comes from the media — which often offer values and goals completely contradictory to those of our parents.

Adolescence, psychologists say, is the time when an individual ought to *critique* all that parents and media have told them to do and not to do, all the pronouncements about what "success" really means, and find which ones square with objective reality and which ones do not. Unfortunately, public schools are not allowed to help young people do that, since they foolishly confuse ethics with religion, and religious schools seem to content themselves with offering lists of do's and don'ts that often seem ludicrous compared to the inducements of the media — and frequently even with the desires of their parents.

Morality has nothing whatever to do with being Christian, or even with being a theist. One has to be moral merely to be a good human being. Each individual has to take possession of his or her own moral choices. The alternative is to be a lifelong victim of "My father always said..." or "Everybody *knows*...."

4. *Transcendence.* An adult life is hugely enriched by a sense of the numinous, of what Bonhoeffer called "the beyond in our midst," by evolving a personal philosophy of life and a personally validated conscience. But as Augustine found, our hearts are still restless. There is in each of us a God-sized hunger. It can be assuaged (momentarily) by "junk food for the soul": the *National Enquirer,* the ball scores, gossip about film stars, and the latest three-inch headlines. It can be palliated (more profoundly) by a genuine encounter with art and nature. But there remains a yearning for... more. For an encounter with the energizing Spirit who is the source of all the aliveness.

For many — perhaps for most — praying means pretty much "saying prayers" or dully dutiful attendance at Mass. That is surely better than nothing, but it is not enough. In order to enliven the divine within us, we have to take time. What is even more difficult, we have to let go — short-circuit the left-brain, calculating intelligence that is our major weapon in getting through the rat-race day, find a quiet place where we will have relatively few distractions, and open ourselves to God. Leave all the questions and requests aside. Sit quietly, not passive but *receptive,* welcoming, "feminine," and merely be-with God. "Be it done unto me according to your word."

Without that, all the theology and all the Scriptures are merely academic: an analysis and a history of Someone we have never met. Theology can tell us a great deal *about* God. But only in personal prayer will we know *God.*

Questions for Reflection and Discussion

1. Do you have much "soul time" in your week outside Mass? If it is not much, what prevents it? If the answer is, "There are so many important things I have to...," then is your relationship with God truly important, or is it quite honestly one of those things you would *like* to believe you hold important?

2. Sum up for yourself *your* philosophy of life. (You might do this first on paper and then, if you are in a group, share it.) What are people for? What does "success" really mean? Is there a purpose for unmerited suffering? Philosophers from Buddha to Karl Marx started with that question; if you haven't started there, you haven't started. How could a good God allow children to suffer?

3. On what do you ground your specific moral decisions in regard to honesty and sexuality? The Bible? The doctrines of the Church? An inherited moral structure? If your reasoned conscience came into conflict with a specific Church doctrine, how would you resolve the disharmony?

Faith in Action

A yogi once concluded a letter, "I bow to the divine in you." Take some "soul time" and consider, slowly, one by one, each of the people who populate your life, at home, at work, and all the places in between. Sense the divine in each one. Then bow to that presence.

Then think of all the "anonymous" people in your life — mail carriers, subway change makers, maintenance folk. Sense the divine in each one, however well hidden. That ought to change the way you deal with them, no?

Prayer

Wellspring of all that lives,
energize my spirit with your Spirit.
Purge me of my fears.
Let everyone I meet
see my freedom, feel my joy. Amen.

5

Scripture and Myth

What has come into being in him was life. (JOHN 1:4)

Read the following dialogue as if every word and phrase were intended as *literally* true.

> JOE: The boss is crazy. Canning Eddie like that? The old man's got a brick for a heart.
>
> SUE: Joe, your boss is a suet-brain. He couldn't find his own ear with a hound dog. Even with a mirror.
>
> JOE: You think I ought to blow the whistle?
>
> SUE: What? And "hoist yourself with your own petard," to quote Hamlet.
>
> JOE: Hamlet, Shmamlet. You know how I always dig my own grave with my own mouth.
>
> SUE: None so blind as those that refuse to see. You stand up for Eddie, you cut your own throat.
>
> JOE: So I leave Eddie out there, swinging slowly, slowly in the wind?
>
> SUE: Your funeral, honey.

Literalists — whether skeptical literalists or credulous literalists — read that interchange and come away baffled. Why would the man work for a boss who is deranged, a man who would put a human being into a can, whose heart is made of brick and, according to his wife, has a brain made of suet? What is a petard? That makes no sense. How long would it take this man to dig a hole six feet by six feet by two feet, with his *mouth*?

Every day, without even thinking, we use figurative language and instantly "translate" it (unless we are hidebound literalists) into perfectly comprehensible communication: "I'm gonna *kill* you, Junior"; "pea-brain"; "motor-mouth"; and on and on. Non-literal language is a perfectly valid way to communicate ideas — even though it might be "parabolic," roundabout. But a great many people — skeptical and credulous — refuse to allow the Bible to use the same kind of verbal roundaboutness.

A great many not-yet-convinced Christians are harmed by well-meaning instructors who leave them with the false impression that the Bible is "nothing but a bunch of myths." The teachers do not seem to have realized — or been able to convey — that there are two quite different (in fact contrary) meanings of the word "myth." In the negative sense, "myth" means a false belief uncritically accepted, as in "Vietnam destroyed the myth that America could never lose a war"; objective facts prove the belief a self-delusion. In the positive sense, "myth" means a story that attempts to express or explain a basic truth, as in Aesop's tale of the turtle and hare; neither Aesop nor his audience believed turtles and hares at one time spoke and made wagers on a race, but they saw *within* the story a real truth: slow and steady wins the race. This is the sense in which a great deal of Scripture is myth: stories trying to embody truths. The author of Genesis, writing about the same time as Aesop, did not expect his audience to believe snakes used to talk to naked ladies in the park, but he was trying to capture a very real truth: only human beings go against God's will for them.

Thus there are two very valid ways of communicating truth: the literal and the symbolic. The very literal dictionary, for instance, takes forty-two lines to define the reality of "love," but when you finish reading, you say, "I wish I knew as little about love as that Noah Webster." On the other hand, a little girl's meticulously corn-rowed hair or a little boy standing in the door with a limp bunch of dandelions "says" love, too, and in many ways far better than Mr. Webster.

All our pictures of realities that exist but cannot be seen are symbols: a dozen roses "says" love; a medal "says" achievement; a flag "says" patriotism. Similarly, all our pictures of God are "false" in the literal sense; God exists outside material reality and thus has no chin for a beard, no right hand, no genitals. If heaven and hell are outside time and space, too, where did they harvest the pearls for the pearly gates; where do they mine all the coal for a hell that has been raging at least since the rise of *homo sapiens?* The problem is not with the reality of heaven or hell but with the inadequacy of our symbols. One could just as easily physicalize the reality of heaven as a beautiful place in the mountains (as C. S. Lewis does in *The Great Divorce*) and hell as an inescapable hotel room inhabited by three people who detest one another (as Sartre does in *No Exit*).

Surely a huge feathery personage swooping into Our Lady's kitchen in Nazareth (as angels do in paintings) would have scared the wits out of her. And if the sky around Bethlehem were literally filled with blazing presences belting out their (non-existent) lungs like the Mormon Tabernacle Choir, *someone* in the area besides the shepherds must have noticed. At the empty tomb in Mark's version of the Gospel, the women are greeted by a young man wrapped in a white cloth; in Luke, it is two young men in white; in Matthew, it is an angel; in John, two angels. Which was it? It does not make any difference! All four are saying precisely the same thing, with different symbols. Young men wrapped in white — or angels — were never literally true in the whole Bible; rather, they are symbols for the real but invisible presence of God. Luke and John, knowing the Law required two witnesses for validity, simply doubled the number of witnesses.

Extreme literalists find a great many more problems in the Scriptures than they need to, and surely more than the original writers intended or the original readers confronted. Skeptical literalists (Scientism) take one look at the Tower of Babel, the star of Bethlehem, Peter and Jesus walking on water and — taking them as if they actually happened — scoff them away as myths in the self-delusional sense. Credulous literalists (Fundamentalism) blithely accept the talking snake, the mass suicide of the Gadarene swine, and the multiplication of the loaves and fishes as if they had the same rock-solid verifiability as the assassination of John Kennedy. Thus they have to keep everything religious in one lobe of the brain, walled off from everything they know to be true from paleontology, psychology, and physics in the other lobe. Literalists, of either persuasion, miss out on a lot in the Bible. They quite often miss out on jokes, too.

Stories can tell very real and important truths about human life without having literally, historically occurred. Aesop's fables tell us — symbolically rather than literally — that it is one thing to propose belling the cat and quite another to execute the proposal. Folktales have been doing the same for centuries: *Cinderella* tells the same truth as Our Lady's Magnificat, the lowly will be raised up; *Beauty and the Beast* says that anything ugly, once it is loved, becomes beautiful; *Jack and the Beanstalk* shows (rather than tells) that every young man, from young David to today's climbing executive, will have to fight the big boys if he wants to get to the top. The whole *Star Wars* saga does the same thing. *Catcher in the Rye* never really happened, but it tells more about male adolescent psychology than any adolescent psychology book.

— ❖ —

There are a few other (not insurmountable) difficulties in understanding the Gospels *as they were intended* to be understood. First, they
were not acted out or written down originally in English. They took
place in Aramaic, a dialect of Hebrew, and were written in Greek —
in neither of which many readers of these pages can boast much pro-
ficiency. Furthermore, they embody customs and ideas that were at
times incomprehensible even to the Greek-speaking translators and
collectors who received them from the Aramaic-speaking disciples.

"Perfect," for instance, could not mean "flawless" to a Jew; that
would be automatically blasphemous, since only God can be perfect in
that sense. Rather, it meant "all-together, whole, at peace with oneself
and with God." Yet literalists, to their peril, have taken it in its Western meaning and crippled their lives (and the lives of those around
them) fretting in an unrealizable perfectionism: "Be perfect as your
heavenly Father is perfect" (Matt. 5:48). Impossible in the English
sense, quite possible in the Hebrew sense.

But a thornier problem is that no stenographer followed Jesus
around, much less a reporter with a trusty tape recorder. If you study
the Gospels of Mark, Matthew, and Luke in parallel (the same episode
in three narrow columns), you will see that — although substantially
the same — they differ quite often: making an editorial judgment to
transfer one complete event to a different chronological time, inserting
words the others do not have and omitting some they do have, inserting stories the others seem ignorant of. It makes a fascinating study to
read the synoptics (Mark, Matthew, and Luke, whose general outlines
are similar yet different from John's) in parallel in order to see the different personalities and viewpoints of the three writers and why they
made the editorial decisions they did. And a good biblical commentary
can resolve most seeming disharmonies. (Except for literalists.)

An even more difficult problem is that the Gospels were not written
till, at the earliest, 65 C.E., thirty years after the events they describe —
and *interpret.* The reasons were that the early community wrongly believed the end of the world was just round the corner (in which case
writing it down would serve no purpose) and the original eyewitnesses
were beginning to die out.

Therefore, the first aspect of the problem is that the final editors of
what we know as the four Gospels were most likely not eyewitnesses.
How reliable is their testimony? The second is that they were written by men who "knew how the story ended" and whose lives had

been profoundly reversed by it: the resurrection and the knowledge that "Jesus is Lord" — that is, Yahweh. How much did the later writers understand about the events that the disciples did *not* realize *as they were going through the events?* How much did the writers read-back-into their description of the events theological elements that the eyewitnesses could not have been aware of? Does their reading-back-into — their interpretation of the events rather than straightforward reportage — render the Gospels as we have them untrustworthy? No. A third aspect of the lateness problem is that, according to most Scripture scholars, at times the Gospel writers show Jesus dealing with problems we know from other sources were not real problems in the Palestine of his day but did in fact become problems for the later community once they moved out into the wider European world. On what authority did that later community insert those episodes showing how Jesus *would* have handled new problems he was unaware of?

The first aspect — the final editors' distance from the actual events — is easily dealt with, provided the reader allows an analogy to modern-day experience. Several years ago, superiors asked an author to write about five Jesuits who had been martyred in 1978–79, one in El Salvador, one in Brazil, and three in what was then Rhodesia. He had never heard of them before; the superiors who had made the request were not about to send him winging off to those places to do research. So he ransacked libraries to find out about those countries; he sent letters to provincials asking for names of Jesuits he could write for information; he went through a whole file drawer of clippings in the national Jesuit office (in Spanish and Portuguese!). When he finished, he had a big carton of notes, clippings, recorded tapes from eyewitnesses to the murders, and pictures, and sat down to write as honestly as he could about these five strangers' lives. Then he sent manuscripts to his correspondents, made suggested changes, and brought out a book that was as near as possible to what had occurred in those tragedies — without being an eyewitness himself. Were he able to go back and rewrite it today, it would be a far better book, but that was the best he could do at the time. And ten years from now, someone else could do an even better job.

The same thing happened with the Gospel writers. Mark (who was the first) was probably Peter's interpreter when preaching to Greek-speaking audiences outside Palestine. A great source of stories there. But Christian Jews were arriving in Rome all the time: more stories, more sayings of Jesus that Peter had forgotten or not been present for (like the crucifixion), perhaps even a short description of the entire final days written by another writer. When he finished, he had about the best he could do at the time.

Later, Matthew comes along with information that did not appear in his copy of Mark; so he writes a new edition of Mark, for a rather different audience, probably Jewish because of Matthew's emphases. Then Luke arrives, with a copy of Mark but not a copy of Matthew, and some sources common to Matthew but not to Mark; and he writes still a third edition of the same story, for a more literate and highly placed Gentile audience, which one can discern from Luke's more elegant Greek style, his explanations of Jewish customs, and his unique concern for kindness (only Luke has the story of the prodigal son, the good Samaritan, Jesus forgiving the one thief on Calvary).

As to the second aspect of the lateness problem, it is unlikely the disciples knew Jesus was the Son of God until after the resurrection. Thus, for instance, Peter probably did not say, "You are the messiah, the Son of the Living God" (Matt. 16:16) when Jesus asked who the disciples believed he was. That statement reflected the later community's understanding rather than what the disciples knew at the time it happened. They were rigidly monotheistic Jews; how could a man be God? In fact, it took the later Church over three hundred years to wrestle with that one, and some are still at it.

Consider another analogy to this kind of reading-back-into. Renaissance painters never tired of picturing Gospel events, and yet their pictures are "false" — when taken in a *literal* sense. Jesus was not white, European, or delicate. Neither he nor his disciples went around swathed in brocade. Our Lady did not receive the Angel Gabriel in the sitting room of an Italian villa. The paintings, however, embodied not what occurred but what the artists had come to *understand* about the people and events they portrayed. The symbols they used tried to capture the invisible *inner* reality of Jesus and his work, not what they literally looked like in actual first-century Palestine.

As for the third aspect (the Gospels showing Jesus solving problems of a later time), some unbelievers cite it to undermine the validity of the Gospels, when it is not really that serious a difficulty. The Church has been doing precisely that for the last two thousand years: interpreting new problems the human Jesus knew nothing about or spoke nothing about — atomic war, genetic engineering, wholesale abortion. The Church says, "To our best mind, this is what Jesus would have said about this question." These pronouncements are not part of the canon of Scripture; they are what is called *tradition,* part of the living teaching of the Church, which remains the physical embodiment of Christ, the Mystical Body, animated by the same Spirit. If we accept that the Church can speak in the name of Jesus in the twentieth century, why not in the first century?

Therefore, in a close reading of the Scriptures, you have to look for three distinct levels of the developing message: first, the original, actually historical events, like the crucifixion; then the obviously fabricated stories that were meant to convey a theological (but not historical) truth, like the parables that Jesus obviously made up, to convey a truth *through* the story, as any good teacher or preacher does; finally, the events that seem to the literalist to be true but that were, in fact, stories the later community made up (just as Jesus had) to portray realities the later writers knew about the real meaning of Jesus but that the persons actually witnessing the events were unaware of at the time, like the arrival of the Magi, Jesus and Peter walking on the water, the transfiguration.

Those three episodes (and others) are unlikely to have occurred historically, and yet each does express a profound truth once one accepts the resurrection and the true nature of Jesus.

The Magi appear in only one Gospel: Matthew's version. Again, we get our ideas of them more from Christmas card art, chic shop windows, and *Amahl and the Night Visitors* than we do from the actual Bible. There is no mention of their being kings, only that they were astrologers; no indication there were three, except for the three gifts, which ten men could have chipped in for; no statement one was white, one black, one Oriental or that their names were Gaspar, Melchior, and Balthasar. Yet even those later, legendary additions to Matthew's basic story are "true" — not in the literal sense, but in the symbolic sense: Jesus came not only for the poor, illiterate, Jewish shepherds but also for rich, learned Gentiles of all races.

The point of the story about walking on the water is not that Jesus walked on the water but that *Peter* did. Any literalist attempt to argue for sandbars or massive lily pads or the sudden upthrust of a whale in a lake misses that whole point: if you forget your own shortcomings and keep your eyes solely on the Jesus who sustains you, you can do what you thought was impossible. Perhaps Peter did not literally walk on water, but the coward who denied Jesus three times early Good Friday morning went on to be crucified upside down for refusing to do so again. That is a *real* miracle.

It is difficult to believe that the three apostles gifted with the searing vision of a literal transfiguration — Jesus clothed in blinding light, Moses and Elijah materializing from the beyond, the voice of Almighty

God thundering — could go back to being the same thick-headed dullards bickering over who would have the first place in this new kingdom. The transfiguration was, after all, quite parallel with Jesus' own realization at his baptism, which changed his entire life. But what the story says is still theologically true; even though they did not realize it at the time, there was an incandescent energy within Jesus that our minds still cannot fully comprehend. Again, the Gospel writers were like renaissance painters: this is what was *really* going on, even if the eyewitnesses were unaware that it was.

All of this is in service of a single insight: if you are going to read the Scriptures on your own — and every Christian should — it is wise to have some help, either a course in delving through the strata of the books or a reliable biblical commentary. As Raymond Brown, S.S., writes in *The Jerome Biblical Commentary*:

> Because Scripture is inspired and presumably this inspiration was for the good of all, there has arisen the fallacy that everyone should be able to pick up the Bible and read it profitably. If this implies that everyone should be able to find out what the sacred author is saying without preparation or study, it really demands of God in each instance a miraculous dispensation from the limitations imposed by differences of time and circumstance.

The primary task of the scriptural authors was to be intelligible *to their own times*. To read the Bible as the authors intended requires that our biblical education be proportionate to our other education. No one would dump *Lear* on adolescents without a welter of notes, yet we blithely dump Luke on them and expect them to fathom it. Just because people know how to read does not guarantee they can read either Shakespeare or Scripture with anything more than the vaguest comprehension.

Reading Scripture takes effort. But it is worth it.

Questions for Reflection and Discussion

1. In the following well-known stories, what is each author trying to tell us *through* the story about the inescapable truths of human life?
     ◆ Hansel and Gretel
     ◆ Little Red Ridinghood
     ◆ Snow White
     ◆ Goldilocks and the Three Bears
     ◆ The Three Little Pigs

2. Whether the following episodes in the Gospels historically oc-
curred or not, what truth is the Jesus community trying to convey
through each?
   - The temptations in the desert (Matt. 4:1–11)
   - The parable of the wedding (Matt. 22:1–14)
   - The rich young man (Mark 10:17–31)
   - Simon's feast (Luke 7:36–50)
   - Raising Lazarus (John 11:26–44)

3. Find a biblical commentary in a library and look up the following
episodes. How is your understanding enriched?
   - A man beset by demons (Matt. 5:1–20)
   - The arrest of Jesus (Mark 14:43–52)
   - Jesus before the Council (Mark 14:53–65)
   - Peter's denial of Jesus (Mark 14:66–72)
   - Jesus and Zaccheus (Luke 19:1–10)

Faith in Action

We cannot "define" the people in our lives, studying them analytically,
writing psychological profiles of them. But we can get to understand
them better (and therefore forgive them more easily) if we try to probe
their stories. Think of someone you find difficult. What irritates you
most about him or her? "No effect can be greater than its causes."
How did they get that way? Do you think they *want* to irritate you?
Do they even know?

Prayer

Hidden God,
you come to us within so many disguises.
Sensitize me to your messages,
in tight spikes of crocus
and in the fierce webs of lightning,
in the breathless stories of children,
and in tragic tales of suffering hearts.
Let the ears of my ears come awake. Amen.

6

Witnessing to Christianity

What you hear whispered, proclaim from the housetops.

When he was in prison, about to be executed, St. Thomas More wrote this letter to his daughter, Margaret:

> Mistrust Him, Meg, will I not, though I feel me faint. . . . I remember how St. Peter with a blast of a wind began to sink for his faint faith, and shall do as he did, call upon Christ and pray him to help. And then I trust he shall set his holy hand unto me, and in the stormy seas hold me up from drowning.

Every "is" implies an "ought." If an object is a clock, it ought to keep time; a human being ought to be moral, recognizably different from a self-absorbed beast; a Christian ought to be in some way different from a good moral Jew, Buddhist, atheist. Not better, just discernibly different.

Interesting question: if we lived in a society in which being Christian were a crime punishable with imprisonment, could they find enough hard evidence against you even to indict, much less convict? More importantly, what would constitute hard evidence that you were Christian?

The four non-negotiables we saw before were: the divinity of Jesus, the resurrection, the anti-materialism of the Gospel, the obligation to worship and serve. Jesus said, "You will know them by what they do" (Matt. 7:16). What we do shouts so loudly no one can hear what we claim. If someone infuriated routinely barks "Jesus!" instead of some other expletive, his or her commitment is at least suspect. Understandable that one laments the death of a loved one, but if it lasts too long, one's faith in Christianity is questionable. If the bottom line is "How much can we make" and not "Who will get hurt? Whom can we help?" there is little chance of an indictment. If one is a loner, wombed in a Walkman, reluctant to worship or serve, unable to find time to pray, there is no case. Such people may claim to be Christian, but they are telling themselves lies and, worse, believing them. They are like those who tell themselves they are good citizens when they fail to vote, cheat on their taxes, and never complain to elected officials.

A priest once received a call from a young man he had taught some ten years before, though he had never had even a Christmas card from him since then. But he knew before the request even came what the young man wanted: to "do" his wedding, even though he had not seen the inside of a church in quite some time. The young man said he was marrying a Jewish woman and had agreed to raise the children Jewish, "not for religious reasons but for ethnic ones." But why did he want a priest (not just "an old friend," but any priest)? He said because he had been brought up Catholic. But was he a Catholic now? Did he ever pray? No. Would this be a truly *religious* ceremony, or was it merely an excuse for the satin and the Purcell Trumpet Voluntary? Could the priest in conscience solemnize these vows with a ritual the young man's consistent behavior proved he no longer held important? He answered that of course he was a Christian; how could anyone live in a big city and witness the human degradation without being Christian?

The young man was confusing being Christian — much less Catholic — with having genuine human compassion, just as some confuse being a moral human being with being Christian. At the bottom line, he wanted a priest for his parents' sake, and in his gut he knew this event was just too important to take place in a J.P.'s office. But the Mass was not important enough to the rest of his life for him to expend any time attending Mass. He had not ceased to be a Catholic, any more than the prodigal son had ceased to be a member of his family when he deserted it. The son on death row is still one's son. But he is like a son who comes home only for a handout, then leaves and never returns.

Attendance at Mass is no proof one is a good Christian, as disgruntled young people never tire of pointing out. But *non*-attendance is a strong piece of evidence that one is not.

In Kurt Vonnegut's *God Bless You, Mr. Rosewater,* the protagonist is asked for a single commandment by which a newborn child should lead her life and, after a pause, he says, "All right. I'll give you a commandment. 'You've got to be kind.'" Not a bad place to start. The Gospel is about healing and forgiveness, so that anyone who routinely walks by those in need or consistently nurses grudges would be hard put to substantiate their claim to be Christian — or even moral.

But good Jews, Buddhists, and atheists want to be kind. The difference in Christian kindness is the one Jesus described in Matthew 25 about the last judgment. The sole question to determine the success or failure of our lives will be: I was hungry, I was thirsty, I was imprisoned. What did you do about that? The point is that the Christian's kindness is doubly motivated: human empathy for a fellow human in need *and* the conviction that somehow Jesus Christ is within that suffering. The young man asking for a Mass that was merely peripheral to his wedding did feel honest compassion for wretched people he saw every day, but he did not see Jesus in them. He did not care about Jesus at all.

Jesus said people could tell we were Christians by the fact that we love one another (with that twofold motivation). Now love is one of the trickiest realities to pin down and a word more misused even than "freedom" or "value." Most people think love is a feeling: palpitations of the heart, warm affection, a yearning to be-with. That is not love; that is romance — being-in-love. Real love is not a feeling but an act of the will. It takes over when the feelings fail, when the beloved is no longer even likable.

When the honeymoon years (or months) begin to wane and being-in-love starts to lose its intoxicating surge, that is when real love has a chance, the love that goes on loving even when there are no kickbacks, when love goes on in other rooms of the house besides the bedroom. Unlike romance, real love is quite undramatic: changing the diapers love, cutting down the drinking love, letting go of the grudge love.

St. Paul put it better than anyone else:

Love is patient; love is kind; love is not envious or boastful or arrogant or rude. It does not insist on its own way; it is not irritable or resentful; it does not rejoice in wrongdoing but rejoices in the truth. It bears all things, believes all things, hopes all things, endures all things. Love never ends. (1 Cor. 13:4–8)

No warm, fuzzy feelings there. A commitment, no matter what. People wonder how they can "love" the stranger, the alien, the repellent outcast — precisely those people Jesus demonstrably sends us to. The reason is that their definition of love is limited to romantic love, affection, the "love" they sing of in "love" songs. Perhaps incandescent, saintly souls can actually *feel* affection for the people they serve. Very often, the best one can muster is, "Well, at least I haven't killed him today." But this is an act of love, a refusal to yield to feelings and a commitment to respect, to go on trying to heal the wound — even when the victim is unaware of a wound.

It may sound unreasonable, but a Christian does not have the option to be shy. Jesus told us we have to shout the good news of freedom from the housetops. The story of Peter walking on the water shows us our shortcomings have no meaning when we are in the hands of an omnipotent God. "But many of us, by our upbringing, are more reserved." But to be "reserved" means you are holding something back, guarding it from harm. But one look at a crucifix shows that the Model of all Christians did not do that. He gave until there was nothing left, not even blood.

Now that does not mean every Christian has to set up a soap-box on a street corner and preach. But it does mean we have to be quite a bit less reticent than many of us would like to be, more intrusive than nearly all of us would want to be. When we see someone obviously in distress, no follower of Christ could pass by in silence: "I don't mean to intrude, but if I could be of any help, you have only to ask." When we listen to someone moaning about the meaninglessness of it all: "I'm on my way to Mass. Would you like to come along?" Most of us move at too fast a pace; even recreation for many is exhausting: "Next month I'm making a retreat. Why not take a couple days off and come along?" The whole Christian Church began because a young carpenter stopped by a couple of beached boats and asked that.

At Baptism, each of us is ordained an apostle of the good news, and at Confirmation each of us (supposedly) personally accepts that role in the Church — as adults and no longer children, shepherds and no longer sheep. Jesus enjoined every Christian, no matter what his or her juridical status within the Christian community, to be yeast in the surrounding culture, no matter how alien. Paul commends laypeople by name at the ends of his letters — Phoebe, Priscilla, Aquila, Ampliatus, Urbanus, Tychicus, and many others, and describes them as "my fellow workers in the service of Christ Jesus" (Rom. 16:3). The Church is — in all its members — the sacrament of Christ in the world, each one a sign that gives grace. Like the One who chose and sent us, we have come "that you may have life, and have it more abundantly."

The mission of Christ — who "came not to be served but to serve" — is ours: "The Spirit has chosen me to bring good news to the poor, to set free captives, to open the eyes of the blind and liberate the oppressed: to declare the Amnesty of God" (Luke 4:18–19, author's translation).

It is not enough simply to sit passively in church of a Sunday and then spend the rest of the week dutifully performing a secular job, caring for a family, or even contributing funds to the parish. No one can be a Christian "on the side." As Karl Rahner said in *The Christian Commitment:* "Everything depends on the lay [person's] understanding that [each] is, as an individual, irreplaceable, with a specifically Christian and moral task to be performed within groups not directly subject to the Church's official control, a task of which [each] will have to give an account before the judgment seat of God."

There are (at least) three ways in which Catholics are called to serve. One is an ecclesial in-house way (hierarchy, clergy, eucharistic ministers, parish councils, etc.). Another is in an ecclesially sponsored way (Catholic school teachers, workers in Church-run soup kitchens, hospitals, half-way houses, etc.) Relatively few of us work in such overtly Catholic apostolates, but every Catholic is ordained an apostle — though only a handful know it or feel a need to exercise it. The third way of serving the good news is precisely as a Christian working in a secular situation completely outside the Church's control, where a black shirt and white tab would be a drawback.

We are used to thinking of "sacred" and "secular" as irreducibly antagonistic. That supposed mutual exclusion gives rise to the death-dealing idea in Central America and elsewhere that the Church's influence should stop at the church door. But it is just as real — not as dramatic, but nearly as deadening — in North America as well. "Church is Church; business is business." When one asks young (and not-so-young) Catholics whether those in business, government, and industry must compromise their own values in order to succeed — or even merely feed a family — the overwhelming majority answer yes. For them, too, Christianity stops at the church door, a conviction that "ghettoizes" the Church even within the individual's own life.

Not only were the original Christians sent out into an unfriendly pagan environment, but — according to Jesus — it must be so: then, now, always. When Peter rebuked Jesus for saying they must go up to Jerusalem, no matter how hostile, Jesus rounded on Peter, fiercely: "Get behind me, you Satan! Your advice comes from human shrewdness, not from God" (cf. Mark 8:33). The risen Jesus asked the disciples on the way to Emmaus, "*Ought* not the Messiah to suffer these things, in order to enter his glory?" (cf. Luke 24:26). Accepting the invitation to be a Christian is not accepting membership in a moral-uplift society. It is a commitment to be an apostle — to be sneered at, misunderstood, perhaps even crucified.

Therefore, to bewail indifference and corruption all around us is to bewail the challenge of God in the way things *are*. No problem with that; prophets have always whined. But nonetheless they set out, grudgingly, to do what God asked of them. So the media and the government are cynical and manipulative; so our students and other potential converts are indifferent or even hostile. "*Ought* not the Messiah to suffer these things?" Since Pentecost, we are the embodiment of Christ; we are the Messiah. We were destined by Jesus to be a stumbling stone, a sign of contradiction to our times. And insofar as we are not, insofar as we preach no more than Hallmark holiness and cheap grace, we are failing at our mandate from the Christ.

We often lipserve the truth that the Holy Spirit speaks to us through history yet too often restrict that to events of the past. Actually, the Spirit speaks to us right now, through the events and trends of this time. One of the loudest statement she makes to us — and has for the last thirty years — is that vocations to the priesthood and religious life are dramatically fewer. Yet priests, nuns, and brothers had been the majority of the church's active apostles for centuries. If the Christian apostolate is to continue, perhaps the Spirit is suggesting we look elsewhere for active apostles. Where? The pews. Galvanize ordinary Catholic laywomen and laymen, nurses, entrepreneurs, domestics, engineers, police, hairdressers. Imbue them with the idealism of the Gospel, ignite their confidence — if not in themselves, then at least in the One who sends them.

There is within each woman and man a God-sized hunger. It is there in our pews; it is there in the fellow workers and clients we deal with every day, people who never darken the door of a church or encounter a cleric. A tinder waiting to be ignited, a potential yet to be actualized. We go to them not with the sunny, sometimes condescending manner of Jehovah's Witnesses at the door: "*I* know something that *you* don't know." It is the manifest joy and freedom of our everyday lives that will make others suspect we know something they do not know.

The usual response to a strong Christian come-on (as even the convinced can testify) is to haul up the drawbridge and look for an escape route. Certainly anyone in the middle of an annual report does not want you to stop by on the way to the coffee pot and plunge into ultimate questions. But there are opportunities aplenty for the ordinary lay Catholic to be a thought-provoking apostle, to lure people to grow: parties, weddings, funerals, after-hours in a pub when people are less suffused in busywork, less guarded. (*In vino veritas* apparently worked for Jesus.)

In a world less ideal than we had expected, when parents and friends begin to die and we ourselves begin to carry sure signs of finitude in our bodies, we are more susceptible to pondering. "Did you ever ask yourself, 'Who am I?'" Well, I'm a salesman; I'm a housewife. I'm this person's spouse, those persons' parent. But who am *I*? Even if (God forbid) I lost my job and my family, who would I be?

Think of Jesus. Think of Socrates. They would amble into a group busy unsnarling their nets or counting up the day's take, and they would merely start to talk about something more important than everyday chitchat, questions we all ponder once in awhile but, finding no answers, stow away in the back of our minds. "Ever wonder what life after death would really be like?" or "I read an article today, and ... " Thoughtful people enjoy being provoked to think.

One way of looking at how an active Catholic might serve is to think of oneself as a talk-show host or hostess, like Ophrah Winfrey or David Letterman. Their purpose (on an admittedly surface level) is to *draw out* the other person. Few of us are so self-effacing we do not rise to "What do you think about ... ?"

It is not exactly shouting the good news from the housetops, but it is plowing before one plants. And it might have a more lasting effect on a soul than filling the same time discussing the ball scores or what film stars just exchanged spouses.

The active Christian confronts the plethora of human problems with an optimism that would seem naive and silly, judged solely from the viewpoint of human shrewdness. We still hold out hope for the world. After all, the whole Christian movement is rooted in the apparent defeat of our Founder; the symbol that embodies the core of our beliefs is Christ on the cross. Yet from that dead body came eternal life.

In the pagan culture to which we are missioned, most of the people we deal with every day seem to believe — or at least act as if — we are all on the *Titanic,* so you are helpless to change anything, and you might as well grab for all the gusto, all the profit, all the youth you can get. They resonate to Kurt Vonnegut's winsome pessimism: "Things are going to get unimaginably worse, and they're never going to get better." The layperson working outside the Church does have a role in the redemption of those souls — redemption not from some future hell but from atrophy here and now, from endless busyness and fluff, and from ultimate meaninglessness at death. We approach them not as Gnostics to bestow enlightenment on the benighted, but as brothers and sisters who say, like the man who returned to Plato's cave: "There's so much *more* than we suspected!" Or like the host at the feast in the parable: "Friend, come up higher."

According to the polls, nearly all Americans have "some kind of" belief in "some kind of" God. But just as with their potential to become more abundantly human, that potential for a life-giving relationship with God gets lost in the pressures and pleasures of the everyday. However, our attempts to insinuate talk of God into our relationships with the people we deal with is not an attempt to indoctrinate them into something alien. Rather, it is an attempt to awaken something that is already within them.

As Paul said to the pagan Greeks in the Areopagus, "That which you worship, even though you do not know it, is what I now proclaim to you." It is what even Freud saw as the drive to life, to challenge, to greater horizons: Eros. We are only trying to erode defenses against the God who is already speaking within their souls. And we work slowly, patiently, like Annie Sullivan drawing signs in Helen Keller's hands.

We must make those wary of God — especially the better educated and thus more skeptical — comfortable with the truth that God will always elude our formulas, just as the horizon will always escape our grasp. The point is going further than we planned.

Christianity cracks open the final horizon: death. "If Christ be not risen from the dead, then our faith is vain." If no one survives death, we are, indeed, all on the *Titanic,* and when we have a flat EKG all our trials and triumphs disappear like a computer file in a power outage. Pfft! Gone. We cease to be real. But if Christ is risen, then we are immortal, now! The darkness can never overwhelm the Light. Every suffering is a birth pain, and even every sin can become a sacramental invitation to rebirth. "Nothing can separate us from the love of God in Christ Jesus" (cf. Rom. 8:39). Everything — without exception — even a lost job, a betrayal, an alcoholic spouse, a child in trouble — is a grace-full invitation to become more like the Victor of Calvary.

Even if a layperson could bring someone that far, it would be a triumph for both spirits. To invite that someone further into the Catholic Church is, to be honest, more difficult. Even to a convinced Christian, a theological posture that seems to make more of obedience and sexual morality than of human fulfillment at least does not appear a likely vessel to carry me to "eternal life."

And yet for those of us still aboard, for all its holes and leaks the Barque of Peter seems still the least leaky of all the Christian vessels, not only because it is the embodiment of a movement going back in an unbroken line to the original Twelve, but also because its sacraments claim an efficacious change within those who receive them.

The Orthodox and the Reformers "broke off" from the Roman vine, not vice versa. That in no way impugns their sanctity or their ability to offer their members more abundant life. It merely means that, for all its faults, the Church of Rome is "the original."

As for the sacraments, Martin Luther himself said, "I'd rather drink blood with the Romans than drink wine with the Zwinglians." The Protestant theologian Karl Barth wrote:

> At those times when the task of being ministers of the divine word, as we of the Reformed Churches say, has oppressed us, have we not all felt a yearning for the rich services of Catholicism, and for the enviable role of the priest at the altar? When he elevates the *Sanctissimum,* with its full measure of that meaning and power which the *material* symbol enjoys over the symbol of the human word, the double grace of the sacrificial death and the incarnation of the Son of God is not only preached in words but actually takes place in his hands.

Some devoted Catholics take strong exception to other Catholics' beliefs that conflict openly with those of the Vatican. Yet they remind us that, as long as we agree on the non-negotiables — the divinity of Jesus, the resurrection, the anti-materialism of the Gospel, and the worshiping and serving community — there is no need of schism, much less excommunication. And they remind us God gave us intelligence before God saw need to give us the magisterium.

Chesterton said that when the lion lies down with the lamb, we oddly believe that the lion should become lamblike, which would be rank imperialism on the part of the lamb. No, let the lion lie down with the lamb and retain his royal ferocity. In the Church we need both the gentle Thérèse of Lisieux and the bellicose Joan of Arc, the fervent conservative and the ardent liberal. As Chesterton writes in *Orthodoxy:* "Christianity was like a huge and ragged and romantic rock, which, though it sways on its pedestal at the slightest touch, yet, because its exaggerated excrescences exactly balance each other, it is enthroned for a thousand years."

And it is some kind of miracle, surely, that a community so passionately attacked from without and so humiliatingly corrupt and rent with factions within has managed to survive for two millennia. Thus, just as we have to forgive God for being unfathomable, we have to forgive the official Church for being what at times at least seems heartless and unreasonable. "Lord, to whom shall we go...?"

A conviction that the Church can be the Church of the faithful would require a profound conversion on the part of a parish, not only of its pastoral staff but of the parishioners in the pews, who would no longer be merely "the audience" who sit politely while the priest and deacons and musical ministers do their thing. Sunday Mass would no longer be "just" a liturgical sacrifice or "just" an insightful homily. It would be a clarion call for the worshiping community to become also a serving community. "I come not to be served, but to serve."

The role of the pastor and parish council in such an enterprise would advance from serving the needs of the community to challenging the community to an active apostolate, to offering opportunities to discover genuine personal prayer and thoughtful reading, armoring them to be Christian apostles "out there on their own" in a non-Christian culture. Such underground agents in the field can no longer have the clergy do their thinking for them. They must be empowered as apostles as resilient and adaptable as Francis Xavier among the Japanese.

We have too long been prisoners of our metaphors. "Pastor" means a shepherd, which implies that the parishioners must be sheep. But they clearly are not. They are human beings, many of them with better degrees than the pastor's and every one of them a unique individual able to think. A more revealing analogy might be to the ideal principal of a school. She is called "principal" because she is the principal *teacher;* he is the head*master.* Ideally, his or her job is to make their staffs into better teachers — not to raise money, nor to get the roof fixed, nor to intrude into the staff's private lives. However, in the less than ideal world we inhabit, bureaucracy becomes an end in itself. The absolute essential in a school — getting young people to learn how to learn — becomes almost ancillary to running a tight ship, filing reports, attending meetings, placating parents, mediating disputes. So too in a parish, administration (which Paul put well below such ecclesial gifts as wisdom, teaching, faith, healing, prophecy, and discernment of spirits) can swamp the pastor's time and energy.

Without assuming the roles of Protestant elders, laypeople can put on many of the "hats" the old-time pastor usually wore: finance, buildings, liturgy, RCIA, Christian adult education, help for single parents, visiting the sick. And let there also be a team to sense out the parishioners' real priorities. Such people ought to be the most capable at those particular tasks — invited, not elected, since popularity is not the primary component of their service but rather commitment, wits, and imagination. Thus, the pastor would be free to do what Jesus did: challenge, encourage, celebrate, forgive — and motivate the rest of us to embrace our mission: to cast fire on the earth.

"Can I *see* your freedom? Can I *feel* your joy?" There is your most profound and least studied witness to our Christianity: our manifest freedom and joy.

Questions for Reflection and Discussion

1. Answer for yourself the question this segment poses: If we lived in a society in which being Christian were a crime punishable with imprisonment, would they find enough hard evidence against you even to indict, much less to convict?

2. Consider the story in this segment of the young man asking for a Catholic wedding when there was strong likelihood the Mass meant little or nothing to him. Is the text's stance too harsh? Would there be a realistic chance a Mass might make the young man rethink?

3. Consider what the segment says about a Christian's not being allowed to be shy. Is that too harsh? Is there an honest way in which a Christian can be "reserved"? Where in yourself do you feel you are "holding back"?

Faith in Action

Think of the pool of talent in your parish: bankers, carpenters, lawyers, realtors, grocers, etc. Now think of a homeless family; picture them, feel their sense of despair. Now think of an abandoned house, perhaps even in the parish. Now what?

Prayer

My crucified Brother,
give me the heart to rise to your challenge.
You have no voice but mine.
You give me the power to heal.
Let me match your gift of mission
with my feeble courage. Amen.

Part Two

The Message: The Nicene and Apostles' Creeds

Mitch and Kathy Finley

---------------------------- *7* ----------------------------

God's Unconditional Love

*But Ruth said [to her mother-in-law, Naomi], "Do not press me
to leave you or to turn back from following you! Where you go,
I will go; where you lodge, I will lodge; your people shall be my
people, and your God my God. Where you die, I will die — there
will I be buried. May the Lord do thus and so to me, and more
as well, if even death parts me from you!"* (RUTH 1:16–17)

Mario and Patricia, a middle-aged husband and wife, were in a reflective mood. "You know," Mario said, "when I look back over the years
we have been married and our years as parents, I can't seem to separate the joys from the sorrows. All in all, it has been absolute heaven.
But sometimes, very clearly, it has been hell on wheels."

"I know what you mean," Patricia replied, "and yet, even when life
has been painful, when we had to struggle with our marriage or put up
with hassles with the kids, still the love has been there. We are blessed,
because both of us have chosen to keep on keeping on. I think that's
what love means, staying true to your promise to be there for the person you marry and for your children. I don't think love means an easy
life free of all pain."

Mario thought about it for a moment. "I guess you're right," he
said. He paused, and Patricia saw tears in her husband's eyes. "You
have given me and our children the greatest gift anyone can give. You
have given us your life. You have stayed with us through thick and
through thin. You have shown me what love really means."

"And you have done the same for me," Patricia said. She and Mario
gave each other a hug, and in the middle of the hug they both said, at
exactly the same moment, "I love you." And then they laughed.

Countless times the Scriptures use examples from ordinary human experience — frequently family relationships — to show us what God's
love is like. The creation narratives in Genesis come to us as stories
about human relationships: Adam and Eve, Cain and Abel, and Abraham and Sarah. The story of Noah and the flood is a family story.
Noah doesn't go aboard the ark alone; he goes with his family and

his married children's families. Even the animals go two-by-two. The Book of Ruth is a story about a widowed woman, Naomi, and her daughters-in-law, Ruth and Orpah. It's about Ruth's loyalty to Naomi, and later it's about the love and respect of Boaz for Ruth.

The Book of Hosea, from start to finish, is a story about a man's persistent love for Gomer, his "wife of whoredom" (1:2). God speaks out of great love, and the author of Hosea couches God's words in terms of loving human intimacy:

> When Israel was a child, I loved him, and out of Egypt I called my son. The more I called them, the more they went from me; they kept sacrificing to the Baals, and offering incense to idols. Yet it was I who taught Ephraim to walk, I took them up in my arms; but they did not know that I healed them. I led them with cords of human kindness, with bands of love. I was to them like those who lift infants to their cheeks. I bent down to them and fed them. (Hos. 11:1–4)

The entire Book of Hosea shows that God's love for His people, Israel, is like Hosea's determined, never-say-die love for the adulterous Gomer. Just as Gomer does not deserve Hosea's love, neither do we deserve God's love, but God loves us all the same. God's love is there for us, in all circumstances, with no strings attached. All we need do is accept.

It is not without cause that one of the best-known lines from the New Testament is a saying of Jesus from John's Gospel that declares God's saving love for everyone and everything: "For God so loved the world that he gave his only Son, so that everyone who believes in him may not perish but may have eternal life" (3:16).

Indeed, Christians believe that God loves people and all of creation; but more than that, God *is* love (see 1 John 4:8). It is of the very essence of who God is to love because what God does is love, only that and nothing else. This is nowhere more evident than in the fact that God "has received human beings into the most intimate communion with himself in love . . . in the sending and incarnation, in the cross and glorification, of his only begotten *Son*" (Karl Rahner). "Father, you so loved the world that . . . you sent your only Son to be our Savior" (Eucharistic Prayer IV).

Because God is love, He brings us to birth. Because God is love, through Baptism we receive the real but invisible gift of union with the risen Christ (see John 3:16), and through this union we are called to love one another as God loves us. Although our love is sometimes weak and sometimes we fail in love, the ideal God calls us to is a love that is unconditional.

Jesus instructed his disciples — and so us, as well — to address God as *Abba,* usually translated "Father" (see Luke 11:1–2). But the meaning of the Aramaic *Abba* is more like "Loving Papa." God is like a Loving Papa who is tolerant of His children's faults, gently but firmly corrects them, and weeps when His children suffer. Our God is like a Loving Papa who rolls on the floor with His children and tickles them.

At the same time, as Pope John Paul I said, God is also like a Mother whose love has no end, who forgives endlessly and whose love for Her children knows no limits. All metaphors have their limits, but metaphors are all we have to understand the unconditional, never-ending love of our God.

Questions for Reflection and Discussion

1. Call to mind one person who has loved you or whom you have loved unconditionally. How does that person image God's love for you?

2. What are some of the conditions we sometimes put on love? How are those *not* present with God?

3. Choose an image to finish the statement "God's love is like...." Why did you choose the image you did?

4. How would you answer someone who said that the only reality they can see in the universe is narrow self-interest?

5. What are the implications for your sense of self-esteem of God's love of you, a love *as is* (unconditional), not *if only* (conditional)?

Faith in Action

God's love for us, as explained by Jesus, is so unconditional as to seem almost foolish, a love that not only takes back a prodigal son who squandered his inheritance, but also an older son who resents his father's generosity (Luke 15:11–32). This love also pays the laborers in the vineyard the same wage at the end of the day no matter how long they worked (Matt. 20:1–16). Because you also receive God's unconditional love, who could *you* be less judgmental and conditional about loving in return? Is the experience of being a parent — or watching those who are — helpful for you to better understand God's love?

Prayer

In order to listen to God's unconditional love more deeply, take some time to calm yourself in a quiet place. Listen to your breathing, then read very slowly one of the following passages, drinking in the richness of God's love for you:

- "Love is patient...." (1 Cor. 13:4–7). In this passage substitute "God" where "love" is mentioned or referred to, since "God is love" (1 John 4:8), and reflect on your relationship with God.
- "Can a woman forget her nursing child?..." (Isa. 49:15–16).
- "O LORD, you have searched me and known me...." (Ps. 139: 1–6).

8

Creation

God saw everything that he had made, and indeed, it was very good. (GENESIS 1:31)

A young man stood in line for nearly an hour in order to view, for a few minutes, treasures from ancient Egypt. Finally inside the exhibit hall, he stood in awe as, with his own eyes, he looked at the brightly colored gold burial mask of King Tutankhamun, a woman's burial garment made of hundreds of small jade tiles, each connected to the others by tiny gold wires, exquisitely fashioned statues of royal cats, and many other wonders.

Back outside the exhibit hall, the young man reflected on how human beings were able to create such beautiful things so long ago. As he walked in the warmth of a sunny spring day, suddenly he heard the loud chirp of a robin sitting in a maple tree overhead. Startled out of his reverie, the young man gazed at the robin, who eyed the young man, chirped again, and flew off. Noticing a bench under the tree, he sat down to continue his reflections.

The works of the ancient Egyptians, amazing and beautiful as they were, could not hold a candle to God's creation, mountains and oceans, insects, animals, and creatures of the sea; sun, moon, and the star-filled night sky. "I am a part of creation, too," the young man thought. "Indeed, God's living creation is a far greater marvel than anything from a dead civilization's mysterious past."

Playing the part of God in the film *Oh, God!* comedian George Burns quipped that when he created the world a few mistakes did slip through, such as making the avocado seed too big. Hollywood humor notwithstanding, Catholicism teaches that God created everything, material and spiritual. Therefore, everything is good and everything is blessed, avocado seeds included: "all your actions show your wisdom and love" (Eucharistic Prayer IV).

In Genesis we read:

> So God created humankind in his image, in the image of God he created them; male and female he created them. God blessed them, and God said to them, "Be fruitful and multiply, and fill the earth and subdue it; and have dominion over the fish of the sea and over the birds of the air and over every living thing that moves upon the earth." (1:27–28)

Sometimes people use God's command to "subdue" the earth to justify abuse of the earth's natural resources, everything from forests to oceans, from rivers to the air we breathe. True, we are to master the earth, but as stewards or caretakers. We are to respect God's creation and our environment. We are to use the earth's natural resources gently and take care that we leave the environment the way we find it. We must guard against spoiling the creation out of greed or thoughtlessness, for our "dominion over inanimate and other living beings granted by the Creator is not absolute; it is limited by concern for the quality of life of [our] neighbor[s], including generations to come; it requires a religious respect for the integrity of creation" (*Catechism of the Catholic Church,* no. 2415).

Questions for Reflection and Discussion

1. What aspects of creation (animals, plants, certain places) help you know God's presence more deeply?
2. Where is it most difficult to see God's presence in creation?

3. Thomas Merton observed, "All creation teaches us some way of prayer." If a tree could speak to you of God, what might it tell you?

Faith in Action

What are some specific actions that you could take to care for the natural world around you, such as recycling, composting, taking time to appreciate the beauty around you, planting a tree, etc.?

Prayer

If possible, go to a park, out in your yard, or to someplace where you can enjoy nature as you take time to praise God for the goodness of creation. Use the following prayer, called the Canticle of the Sun, given to us by St. Francis of Assisi:

Most High, omnipotent, good Lord,
to you alone belong praise and glory, honor and blessing,
no one is worthy to breathe your name.
Be praised, my Lord, for all your creatures.
In the first place for the blessed Brother Sun,
who gives us the day and enlightens us through you.
He is beautiful and radiant with his great splendor,
Giving witness to you, most Omnipotent One.
Be praised, my Lord, for Sister Moon and the stars
formed by you so bright, precious and beautiful.
Be praised, my Lord, for Brother Wind
and the airy skies, so cloudy and serene;
for every weather, be praised, for it is life-giving.
Be praised, my Lord, for Sister Water,
so necessary, yet so precious, humble, and chaste.
Be praised, my Lord, for Brother Fire, who lights up the night.
He is beautiful and carefree, robust and fierce.
Be praised, my Lord, for our sister, Mother Earth,
who nourishes and watches us
while bringing forth an abundance of fruits
with colored flowers and herbs....
Praise and bless the Lord. Render thanks.
Serve him with great humility. Amen.

9

The Dignity of Human Beings

Then God said, "Let us make humankind in our image, according to our likeness; and let them have dominion over the fish of the sea, and over the birds of the air, and over the cattle, and over all the wild animals of the earth, and over every creeping thing that creeps upon the earth." So God created humankind in his image, in the image of God he created them; male and female he created them. (GENESIS 1:26–27)

"It's a girl!" Peg, the nurse-midwife, exclaimed joyously, the slippery but peaceful newborn in her latex-gloved hands. Clara, her face covered with perspiration, felt an enormous sense of relief now that her hours of labor were over. Her husband, Tim, hovered close. His hand shook as he took the surgical scissors Peg offered him.

"Cut right here," Peg directed, and Tim cut the sturdy umbilical cord that had been the lifeline of his and Clara's first-born for the last nine months.

"We have a beautiful baby girl," Clara said, her face lit up with an enormous smile as she watched Peg give the baby a quick post-partum check-up.

"Ah," Peg said quietly, examining the infant's hands. "Here," she said, gently placing the baby in Clara's arms. "Let's see if this little girl is hungry." Instinctively, the baby took Clara's nipple into her mouth and began to nurse hungrily.

"Peg..." Clara said. "Is she okay? I'm almost forty, you know, and, well, naturally we're concerned...." I refused to have an amniocentesis done while I was pregnant....I saw you checking her hands...."

"Clara and Tim," Peg said softly. "It's possible your baby has Down's Syndrome. She seems to have the single crease in her palms. But we can't be sure until the pediatrician has a look...."

Tim was shocked into silence. Tears ran down Clara's cheeks. "Oh, my poor, precious little baby girl," she said, holding the baby close.

"My God," Tim said, finally able to speak. "What now?"

"We won't know anything for sure until later," Peg said.

Clara took a deep breath and wiped the tears from her face. "We'll take it one step at a time," she said, looking into Tim's eyes. "The important thing is that our baby needs to be loved by her parents. We are her parents and we will love her."

"Believers and unbelievers are almost at one in considering that everything on earth is to be referred to humanity as its center and culmination" (Vatican II, Pastoral Constitution on the Church in the Modern World, no. 12). All human beings have a special God-given dignity because they are created in the image of God. "You formed man and woman in your own likeness and entrusted the whole world to their care, so that in serving you alone, their Creator, they might be stewards of all Creation" (Eucharistic Prayer, proposed ICEL translation).

As Christians, we also believe that through Baptism we are identified in a real but invisible way with the risen Christ. "For you did not receive a spirit of slavery to fall back into fear, but you have received a spirit of adoption. When we cry, 'Abba! Father!' it is that very Spirit bearing witness with our spirit that we are children of God, and if children, then heirs, heirs of God and joint heirs with Christ" (Rom. 8:15–17).

Human dignity derives from how we are created by God, gifted with capacities not found in the rest of creation, thus called by God to responsibilities not delegated to any other part of creation. "Endowed with a spiritual soul, with intellect and with free will, the human person is from his [or her] very conception ordered to God and destined for eternal beatitude" (*Catechism of the Catholic Church,* no. 1711).

At the same time, belief in the God-given dignity of all human beings has consequences, it is not just a pleasant idea. Every person must consider all other persons as their neighbors, without exception. The other person is my other self. "Today particularly there is a pressing obligation on us to be a neighbor to every single individual and to take steps to serve each individual whom we encounter, whether she or he be old and abandoned, or a foreign worker unjustly despised, or an exile" (Vatican II, Pastoral Constitution on the Church in the Modern World, no. 27).

Note, too, that according to Genesis God created male and female *together* in the divine image. Woman and man share equally in the image of God; it is their shared humanity and their sexual differentiation that reflects the likeness of God. There is no basis in Scripture to attribute a greater dignity to either sex. Rather, male and female are clearly gifts of God to each other, meant to complement and complete each other.

We take for granted that all human beings are equal in dignity before God, and so they have the same rights. This short-circuits any inclination we may have toward prejudice, discrimination, and injustice. "But every type of discrimination affecting the fundamental rights of the person, whether social or cultural, on grounds of sex, race, color, class, language or religion, should be overcome and done away with, as contrary to the purpose of God" (Vatican II, Pastoral Constitution on the Church in the Modern World, no. 29; *Catechism of the Catholic Church,* no. 1935).

Thus, we must combat all forms of human inequality, regardless of where they may be found. "The equal dignity of persons demands access to more human and equal conditions of life. And the excessive economic and social inequalities among members or peoples of the same human family are a scandal and are at variance with social justice, equity, the dignity of the human person and, not least, social and international peace" (Vatican II, Pastoral Constitution on the Church in the Modern World, no. 29; *Catechism of the Catholic Church,* no. 1938).

Because each person is created in the image of God, each individual deserves infinite respect. To paraphrase André Gide, a Nobel prize-winning twentieth-century French Catholic author: God made each person, not humanity, in the divine image. "Each one is more precious than all," Gide said.

Questions for Reflection and Discussion

1. Name some public figures who have helped you see the dignity of the human person more clearly and explain why. Some examples might be Helen Keller, Martin Luther King, Jr., Dorothy Day, Cesar Chavez, and Maximilian Kolbe.

2. What are some of the basic aspects of your God-given human dignity, to which you and every other human person have a right? How do you see these sometimes abused today? Where do you see these respected and enhanced?

Faith in Action

Think of several local groups that help enhance the dignity of others, such as the Red Cross, the St. Vincent de Paul Society, the local food bank, or shelter for the homeless or battered women. What are two specific ways that you could help in the work of these groups, such as volunteering some of your time?

Who could you help to feel special and be more aware of their God-given dignity today, either through a card, a visit, a call, or a kind word?

Prayer

In a quiet place take some time to be thankful for your existence and the unique gifts and dignity that you were given by God. Then slowly read the Magnificat (Luke 1:46–55), realizing that just as it refers to Mary, it also applies to you.

10

Trinity

Those who love me will keep my word, and my Father will love them, and we will come to them and make our home with them. Whoever does not love me does not keep my words; and the word that you hear is not mine, but is from the Father who sent me.

I have said these things to you while I am still with you. But the Advocate, the Holy Spirit, whom the Father will send in my name, will teach you everything, and remind you of all that I have said to you. . . . (JOHN 14:23–26)

Maria and Bill sat watching television. The children were in bed for the night, and they both were tired. All day, off and on, Maria had been thinking about what she wanted to say. She took a deep breath, then cleared her throat. Bill recognized the signal. "Hm?" he said.

Maria took another deep breath. "Um...you know, I've been feeling lately like everything is closing in on me. I work all day, and then I come home and the kids seem to take up whatever energy I have left. I appreciate that we take turns when it comes to fixing dinner, but even on the days when I don't have to do that I end up beyond exhaustion by the time we head for bed."

Bill glanced away from the TV and looked at his wife. "I know. We're both dead tired by the end of the day."

"Yes," Maria said. "Well, I was thinking. Remember there was a notice in the bulletin at church last Sunday? About a silent weekend retreat next month? I was wondering if you would mind if I went. I think it's just what I need to recharge my batteries and get caught up on some rest. There will be another retreat sometime, and you could go then...."

Bill frowned. A whole weekend alone with three kids between the ages of three and ten. Yikes! "Gosh," he said. "I don't know. That sounds like a long time to be away...."

Maria held her breath. She didn't want to get into an argument about this, but she was determined to go. "Hey," she said, leaning over to give Bill a kiss on the cheek. "Tell you what. I'll fix lasagna and freeze it, and all you'll need to do is put it in the oven for dinner Friday evening. Saturday you can take the kids out for hamburgers, and I'll be home to fix dinner by Sunday evening...."

Settling herself into her room at the retreat center a few weeks later, Maria unpacked her overnight bag and hung up the change of clothes she brought with her. She lay on the neatly made bed, and in less than a minute she was in a sound sleep. How long had it been since she took an uninterrupted nap in the afternoon?

A couple of hours later, refreshed by her rest, Maria joined fourteen other men and women in the retreat center's dining room for dinner. Afterward, they would gather for the first talk of the retreat by a woman who wrote books on spirituality. Maria chatted happily with those at her table, and as she did so she realized that each person, herself included, talked about his or her family. She heard about husbands and wives, children and grandchildren. It was a small revelation.

"For heaven's sake," Maria thought. "Each person is here alone, but it's like they all brought their families with them. Each person is one person, but each person is also a bundle of relationships. It's like we are who we are because of our closest relationships. We can't leave our families behind, they're a basic part of who we are...."

— ❖ —

We are familiar with the doctrine of the Trinity. In the eucharistic liturgy, for example, we hear: "The grace of the Lord Jesus Christ and the love of God and the fellowship of the Holy Spirit be with you all."

When a person is baptized, he or she receives this basic sacrament "in the name of the Father, and of the Son, and of the Holy Spirit" (Matt. 28:19). There are in the Trinity, the Church teaches, three "persons" in one God. "We do not confess three Gods, but one God in three persons.... The divine persons do not share the one divinity among themselves but each of them is God whole and entire" (*Catechism of the Catholic Church,* no. 253).

Yet we need to be honest. We may puzzle over such concepts till the cows come home, and we may still feel confused. There is no mystery of Christian faith that boggles the human mind more completely than the mystery of the Trinity. No matter whose words we listen to, reflecting on the meaning of the Trinity, we seem to know little more than we did to begin with. Sample the following remarks by great Christian thinkers ancient and modern:

> We confess the Father and the Son and the Holy Spirit to be consubstantial, three hypostases [persons], one essence, one divinity.
>
> — St. Epiphanius of Constantia (4th c.)

> The divine nature is really and entirely identical with each of the three persons, all of whom can therefore be called one: I and the Father are one.
>
> — St. Thomas Aquinas (1225–74)

> Tell me how it is that in this room there are three candles but one light, and I will explain to you the mode of the divine existence.
>
> — John Wesley (1703–91)

> In God there can be no selfishness, because the three selves of God are three subsistent relations of selflessness, overflowing and superabounding in joy in the perfection of their gift of their one life to one another.
>
> — Thomas Merton (1915–68)

When Jesus, in John's Gospel, prays to the Father "that they may all be one ... as we are one" (17:21–22) he opens up what Vatican II called "prospects unattainable to human reason" (Pastoral Constitution on the Church in the Modern World, no. 24). Jesus implies a similarity between the union of the divine Persons and the union of God's people in truth and love. The mystery of the Trinity is a mystery of love. It means that a human person can discover his or her true self only by the sincere gift of self to others.

Contemporary theologies of spirituality suggest that all Christian spirituality is Trinitarian. This simply means that the Christian life emphasizes human relationships rather than human individuality. Thus, the goal of a Christian life is to live always in the context of loving relationships with others. The Christian life cannot be lived in isolation from others but only in community. There is no "God and me" apart from "God and us."

In the end, when we reflect on the mystery of the Trinity we are left with six conclusions, ones that are true but may shed more light on the soul than on the intellect:

1. The mystery of the Trinity is the central mystery of the Christian faith. This mystery we can experience but never completely comprehend, but it means that God is committed to humankind and its history.

2. Jesus' coming into the world as a human being shows that, to use traditional Trinitarian terms, he and the Father are one (see John 10:30).

3. The Holy Spirit is sent by the Father in the name of the Son (John 14:26) and by the Son "from the Father" (John 15:26). Therefore the Spirit is the same God.

4. The Holy Spirit comes from the communion of Father and Son and draws us into communion with one another.

5. When we are baptized "in the name of the Father, and of the Son, and of the Holy Spirit," we begin to share in the divine life of the Trinity here on earth, which leads to full sharing after death.

6. The divine persons, Father, Son, and Holy Spirit, are inseparable in being and in what they do, yet each has a special work aimed at the healing and well-being of all creation.

Questions for Reflection and Discussion

1. Who do you "take with you" in your life, that is, who forms your basic community of life and of faith?

2. When have you felt so close to others that there was very little sense of separateness from them? How might the love you felt, which bridges the gaps between persons, be a little taste of God's presence that we celebrate in the Trinity?

3. Which person of the Trinity is easiest for you to pray to — Father (Creator), Son (Redeemer), or Holy Spirit (Sustainer) — and why?

Faith in Action

How could you tell some of those people whom you "take with you" how important they are in your life, perhaps not only with words? How might you have been different if the people you share your life with would have been different?

Prayer

In a comfortable place take a few minutes to bask in the presence of the three divine Persons whose love for one another overflows into an unconditional love for you, a love that has no end and delights in you just because of who you are. Then slowly read one of the following passages, listening for the fullness of love between the Divine Persons:

- ◆ The baptism of Jesus (Mark 1:9–11).

- ◆ Jesus' prayer for unity (John 17:20–23).

- ◆ Paul's prayer for the Ephesians (Eph. 3:14–19).

11

Mystery of Sin

Sin came into the world through one man, and death came through sin, and so death spread to all because all have sinned.
(ROMANS 5:12)

Folk humorist Garrison Keillor tells a marvelous story about sin. Sometimes we think of sin as a private matter, but this story, told with a light touch, illustrates how mysteriously social sin really is. Garrison Keillor reads a letter from an old friend, Jim, who becomes the narrator of the story.

Jim writes that not long ago he lost his job as a professor at a small-town college. A few weeks later, he was offered a job at the same college as an admissions counselor, which he gladly accepted. Jim's wife and three children were greatly relieved.

Jim's fellow counselor was a beautiful young woman named Barbara. "She and I began to counsel each other," Jim said. "She was lonely in our little town, so I advised her to make friends. She made friends with me. She advised me that I was funny and smart and stylish and handsome. To my family, I seemed to be Daddy the old drudge. But to this quiet woman I was valuable for being myself."

A week after Christmas, Barbara offered to give Jim a ride to a counseling conference in Chicago. "I don't know what she was thinking," Jim said, "but I had adultery in my heart. I thought, 'So this is what adultery is like: simple.'"

Some time later, Jim sat in his front yard, under a spruce tree, and waited for Barbara. Having left his parents for his wife twenty years ago "because she appreciated me and they didn't," now Jim sat in his front yard waiting to join a woman who appreciated him more. "So this is what adultery is like," Jim thought: "it's just horse trading."

Looking up and down the quiet street he lived on, Jim realized that "although I thought my sins could be secret, they would be no more secret than an earthquake. All these houses, and all these families," Jim thought, "my infidelity will somehow shake them. It will pollute the drinking water; it will make noxious gasses come out of the ventilators in the elementary school. . . . If I go to Chicago with this woman who is not my wife, somehow the school patrol will forget to guard an intersection, and someone's child may be injured. A sixth-grade teacher will think, 'What the hell,' and eliminate South America from Geography. Our minister will decide, 'What the hell, I'm not going to give that sermon on the poor.' Somehow my adultery will cause the man in the grocery store to say, 'To hell with the Health Department, this sausage was good yesterday, it certainly can't be any worse today. . . .'

"We depend on each other more than we ever know. . . . "

In Scripture, the word "sin" means "to miss the mark." At its most basic, a sin is any act that breaks or damages our relationships with God, other people, the world, or oneself. We find the classic example in Genesis. In the story of Adam and Eve, after they sin they hide themselves from God (3:8). God banishes them from Eden (3:23–24) because their relationship with their Creator has been broken; a trust is violated.

Our relationships with one another cannot be separated from our relationship with God. Adam and Eve violate their relationship with God, and human relationships are broken as well. Adam blames Eve for the sin (3:12), and later one of their two sons kills the other one (4:8).

Other relationships break down, too. Because of their sin, Adam must now work by "the sweat of [his] face" (3:19), and for Eve the experience of childbirth will be "in pain" (3:16). Humanity's original relationship with creation is now disrupted. When Adam and Eve realize they are naked, they feel ashamed (3:10): complete comfort with the self is also damaged. Both Scripture and human experience witness that none of these relationships can be separated from the others — our relationships with God, other people, self, and creation are one, and to nourish or harm one is to nourish or harm them all.

The Gospels make this unity of relationships clear with regard to our relationships with God and those with whom we live most closely. "You shall love the Lord your God with all your heart, and with all your soul, and with all your mind," Jesus says in Matthew's Gospel. "This is the greatest and first commandment. And a second is like [the Greek word means "the same as"] it: 'You shall love your neighbor as yourself' " (22:37–39).

In the Synoptic Gospels (Matthew, Mark, Luke) the word "sin" appears almost always in a narrative about the *forgiveness* of sins. Jesus hangs around with sinners and invites them to change their ways. The

Johannine tradition portrays the evil of sin more explicitly. To sin is to violate divine laws (1 John 3:4) or engage in works of darkness (1 John 3:9–11). Yet Jesus conquers sin (John 8:46), and he is "the Lamb of God who takes away the sin of the world" (John 1:29).

In the Letter to the Romans, Paul explains that it is not observance of the Mosaic Law — or, by extension, any set of religious rules or laws — that gives victory over sin. Laws only help us to become aware of our sin. In Baptism, we die to sin. Since we are now new creatures in the risen Christ we should act in ways consistent with our new identity. Yet we do sin; we damage our relationships with God, neighbor, the world, and self. Still, "The Spirit helps us in our weakness and makes intercession for us" (Rom. 8:26). "If God is for us, who is against us?" (8:31).

Vatican II declared that although "constituted in righteousness by God, humanity...at the dawn of history abused its freedom" (Pastoral Constitution on the Church in the Modern World, no. 13). Sin — more often small, petty, and mean than spectacularly evil — is woven into the fabric of our lives. But life in Christ is our ultimate victory over sin. "Father, you so loved the world that in the fullness of time you sent your only Son to be our Savior" (Eucharistic Prayer IV).

Traditionally, Catholicism has distinguished between "mortal" and "venial" sins, a distinction meant to evaluate sins according to how serious they are. Indeed, we easily realize that some sins are more serious than others. Murder is more serious than petty theft. Mortal sin — more likely to be a condition of cumulative human corruption than a single isolated act — is so serious that it obliterates the human capacity for love and compassion. If we do think of a single act as a mortal sin, however, it must meet three criteria. It must be a grave matter "committed with full knowledge and deliberate consent" (*Catechism of the Catholic Church,* no. 1857). Since "unintentional ignorance can diminish or even remove" the blame due to such an act, single actions that are mortally sinful are probably rare.

Venial sin coexists with the capacity to love and care for others, but we do so "with a limp," imperfectly. In this sense, we are almost always "venial sinners" because we choose so often to act in selfish or mean-spirited ways. We might say that the human condition is one of venial sin, but God's saving love is stronger if we accept that love in faith, asking forgiveness.

Questions for Reflection and Discussion

1. How would you answer someone who told you that from what they see people are basically evil?

2. How can God love us when we selfishly turn away? Does your experience or observation of parenthood help you answer this?

3. How does accepting your own sinfulness have an impact on how forgiving or judgmental you are of others?

Faith in Action

In the Twelve Steps of Alcoholics Anonymous, step number 5 states, "[We] admitted to God, to ourselves and to another human being the exact nature of our wrongs." This is a valuable process for anyone. Whom may you have hurt that you may need to make amends to?

Whom do you need to forgive who has hurt you? Are you ready to forgive them or are you working on that forgiveness?

Prayer

Take some time to review your day. Become aware of some of the blessings that the day held and some ways in which you did not respond to others at times with the forgiving love that God has for you. After slowly reading one of the following passages, thank God for the forgiveness that God offers you and ask for the ability to forgive others more readily.

+ St. Paul speaks of his experience of sin (Rom. 7:18–8:2).

+ The Lord's Prayer (Matt. 6:9–15).

12

Redemption: Incapable by Ourselves

But now, apart from law, the righteousness of God has been disclosed, and is attested by the law and the prophets, the righteousness of God through faith in Jesus Christ for all who believe. For there is no distinction, since all have sinned and fall short of the glory of God; they are now justified by his grace as a gift, through the redemption that is in Christ Jesus, whom God put forward as a sacrifice of atonement by his blood, effective through faith. He did this to show his righteousness, because in his divine forbearance he had passed over the sins previously committed; it was to prove at the present time that he himself is righteous and that he justifies the one who has faith in Jesus.

(ROMANS 3:21–26)

- "We'll be right back after these messages. Don't go away!"
- "Just how strong is *your* instinct for self-preservation? Of course, you know that exercise and a nutritious, low-fat diet are important. You also know the importance of vitamins. But are you choosing an inexpensive brand that may be high in artificial ingredients and low in potency? Or are you willing to spend a little more for something better? At Solbar, we've earned a reputation for making the highest quality vitamins available. When it comes to your health, there will always be a cheaper, easier way to go. But what do your instincts tell you?"
- "Redeem yourself. Now, you can hold on to your brilliant blonde, your ravishing red or your sensational brunette with Klaritee.... Gorgeous hair is the best revenge."
- "Make your body all you've ever wanted. You feel great on the inside. Now you can look the same on the outside. The Fit Over 40 System."
- "Salvation is here. Save yourself from embarrassment and feel cool all the time with Starburst anti-perspirant deodorant."
- "Welcome back! Our next guest is one of the country's most widely respected psychologists, who will show us how to find more peace

of mind and leave anxiety behind by getting in touch with our inner child. . . . "

'Round and 'round we go, spiritually unbalanced from the influence of mass media advertising, much of it designed to capitalize on our feelings of emptiness or anxiety, much of it promising, in effect, various kinds of redemption. Station wagons and vans offer redemption from the stress, insecurity, and conflict that come with family life. Cosmetics, nutritional aids, weight-loss programs, and exercise equipment offer redemption from growing older. Beer commercials promise to redeem us from loneliness by bringing us friends by the dozens.

Basic to our Christian faith is the conviction that God loves us, and Jesus came to show us that love. Jesus came to begin the reign of God by doing the will of his *Abba* (loving Papa), and he invites us to follow him by saying yes to his path of death and resurrection. When the early Christians wanted a metaphor to convey the liberation they experienced through faith in Christ, they hit upon the metaphor of redemption from slavery. When a slave was freed by his or her master, the slave was said to be "redeemed." So, by his death and resurrection, Jesus "redeemed" or "ransomed" us from slavery to our sinful condition.

This metaphor has its limits, however. Jesus did not redeem us by dying on the cross to satisfy the wrath of an angry God, as if God demanded payment. Rather, "the redemption that is in Christ Jesus" is "a gift" of God (Rom. 3:24).

We are never satisfied. We always want something else, and ultimately that "something else" is God. In St. Augustine's famous words, "you have made us for yourself, and our heart is restless until it rests in you." Endless commercial messages to the contrary, we can never redeem, save, or completely satisfy ourselves. Rather, it is God who "redeems" us as a pure gift. "They remembered that God was their rock, the Most High God their redeemer" (Ps. 78:35).

Redemption is not a casual act of God, something of minor importance. "You were bought with a price," St. Paul says (1 Cor. 7:23). The life and death of Jesus in some way, mysteriously, served God's intention to redeem humankind from slavery to sin, nothing less. The life, death, and resurrection of Jesus showed God's love given without cost or obligation. Jesus offered a share in God's life that we can have by saying yes, by accepting Jesus' offer of friendship, by believing in him and by joining with him in the total giving of ourselves to God and His will. When we do this we join Jesus in the establishment of the kingdom, or reign, of God in this world.

The early Church's faith in the redemption brought about by Jesus' death came from its faith in his resurrection, not from an exclusive focus on his death on the cross. Jesus' death was seen as redemptive *in the context of his resurrection.* As Jesus says in the Fourth Gospel: "Very truly, I tell you, unless a grain of wheat falls into the earth and dies, it remains just a single grain; but if it dies, it bears much fruit. Those who love their life lose it, and those who hate their life in this world will keep it for eternal life" (John 12:24–25).

The mystery at the heart of our redemption is the cross and resurrection of Jesus. Through this paschal mystery, God's salvation was accomplished "once for all" (Heb. 9:26). There is also a connection between the redemption accomplished by Christ and his relationship with the people of God, the Church. For the redemption Christ brought about is the source of the authority he exercises over the Church, an authority to which all in the Church are subject, regardless of vocation or position of authority.

Christ continues the task of redemption in a special way through the eucharistic liturgy or Mass. "Through the liturgy Christ, our redeemer and high priest, continues the work of our redemption in, with, and through his church" (*Catechism of the Catholic Church,* no. 1069). No wonder, then, that regular participation in the Eucharist is so important to the disciples of Jesus.

No matter how much light we may shed on the nature of redemption, however, eventually we come face to face with a tremendous mystery. Here "mystery" does not mean an unsolved riddle, but a reality of faith that only the heart, not the intellect, can fully grasp.

Questions for Reflection and Discussion

1. Where do you see appeals for salvation in the advertising around you, e.g., "Calgon, take me away," or "You deserve a break today?"

2. Which are most enticing for you?

Faith in Action

Make a list of the fears, worries, and sins you are aware of that you would like to be redeemed from. Then make a list of all the ways that you try to redeem yourself from them, e.g., talking to friends about your concerns, hobbies, music, or other leisure activities to get your mind off your concerns. By each item in the second list make a note about the limitations of that source of personal salvation, compared to Jesus. For example, friends don't always understand me or can't always be there for me like Jesus can.

Prayer

Keeping in mind a sense of how God saves us from our fears, confusion, and the chaos of our lives, spend a few minutes giving God all those things that can get in the way of real trust in God. After doing that, read one of the following passages slowly, giving thanks as you do for the ways that God is present and saving you from what otherwise might feel overwhelming:

- "If God is for us, who is against us?" (Rom. 8:31–39).
- "The LORD is my shepherd" (Ps. 23:1–6).

13

God's Kingdom/Reign

Now after John was arrested, Jesus came to Galilee, proclaiming the good news of God, and saying, "The time is fulfilled, and the kingdom of God has come near; repent, and believe in the good news." (MARK 1:14–15)

"I have good news, and I have bad news," Margo said. "You want the good news first or the bad news first?" Margo's right eyebrow lifted as she glanced sideways at her husband, Jake, who sat in the passenger seat of the car.

"Whatever," Jake said. "Just please don't keep me in suspense."

"Okay," Margo said. "The bad news is that I lost my job. The good news is that I was offered a new job immediately after losing my old job." The midday traffic was heavy, and Margo kept her eyes on the road, lifting her vision to the rear view mirror now and then.

"You lost your job? That's terrible. What happened?"

"The company was bought out by another company, and they decided to eliminate the entire department I was in charge of. Here's the notice I got." Without taking her eyes from the road, she felt for an envelope on the seat beside her and handed it to Jake.

"Atkinson and Company has been purchased by the Big Corporation," Jake read aloud, "and the Big Corporation has determined that the Public Relations Department of Atkinson and Company will be closed in thirty days. All the responsibilities of this department will be assumed by the corporate headquarters of Big Corporation, in Houston, Texas. We regret the inconvenience this will cause you. You will be contacted by the Personnel Department with further details."

"Very personal and all," Margo said sarcastically.

"No kidding.... But you said you were offered a new job right away? What is it?"

"The Big Corporation just lost the head of its Public Relations Department, in Houston. They offered me the job...."

"Houston? This is the *good* news? Margo, it's a long way from Springfield to Houston. I have my job here, the kids are just into a new school year, ... and the cat just had kittens! We can't move now. In fact, I'm not sure I want to move at all. I think I'm getting a headache." Jake closed his eyes and massaged his temples with his fingertips.

Margo stomped on the brakes, screeching to a stop behind the car in front of them. "Jake," she said, "we both know we can't live on your income alone. We both have to work, and new P.R. jobs are non-existent around here. You have your own business, you work out of our home, and you can do what you do just about anyplace. We wouldn't have to move until the end of the year, and we could do it so the kids can switch schools over the Christmas vacation. The Big Corporation will buy our house here and pay our moving expenses, so that won't be a problem, and we can buy a new house in Houston. When you think about it, this job offer, and all that goes with it, is a God-send. It could be so much worse."

Jake said nothing for a minute, then heaved a deep sigh. "I suppose you're right. I just have a hard time with the whole idea of moving, of being a stranger in a strange land."

"I love you," Margo said.

"I love you, too," Jake said. "Watch out for that car on your left."

Many people find the "kingdom" or "reign" of God a difficult idea to understand, but as this story illustrates, it is not a "religious" concept in a "churchy" sense. Rather, the reign of God is a reality that goes beyond time, space, and institutions. The kingdom of God is a reality characterized by love, peace, truth, and justice that slips in small ways into the fabric of our ordinary, everyday lives, often unnoticed, sometimes when we least expect it. The reign of God exists where God is; it's as simple as that. God's reign brings newness and change, and these are often not easy to accept, but God's kingdom also brings the grace we need to take the risks required by faith.

Jesus talks about "the kingdom of God" frequently in the Gospels, and he uses examples from everyday "non-religious" situations to explain it. In fact, Scripture scholars tell us that "the kingdom of God" was the heart of Jesus' message and preaching.

Jesus teaches his disciples to "strive first for the kingdom of God" (Matt. 6:33). He compares the kingdom/reign of God to scattering seed on the ground (Mark 4:26), to a mustard seed (Mark 4:31), and to yeast in bread (Luke 13:21). Jesus insists that "it is easier for a camel to go through the eye of a needle than for someone who is rich to enter the kingdom of God" (Luke 18:25), and St. Paul declares that "the kingdom of God is . . . righteousness and peace and joy in the Holy Spirit" (Rom. 14:17).

"Kingdom/reign of God," like many religious terms, is a metaphor for a reality the human mind cannot fully grasp. It refers to a condition, or state of affairs, affecting all of creation, when God will be "all in all" (1 Cor. 15:28). The reign of God, according to the New Testament, is already in our midst but not yet fully accomplished. We experience the beginnings of the kingdom of God in many ways, wherever life, peace, goodness, truth, justice, joy, and beauty are present. Whenever people truly love one another, the reign of God erupts in human history. Whenever human institutions make human needs a priority and people take risks to live according to the Gospel, the kingdom/reign of God breaks into human history.

Obviously, the reign of God is not yet completely present. We live in the tension between the "already" and the "not yet." We are "looking forward to [Jesus'] coming in glory" (Eucharistic Prayer IV), yet the final coming of the kingdom of God cannot be predicted. "Keep awake," Jesus says, "...for you know neither the day nor the hour" (Matt. 25:13).

Neither, by our own efforts, can we build the kingdom of God. We can prepare for the reign of God and, by cooperating with God's self-gift, or grace, we can allow it to come into our lives and into our world.

Earlier generations sometimes thought of the Church itself as the kingdom of God, so that the object was for the world to catch up with the Church. Such a perspective fails to take seriously the imperfections of any institution filled with imperfect human beings. The Church is in the service of the reign of God, and in the Church we benefit from God's self-gift, or grace. The Church is both a sign of the kingdom of God and a means for its emergence in human history, but we may not identify the Church with the kingdom of God as if they are one and the same.

The "kingdom/reign of God" is a scriptural metaphor that refers, most basically, to God's transforming presence in each human heart, in communities and groups, in the world and all of creation, bringing all to birth, healing, reconciling, establishing peace and joy. The mystery of the "kingdom/reign" of God is simultaneously the process that leads to all this and the goal toward which the process is moving. Thus, the "kingdom/reign" of God is in our midst but not yet fully accomplished. For that we await the final consummation of all things in Christ.

Questions for Reflection and Discussion

1. If someone asked you to explain the reign of God, what would you say?

2. How does your idea of an ideal world intersect with the reign or kingdom of God as Jesus talked about it, e.g., the poor are especially welcome, and the care and service of others is primary?

3. If we think of the kingdom of God as a set of values and statements about what's really important in life, what would the values of the "kingdom" of our culture look like, e.g., efficiency, greed and materialism?

4. Therefore, what do you see as the most difficult part of the reign of God for our culture to accept?

Faith in Action

Name one specific way in which you feel called to live each of the following qualities of the reign of God so that it is beginning already: truth, forgiveness, service, care of the poor, peace, justice, hope.

Prayer

God, who loves us with a complete and unconditional love, has in effect told us through Jesus, "I have a dream." That dream we call the "reign" or "kingdom" of God. Listen carefully to that dream as you read one of the following passages and then close with the Our Father, where you pledge yourself to live this dream when you say, "Thy kingdom come":

- The Beatitudes (Matt. 5:2–10).
- The Last Judgment (Matt. 25:31–46).

14

Redemption: Begun through Baptism

Do you not know that all of us who have been baptized into Christ Jesus were baptized into his death? Therefore we have been buried with him by baptism into death, so that, just as Christ was raised from the dead by the glory of the Father, so we too might walk in newness of life. (ROMANS 6:3–4)

It was an old, old story. As a college student, Camilla was a "social drinker." At parties she often drank heavily, but no more than her drinking buddies. Waking up the next morning, her head throbbing with a hangover, she would mutter to herself, "This is crazy. I've really got to stop drinking so much at parties." But the next party would come along, and Camilla would be three sheets to the wind. Again. And the next morning her head would pound. Again.

After she married, Camilla drank when she and her husband, Scott, went out for the evening. If Scott had two drinks, she would have four. Sometimes when she had been drinking, Camilla was very funny, and people laughed at her affectionately. "Good old Camilla, she's always good for a laugh." On her lunch break at work, Camilla often joined a few of her fellow employees at a nearby pub, and she would drink a couple of beers with her sandwich. To "unwind," Camilla often stopped after work with a friend for a drink. Or three or four.

Camilla took a leave of absence from her job after her first child was born, a boy. Two weeks after the birth, she felt frustrated being home all day with the baby. Scott left for work each weekday at 7:30 and returned at 6:00, and Camilla began to drink. One day Scott came home and found Camilla passed out on the living room floor, the baby in his crib crying and neglected. Scott changed the baby's diaper, fed him a bottle of formula, rocked him to sleep, and then went back to the living room and dragged Camilla onto the couch where he left her for the night.

The next day, after Camilla had a hot shower and ate a bite of breakfast, Scott confronted her with what he now knew was a serious problem. Camilla cried and agreed to go to a treatment center. "I feel so ashamed," she said. Camilla's mother offered to come and care for the baby during the day while Scott was at work. The morning Camilla left, her mother hugged her and wept.

Camilla's first few days in treatment were agonizing, and a few times she thought she might die. Her body screamed for alcohol. Camilla cried and used language she never used. At the end of the first week, she woke up that morning feeling like she had been run over by a large truck. At the same time, she felt better. "It was like I had died," she recalled later, "and now I was, very gradually, coming back to life. I remember lying in bed staring at a crack in the ceiling and thinking, 'Hm, interesting crack.'"

A counselor at the treatment center told Camilla, "It's just the beginning, and there's a lot of hard work ahead. In fact, you — and your Higher Power — are going to be working at it for the rest of your life. It's a lifelong process, but you have taken the first step, and the sun is shining."

A technical definition of "magic" is "to attempt to control supernatural forces with verbal formulas and ritual actions." Baptism is *not* magic. We do not perform the ritual of water, words, and anointing

with holy oil to force God to "save" or forgive the person being baptized. Rather, like all the sacraments, Baptism is a visible sign of an
invisible reality. The community of faith baptizes as a way to initi-
ate and welcome new members into its midst. Since the beginning of
the Church, through Baptism people have been "reborn" and become
members of the Church and new creatures in Christ.

Neither is Baptism "magic" in the sense that simply going through
the ritual automatically guarantees something. In the case of infant
baptism, for example, the community presumes that the parents of
the child will raise him or her in a Christian home environment and
teach the child what it means to be a follower of Christ. In this
sense, Baptism liberates the child from bondage to "a fallen human
nature [that is] tainted by original sin." It frees the child "from the
power of darkness" and brings him or her "into the realm of the
freedom of the children of God" (*Catechism of the Catholic Church,*
no. 1250).

The "original sin" from which Baptism frees us is perhaps best
understood not as a personal sin committed by a historical first man
and first woman (Adam and Eve). Rather, the point of the Adam and
Eve narrative in Genesis — and the concept of "original sin" — is to acknowledge and explain the mystery of evil in human existence and in
the world and its impact on us. Sin was with human beings from the
beginning. In this sense, Baptism liberates us from bondage to original sin. In the case of adult baptism, the sacrament liberates the new
Christian from all personal sin as well.

Baptism is a "mystical" experience. That is, it relates to a spiritual
reality that is not apparent to the senses. Not only that, but when a
person is baptized "Christ himself is baptizing" (Vatican II, Constitution on the Sacred Liturgy, no. 7). St. Paul talks about Baptism as
a kind of death. To be baptized, he says, is to die and be raised to
new life: "When you were buried with [Christ] in baptism, you were
also raised with him through faith in the power of God, who raised
him from the dead" (Col. 2:12). The death we experience in Baptism is a sharing in the death of Christ so that we might share in his
resurrection, too, and "walk in newness of life" (Rom. 6:4).

Baptism does not accomplish redemption once and for all. Rather,
it is the beginning of a lifelong pilgrimage of faith, hope, and love. To
the biblical fundamentalist query, "Are you saved?" Catholics reply,
"Yes and no." Baptism is the *beginning* of our redemption, a process
whereby we "grow into salvation" (1 Pet. 2:2).

We are all sinners — people who choose to damage and break our relationships with God, other people, the earth, and ourselves. But through Baptism we share in the death and resurrection of Christ, which means that we share in the gift of God's own "divine nature" (2 Pet. 1:4). Through Baptism, all along the way we "have eternal life" (John 3:15).

Baptism — along with Confirmation and the Eucharist — forms the foundation of a Christian life. "Holy Baptism is the basis of the whole Christian life, the gateway to life in the Spirit . . . and the door which gives access to the other sacraments. Through Baptism we are freed from sin and reborn as sons [and daughters] of God; we become members of Christ, are incorporated into the church and made sharers in her mission" (*Catechism of the Catholic Church,* no. 1213).

Every Christian vocation or way of life is a way to live out one's baptismal commitment. Thus, those called to marriage are called to be disciples of Christ *by being married* and, typically, *by being parents.* Those called to priesthood or religious life are called to follow Christ *by being priests or religious.* Those with a vocation to a single life are to be disciples of Christ *by being single.* In all cases, Baptism radically conditions the ways we live in the world, making of all ways of life ways dedicated to love of God and neighbor in the service of the kingdom/reign of God.

Questions for Reflection and Discussion

1. Think of some of your own personal experiences of death and rebirth — perhaps a disappointment, a loss of a job or friendship, or the death of a loved one.

2. Where did you find new life then? Where do you find new life now in your life?

3. How could you explain what Baptism means in your life?

Faith in Action

Who do you know who is struggling with the passage from a kind of death to a new life? How can you help support them in that struggle? As you grow in your own life, can you ask for the grace of your baptism to help you "from death to new life"?

Prayer

As one who shares new life in Jesus through Baptism you are called to
a new way of living, one that begins the reign of God now. Take some
time to reflect on how you can respond to the love God offers you. As
you read one of the following passages, listen for where God may be
calling you to further grow and change in your life:

- John the Baptist teaches the implications of Baptism (Luke 3:7–14).

- Paul teaches the consequences of sharing a new life in Christ (Col.
  3:9–17).

15

Jesus: Promised through the Prophets, the Jewish People

*Long ago God spoke to our ancestors in many and various ways
by the prophets, but in these last days he has spoken to us by
a Son, whom he appointed heir of all things, through whom he
also created the worlds. He is the reflection of God's glory and
the exact imprint of God's very being, and he sustains all things
by his powerful word.* (HEBREWS 1:1–3A)

"In the darkest days of July 1944," wrote Michael Nicholson and
David Winner in *Raoul Wallenberg* (Morehouse Publishing, 1990),
"an obscure Swedish diplomat abandoned the comfort and safety of
home for an impossible rescue mission in one of the most dangerous
places on earth."

The man was Raoul Wallenberg — a non-Jew, or Gentile — and his
destination was Hungary, where the Nazis planned to murder all of the
country's 750,000 Jewish men, women, and children.

United States officials asked Sweden, the most influential of the neutral countries left in Europe, for help. Sweden was still on speaking terms with the Nazi government, and Swedish leaders agreed to do what they could to save Jews.

Raoul Wallenberg gladly traveled to Budapest. His government gave him money to provide "safe houses" and food for thousands of Jews, plus money to bribe Nazi officials. It was Wallenberg versus Adolf Eichmann, the mastermind behind the Nazi plan to murder all Jews in Europe. Both knew the war was winding down and that the Nazis would lose. "For Wallenberg," Nicholson and Winner said, "the question was: how many Jews could he rescue before the capital was liberated?"

Wallenberg designed a document that looked like a Swedish passport, but it was actually a marvelous fake. Wallenberg's *Schutz-pass* (protection pass) had no legal status at all. But because it looked so genuine the Nazis accepted Jews who held it as Swedish citizens.

Wallenberg's staff — including many of Budapest's most outstanding community and business leaders, some of whom were Jews — produced *Schutz-passes* at a terrific rate. Raoul got permission from the Hungarian Foreign Ministry to issue fifteen hundred *Schutz-passes,* then by bribery, clever threats, and cajoling the number increased to five thousand and Wallenberg actually gave away more than three times that many. Within weeks many thousands were saved by these fake documents.

Finally, when he couldn't get any more *Schutz-passes* printed, Wallenberg gave away a simplified document. Even though it was printed on poor quality paper, often it worked to protect the holder. Other foreign embassies in Budapest, seeing Wallenberg's success, issued their own phony passes.

In the final days of the war, Eichmann decided to kill all the inhabitants of Budapest's Jewish ghetto. When Wallenberg heard this news, he sent a message to the Nazi general who had been ordered to carry out Eichmann's directive. "If you do not stop this now," Wallenberg wrote, "I can guarantee you will be hanged as a war criminal." The general thought it over, and then backed down.

When the Soviets entered Budapest they saw Raoul Wallenberg as dangerous because he was on friendly terms with the United States and had American money to spend. On January 17, 1945, as he made plans to help Jews after the war, Soviet authorities arrested Wallenberg, and he was never heard from again.

"Raoul Wallenberg...fought evil because it was there," according to Danny Smith in *Wallenberg: Lost Hero* (Templegate Publishers,

1987). "There was no other choice. He risked his life because the Jews, 'his people,' God's people, had to be saved."

Jesus was born and raised in Judaism. In the Gospels, especially John, people address Jesus as "Rabbi." For example: "When Jesus turned and saw them following, he said to them, 'What are you looking for?' They said to him, 'Rabbi' (which translated means Teacher), 'where are you staying?'" (John 1:38).

The New Testament as a whole understands Jesus as the fulfillment of Jewish messianic prophecies. Of the Gospels, Matthew especially emphasizes this tradition of fulfillment. "But all this has taken place, so that the scriptures of the prophets may be fulfilled" (Matt. 26:56a).

"But now," St. Paul writes, "...the righteousness of God has been disclosed, and is attested by the law and the prophets, the righteousness of God through faith in Jesus Christ for all who believe" (Rom. 3:21–22a).

Catholicism believes that the prophets of ancient Israel foretold the coming of the Messiah, and we believe that Jesus is that Messiah. "Again and again...through the prophets [God] nurtured the hope of salvation" (Eucharistic Prayer IV, proposed ICEL translation). This should not, however, lead us to think of Judaism as a second-class religion, and by no means may it be used to justify anti-Semitic prejudice. "Although the church is the new people of God, the Jews should not be represented as rejected by God or accursed, as if that follows from holy scripture" (Vatican II, Declaration on the Relation of the Church to Non-Christian Religions, no. 4).

Throughout the New Testament, it is true, we find certain types of anti-Jewish polemic. For example, the New Testament frequently echoes the belief that Judaism has been superseded or rendered irrelevant by Christianity. Historically, this happened — it reflects the early Christian community's struggle to differentiate itself from the Judaism of the time. Today, however, it is both possible and necessary for Christians to reject any such belief. We can do this, writes Norman A. Beck, in *Mature Christianity in the 21st Century* (Crossroad Publishing Co., rev. ed., 1994), "without any damage to our Christianity or to our Christian theology." Indeed: "By doing this, we shall enhance our religion and our theology."

Jesus was an observant Jew ("He went to the synagogue on the sabbath day, as was his custom" [Luke 4:16]); thus Christianity's roots are in Judaism. Jesus is the fulfillment of the Mosaic Law and the prophets (see Matt. 5:17), but Judaism remains a valid religion in its own right. Indeed, as Pope John Paul II said, the Jewish people are, in truth, our elder brothers and sisters.

In fact, we must insist that in a way the Jewish people are part of the people of God. The Church "cannot forget that through that people with whom God out of his ineffable mercy deigned to enter into an ancient covenant, it received the revelation of the old Testament and is nourished from the root of the good olive tree, onto which the branches of the wild olive tree of the gentiles have been grafted. For the church believes that Christ our peace reconciled Jews and gentiles and made us both one in himself through the cross" (Vatican II, Declaration on the Relation of the Church to Non-Christian Religions, no. 4).

Questions for Reflection and Discussion

1. From the Jewish tradition Christianity received many important gifts, such as an awareness of God as greater than all our concepts and ideas, a strong reverence for God and God's name, a need to live out one's faith in actions (the Law) and not just in theory and words, the importance of justice especially toward the poor, and the family as the most basic place where faith is learned and expressed. Out of this list — or others — what qualities especially strike you and why, and which if any do you think Catholicism needs to relearn?

2. If you've had any contact with those of the Jewish faith, which of these strengths did you notice?

Faith in Action

Name some people you know, or know of, who have been prophetic like Raoul Wallenberg. For each, name at least one important quality that they possess and at least one way in which you can live out that quality in *your* life. For example, Dorothy Day stayed very faithful to daily prayer and Mass while helping to feed and house hungry street people and demonstrate for causes of justice. How can you be faithful to daily prayer and listen for the ways that that may call you to serve others around you?

Prayer

In the season of Advent we especially remember Israel's longing for a Messiah and our longing for Jesus' coming. As you read one of the following, join your own personal longing for Emmanuel (God-with-us) to that of the people of God:

- Zechariah's song at the birth of John the Baptist (Luke 1:69–79, the Benedictus).

- The "O" antiphons are read during the last seven days of Advent (December 17–24) and are a beautiful expression of the Church's longing for Jesus' coming:

    O Wisdom, that proceeds from the mouth of the Most High, reaching from end to end mightily, and sweetly disposing all things: come and teach us the way of prudence.

    O Adonai, and Leader of the House of Israel, who appeared to Moses in the burning bush, and gave him the Law of Sinai: come and redeem us by your outstretched arm.

    O Root of Jesse, who stands as the emblem of the people, before whom kings shall not open their lips; to whom the Gentiles shall pray: come and deliver us; delay no more.

    O Key of David, and Scepter of the House of Israel; who opens and no one shuts: come and lead the captive from the prison, and the one who sits in the shadow of darkness and in the shadow of death.

    O Orient, Splendor of the eternal Light, and Sun of Justice: come and enlighten those who sit in darkness and in the shadow of death.

    O King of the Gentiles, and their very desire, the Cornerstone that makes both one: come and save humanity, whom you have made out of the dust of the earth.

    O Emmanuel, our king and lawgiver, the expectation of all the nations, and the Savior: come and save us, O Lord our God.

16

Jesus: God Become Human

And the Word became flesh and lived among us, and we have seen his glory, the glory as of a father's only son, full of grace and truth. (JOHN 1:14)

One of the most delightful and spiritual novels of our time is *Wonderful Fool,* by Shusaku Endo, a Japanese Roman Catholic writer. In *Wonderful Fool,* an awkward, "horsefaced," but enormously likable young Frenchman, Gaston Bonaparte, arrives in Tokyo. Gaston's hosts are Takamori and Tomoe, an adult brother and sister who live with their mother, Shizu, in a typical middle-class Tokyo neighborhood.

Gaston — whom everyone calls "Gas" — is a Christ figure who can't resist reaching out to help victims, the poor, and the downtrodden in Japanese society. He adopts a stray dog, names it "Napoleon *san,*" and loves it like a brother. Gaston saves the life of a good-hearted prostitute caught stealing a client's money in a flea-bag hotel and befriends an old hermit and fortune teller.

Gaston is kidnapped as a hostage by a cold-blooded killer who, ironically, has the same name as the author: Endo. When Gaston learns that Endo is very ill with tuberculosis, he refuses to leave him, even when he has a chance to escape. Endo is traveling to a distant town to find a man named Kobayashi, and kill him in revenge for the death of Endo's brother years before. When Endo finds Kobayashi he leads him and Gaston to a place called Big Swamp, where they clash in the rain and the mud, and Endo accidentally drops his pistol. When Gaston tries to prevent the two men from fighting, Kobayashi beats Gaston in the head with a shovel. Endo retrieves his gun and shouts, "Now I'll be revenged for my brother's death."

Raising himself up from the muddy swamp he has fallen in, blood gushing from wounds in his head, Gaston cries out in French, *"Non. Non. Non."* He shakes his head violently and with all the strength in him makes a gesture of appeal for clemency. "I...ask you." Then Gaston falls back into the water.

Endo aims the gun at Kobayashi, but Gaston's words echo in his ears insistently, and Endo falls unconscious into the water next to Gaston. When Kobayashi raises the heavy shovel over his head to kill

Endo, Gaston raises himself once more from the swamp and cries, "Stop!" And this strange monster of a man stretches his huge hands over the fallen body of his friend in a protective gesture.

"Shovel upraised, Kobayashi stared at Gaston in astonishment. This time chills of fright ran up and down his spine. He dropped the shovel and scurried with rat-like speed toward the road."

Three days later, from a hospital bed Endo relates the story to Takamori and Tomoe, who have come looking for Gaston. "He told how Gaston had taken Kobayashi's blows on himself in order to save him, and how finally, seriously injured, he had collapsed in the shallows of the swamp." No trace of Gaston could be found.

"Then [Endo] remembered that some time after he lost consciousness he had felt the driving fog wet on his cheeks and had opened his eyes slightly. One corner of the sky was a cloudless blue and he saw a lone egret, flapping snow-white wings, heading in that direction."

On the train ride back to Tokyo, as Takamori gazes at the mountain peaks surrounded by clouds in the distance, he imagines that he sees Gaston slowly climbing the mountains, just below the highest peak. "He was waving his hat at him, a smile on his horseface...."

"Takamori *san,* I'm going."

"Where are you going, Gas?"

"Anywhere, everywhere...wherever there are people."

Back home, Takamori and Tomoe find a tattered notebook in Gaston's duffel bag. Only a few words are written in the notebook: "I've failed three times to pass the entrance examination to the Mission Seminary. So I won't be able to become a missionary priest. Still I must go to Japan."

From stories such as this one we may learn to take the humanity of Jesus more seriously, for it was in and through his humanity that Jesus' divinity was revealed. In a very real sense, if we don't take Jesus' humanity seriously we won't be able to experience the meaning of his divinity.

Jesus was fully, wonderfully human. He came into human existence through nine months in his mother's womb, was "born of a woman" (Gal. 4:4) in the usual manner, sucked milk from his mother's breasts, and had a human infancy and childhood. His diapers (or whatever the first-century Palestinian equivalent may have been) had to be changed, and later he learned to control his bladder and his bowel movements. Mary and Joseph had to teach him his table manners and his prayers.

If Jesus was as human as we are, then he felt all that we feel and knew all that we know. He knew hunger and thirst, loneliness, joy, sexual feelings, frustration, anger, love, laughter, and friendship. John's Gospel clearly implies all this when it says: "And the Word became flesh and lived among us" (John 1:14). Anyone who is embarrassed or scandalized by this fails to understand who Jesus was and is.

Jesus' mission included showing us how a human life should be lived. It's as if God said, in Jesus, "Here is what a human life should look like — love of God and neighbor is the meaning of it all. At the same time, it is not always easy to do this. In fact, if you do it right you can get killed for it. But don't be anxious about that, because my love conquers even death."

When we say that Jesus was also fully divine we mean that in him God was made present in a personal, visible form. As the Letter to the Hebrews puts it:

> Long ago God spoke to our ancestors in many and various ways by the prophets, but in these last days he has spoken to us by a Son, whom he appointed heir of all things, through whom he also created the worlds. He is the reflection of God's glory and the exact imprint of God's very being, and he sustains all things by his powerful word. When he had made purification for sins, he sat down at the right hand of the Majesty on high, having become as much superior to angels as the name he has inherited is more excellent than theirs. (1:1–4).

Jesus is "the exact imprint of God's very being." No one is likely to do better than this in describing what it means to say that Jesus was fully divine. With the apostle Thomas we say to Jesus, "My Lord and my God" (John 20:28). Ultimately, the union of full humanity and full divinity in Jesus is beyond the grasp of the human intellect. But is this so remarkable? Any human being is a mystery, so why should we expect to be able to understand the one Scripture calls "Son of God" (e.g., Mark 1:1) — a title applied to Jesus no less than sixty-three times in the New Testament?

The perfect union of humanity and divinity in Jesus raises almost endless questions, but one of the main ones is: Was Jesus conscious of his divine nature, his identity as the Son of God? The best response to this question, from a scriptural perspective is: yes and no. Many New Testament passages suggest that Jesus had unlimited knowledge about himself (e.g., Matt. 9:20–22 and John 6:5–6). On the other hand, many other passages suggest just the opposite (e.g., Mark 5:30–33 and Luke 2:46). It is true that Jesus spoke often of God as his *Abba,* or loving Papa. Still, there seems to be no absolute proof, in Mark's Gospel, for example, that Jesus understood himself to be a unique Son of God. Jesus says, "No one is good but God alone" (Mark 10:18). It is also true that in John's Gospel Jesus clearly claims to be the Son of God, but we need to keep in mind that this Gospel was written in order to make exactly this point.

In the end, we are left with the understanding of the Church that is based on the life, death, and resurrection of Jesus, plus some two thousand years of loving communion with the risen Christ in the power of the Holy Spirit in the midst of God's people, the Church:

> Jesus Christ possesses two natures, one divine and the other human, not confused, but united in the one person of God's Son. Christ, being true God and true man, has a human intellect and will, perfectly attuned and subject to his divine intellect and divine will, which he has in common with the Father and the Holy Spirit. The Incarnation is therefore the mystery of the wonderful union of the divine and human natures in the one person of the Word. (*Catechism of the Catholic Church,* nos. 481–83)

Questions for Reflection and Discussion

1. How do you see Gaston as a Christ figure?
2. Do you know anyone who is a Christ figure for you, one who helps make God more real in the world?

Faith in Action

How are *you* called to be a Christ figure to those around you, to love more than may be "sensible"? Make a list of who those people are and how you can be Christ's love for them.

Prayer

A preschooler once had an excellent insight into Jesus' Incarnation, his becoming human for us. She said with delight, "I get it! Jesus is God's Show-and-Tell!" In thanksgiving for such a wonderful "Show-and-Tell," recall some of the ways in which Jesus loved tenderly, truthfully, and with an authority and a healing touch that seemed very new to those who heard and saw him. Then read the following:

- Jesus in the Synagogue: "The Spirit of the Lord is upon me" (Luke 4:16–21).
- A prayer of St. Bernard of Clairvaux:

    Jesus, hope of the penitent,
    how kind you are to those who ask,
    how good you are to those who seek.
    What must you be to those who find?

17

The Mission of Jesus: Teaching, Healing, Forgiving, Serving

Jesus went throughout Galilee, teaching in their synagogues and proclaiming the good news of the kingdom and curing every disease and every sickness among the people. (MATTHEW 4:23)

Martha and Ben were in their late thirties when they married. A couple of years later, Martha gave birth to a daughter they named Ann. Ann was a remarkably beautiful baby, and as she grew she became such a strikingly beautiful toddler that strangers would remark about her appearance. When Ann was eighteen months old, she began to act in rather odd ways. She would jump up at unpredictable times and scamper about uttering strange, guttural sounds, not at all like a little girl just learning to talk. She also seemed sluggish and didn't seem to take enough nourishment.

"Ann has an incurable disease called Gallo's disease," the medical specialist said. "She is going to need a lot of love for the next few years or so. She will have special needs, but love is what life is for, after all, and when Ann is gone you'll both say that you're glad you had her with you."

When Ann was ten years old, she died. Ben and Martha wrote a eulogy that Ben read at the graveside service following the funeral Mass. "Ann was a great blessing to us," he said, "but Ann's disease was no blessing. The gradual destruction of our beautiful little girl was a terrible thing to watch. She experienced pain and anguish in her last months that only heavy doses of drugs could relieve, and the look in her eyes when we could do nothing more was heartbreaking. Ann's cross was our cross, too."

Ben said that Ann was a sign of how delightful God is, but she was not a sign of God's all-powerfulness. "The God we knew in Ann was a kind and happy God who suffered with us the sorrow and pain of Ann's disease."

Ann's life was a sad mystery, Ben continued, but it was also a beautiful life. "For Ann taught us things, and she brought healing, and she helped us learn what forgiveness means. Ann taught us that people and relationships are what matter most. In spite of her disease, she healed us with her smiles, and when our patience wore thin and we spoke harsh words to her she would forgive us in a second and get right back to living the only life she had.

"Faith, hope, love, and joy — these were Ann's gifts to us, and the greatest of these was joy. Instinctively, she knew that our human destiny is ecstasy. For as long as she could, she met each day with joy and wonder. In this sense, Ann was a genius in spite of her mental retardation."

Ben called this "the Gospel according to Ann." He said: "This is a Gospel this tired old world needs so much."

In the Gospels, we find four unique presentations of the meaning of Jesus the Christ. But in each Gospel we find a Jesus who teaches, who goes to Jerusalem, who brings healing, forgiveness, and service to others. By doing this he brings the beginnings of the kingdom of God, where everyone and everything is whole, where nothing and no one is broken, and where there is complete unity of people with one another, with God, with themselves, and with creation.

In the Gospels when Jesus teaches, the people are astounded and astonished, because he teaches "with authority" (Mark 1:22). He heals Simon's mother-in-law (Mark 1:31) and many others as well. He forgives sins and heals as proof of his power to forgive (Matt. 9:6).

Jesus teaches not as philosophers teach, with abstractions, but as one with a message on how to live in harmony with God, neighbor, self, and the earth. His message addresses people "where they live." "To the poor he proclaimed the good news of salvation, to prisoners, freedom, and to those in sorrow, joy" (Eucharistic Prayer IV).

You will have peace of heart, Jesus teaches in the Beatitudes (Matt. 5:3–11), if you depend on God alone; turn to God for comfort when you are sorrowful and distressed; act with humility rather than arrogance; desire to know and follow God's will above all things; show unbounded mercy to others; have no room in your heart for duplicity, deceit, or acts of darkness; and strive to work for peace using peaceful means. Jesus adds that God blesses those who are treated badly by others for trying to live such a life.

When Jesus heals, teaches, and continues on to Jerusalem to his destiny with cross and resurrection, he does so as a manifestation of God's presence — the kingdom/reign of God — in human history even here and now, and he directs his disciples to do likewise. "Then Jesus called the twelve together and gave them power and authority over all demons and to cure diseases, and he sent them out to proclaim the kingdom of God and to heal" (Luke 9:1–2).

Jesus forgives sins, but he insists that we must forgive one another if we hope to have God forgive us. "Whenever you stand praying, forgive, if you have anything against anyone; so that your Father in heaven may also forgive you your trespasses" (Mark 11:25).

"As the Father has sent me," Jesus says in Matthew's Gospel, "even so I send you" (10:40). Thus, the teaching, healing, service, and forgiveness of Jesus exemplify what we are to do, as well — namely, bring the teaching, healing, service, and forgiveness of God to the world. In a nutshell, that is our mission as followers of Jesus. The shape this will take differs from one era to another, of course, and from person to person.

The people of God, the Church, is a missionary Church. Down through history we remain in communion with our origins in Jesus and in the early Christian communities. The heart of Jesus' message was the coming of the kingdom, or reign, of God as both a dream and a reality open to all, including the poor, those afflicted with the most terrible diseases, social outcasts, and sinners of all kinds.

Therefore, in all the forms of ministry in the Church the fundamental aim is to proclaim, prepare the way for, and cultivate the kingdom, or reign, of God. Since "the kingdom of God is among you" (Luke 17:21), we do not merely prepare for a future reality. Rather, we strive to bring about conditions that allow the present reality of the kingdom of God to exist here and now in particular circumstances. Although the fullness of the reign of God will exist only at the end of time, even now we begin to experience it and can make way for it — in the world and in the Church — through our efforts on its behalf.

Questions for Reflection and Discussion

1. If Jesus stood before you right now, what would he teach you that you need to learn? How would he heal you? How would he challenge you to serve others? What would he forgive you for?

2. If you had to describe the core of Jesus' message in a few sentences, what would you say?

3. How is forgiveness different from forgetting or excusing?

Faith in Action

Keep in mind that the reason Jesus was such an effective teacher — but also such a dangerous one as far as the Jewish officials were concerned — was that he *lived* what he spoke about, and his example taught even more loudly and more effectively than his words. What are the daily opportunities *you* have to teach, heal, and forgive as Jesus did? Make a plan for what you will actually do this week.

Prayer

As we listen to Jesus teach, offer the gift of himself, forgive, and heal in the Gospels, it is important to remember that the healing was more than a physical reality; today we might call it "holistic." Also we need to remember that Jesus' words are directed to *us* as we read the Word of God, that the healing and forgiveness are also offered to us. Listen to Jesus' words and actions as you put yourself in his presence:

- True disciples: "You will know them by their fruits" (Matt. 7:20–29).
- Cure of the paralytic (Matt. 9:2–8).

18

The Paschal Mystery

For if we have been united with him in a death like his, we will certainly be united with him in a resurrection like his. We know that our old self was crucified with him so that the body of sin might be destroyed, and we might no longer be enslaved to sin. For whoever has died is freed from sin. But if we have died with Christ, we believe that we will also live with him. (ROMANS 6:5–8)

Martin was an ordinary enough young man. A third-generation Mexican-American, he grew up in a standard issue suburban home in western Washington state.

Martin earned good grades in high school and attended a Catholic university, where he majored in electrical engineering with a minor in religious studies. After graduation in the early 1970s, jobs were scarce, so Martin interviewed with any company who would talk to him. He received a job offer from a large corporation that had government contracts to help build nuclear submarines. Martin's academic background in religious studies made him sensitive, on the level of his faith, to the idea of working for such a company, but jobs were so few and far between that he accepted the offer.

When Martin reported for work, he was assigned to design guidance systems for missiles meant to carry nuclear warheads. He learned of the devastating destruction just one missile could cause. Each morning he went to work, and the pay was excellent. Martin bought a small house, he bought a new car, and he filled his house with nice things — furniture, appliances, stereo equipment, and the like.

But Martin was never comfortable with what he was doing. His conscience bothered him. He earned far more money than he ever had before, and as long as he didn't think too much about the purpose of his work, he enjoyed his job. He attended Mass on Sundays, joined a young adults group in his parish, and helped out with the youth group's activities. Then one Sunday, about a year after Martin began work on his new job, something happened. The pastor of Martin's parish gave a homily on the connection between the peace Christ came to give and the experience of the cross in everyday Christian spirituality.

The priest quoted from *Pacem in Terris,* an encyclical issued in 1963 by the late Pope John XXIII: "Justice, right reason and humanity... urgently demand that the arms race should cease; that the stockpiles which exist in various countries should be reduced equally and simultaneously by the parties concerned; that nuclear weapons should be banned."

Martin sat in his pew stock-still, touched to the core of his being. The pastor continued quoting Pope John's encyclical: "Human beings, in the intimacy of their own consciences, should so live and act in their temporal lives as to create a synthesis between scientific, technical and professional elements on the one hand, and spiritual values on the other."

The pastor commented: "To take such words to heart and act on them will require one to embrace the cross and to make the sacrifices necessary to follow Christ in the way of truth and peace."

If the pastor had stepped down from the lectern with a wooden mallet in his hand and given Martin a whack on the head with it, he could not have had more of an impact than he did with his homily. Martin went home a shaken man. He knew that he had to leave his job; he was helping to make instruments of terrible destruction. Yet there would be a cost.

Martin was not married and had no family to support, so that was a relief. He could simply quit. Still, he regretted giving up the fat check he received each month, and what if his house didn't sell right away? He had saved a little money, but what if he didn't find another job soon? The more he thought about it, the more anxious Martin became. In the end, however, he screwed up his courage, left his high-paying job, sold his house, moved to another city, and found other work. "It was worth it," he said. "The minute I left that job I slept better at night, and everything worked out eventually. That was one of the few times when I felt like I really lived my faith."

The paschal mystery — Jesus' death and resurrection — is at the very heart of Christian existence and Christian spirituality, because the heart of what it means to be Christian is our participation in that mystery: "He gave himself up to death, and by rising from the dead he destroyed death and restored life" (Eucharistic Prayer IV).

In Baptism we dedicate ourselves to love God and other people above all else, regardless of the specific shape our life may take — the work we do, whether we are married or single, and so forth. Our faith frees us to make of our work a way to love God and neighbor. Our faith frees us to make being married or single a way to love God and neighbor. Of course, love is not always as pleasant an experience as the popular culture makes it seem. As Dostoevsky wrote in *The Brothers Karamazov,* "Active love is a harsh and fearful thing compared to love in dreams." Indeed, "active love is labor and perseverance." Authentic love is "to will the good of the other" (St. Thomas Aquinas), and often this requires that, like the grain of wheat, we die to self in order to "bear much fruit" (John 12:24). "The good of the other" may demand that we sacrifice our own good.

Unpopular though it may be in an era enthralled with the idea of self-fulfillment, "Those who love their life lose it, and those who hate their life in this world will keep it for eternal life" (John 12:25). To embrace the paschal mystery means to say no to self-centeredness on one level in order to rejoice on another level.

Husband and wife, in the midst of a conflict, will need to give up defensiveness in order to make peace. "To have a successful marriage," a wise marriage counselor said, "often you must want to be married more than you want to be right." Friends, if their friendship is to survive, will need to overlook the ways they irritate each other unintentionally. Such constitute the small but vital ways we participate in the paschal mystery, the death and resurrection of Christ.

"The Paschal mystery of Christ's cross and Resurrection stands at the center of the good news that the apostles, and the Church following them, are to proclaim to the world. God's saving plan was accomplished 'once for all' [Heb. 9:26] by the redemptive death of his Son Jesus Christ" (*Catechism of the Catholic Church,* no. 571).

It is important to keep in mind that when we speak of the mystery of Jesus' resurrection we refer to an event that really happened and was historically verified. At the same time, apparently there were no eyewitnesses to the resurrection, so we don't know what an eyewitness would have seen. For certain we are not talking about a merely resuscitated corpse but a body transformed in ways beyond the grasp of the human mind and imagination.

Therefore, our own experience of resurrection, even here and even now, transforms us in real but mysterious ways as well. Our participation in the paschal mystery, through Baptism and Holy Eucharist and through daily life in Christ, is an experience that the heart can accept when the intellect reaches its limits.

Questions for Reflection and Discussion

1. Name as many ways as you can that death and rebirth happen in daily life. Some examples are: sleeping and waking, learning something new and "dying" to your former ignorance, saying goodbye and hello, watching the seasons change, going from messy to clean, illness, moving, etc.

2. What would you say to someone who said that they could not understand why Jesus had to suffer and die before he rose?

Faith in Action

How does an awareness of the paschal mystery, Jesus' death and resurrection, help you cope with disappointment, sickness, or loss? How could it, or has it, helped you comfort others in their suffering?

Prayer

St. Paul reminds the Christians at Corinth and us that "if Christ has not been raised, then...your faith has been in vain" (1 Cor. 15:14). Although we live in a society that wants to avoid death and pretend that it's not there, we know that the Christian life says that in the death and suffering that comes with any real love is the beginning of *real* life that can't die. In light of that hope, read one of the following:

- ◆ "God's foolishness is wiser than human wisdom" (1 Cor. 1:18–25).

- ◆ This prayer, attributed to St. Francis of Assisi, is a favorite of many and describes the paschal mystery in our lives:

  Lord, make me an instrument of your peace.
  Where there is hatred, let me sow love;
  where there is injury, pardon;
  where there is discord, unity;
  where there is doubt, faith;
  where there is despair, hope;
  where there is darkness, light;
  where there is sadness, joy.
  O Divine Master,
  grant that I may not so much seek
  to be consoled as to console;
  to be understood as to understand; to be loved as to love.

For it is in giving that we receive;
it is in pardoning that we are pardoned;
and it is in dying that we are born to eternal life. Amen.

19

The Sending of the Spirit

When the day of Pentecost had come, they were all together in one place. And suddenly from heaven there came a sound like the rush of a violent wind, and it filled the entire house where they were sitting. Divided tongues, as of fire, appeared among them, and a tongue rested on each of them. All of them were filled with the Holy Spirit and began to speak in other languages, as the Spirit gave them ability.

Now there were devout Jews from every nation under heaven living in Jerusalem. And at this sound the crowd gathered and was bewildered, because each one heard them speaking in the native language of each....

All were amazed and perplexed, saying to one another, "What does this mean?" But others sneered and said, "They are filled with new wine." (ACTS 2:1–6, 12–13)

David James Duncan's novel *The Brothers K* tells the story of the Chance family. The "K" in the title is the one baseball scorekeepers put in the record book when a pitcher strikes out a batter. The four Chance boys must attend an Adventist summer camp. Kincaid Chance, narrator of the story, explains that a young minister, Brother Beal, is in charge, and a softball game is in progress. Brother Beal, who was a star on his college baseball team, has been bunting so the kids won't have to chase the ball so far. Then along comes sweet Nancy Durrel, Brother Beal's assistant, to whom the kids must recite their Bible verses once they have them memorized. Brother Beal smiles a cocky grin at Nancy, and she gives him a big beautiful smile in return. Brother Beal steps to the plate and says, "This one's for *you*, Nancy."

Kincaid is pitching, and he just can't stand it. "I decided to wipe the grin right off his face." He throws Brother Beal a fast, overhand pitch, which is illegal in Adventist summer camp softball. "Winding up fast to increase the surprise, I blazed a perfect strike in there — and Beal's grin *did* vanish. The problem was, so did the softball."

The ball flew "so far beyond anything we had considered 'outfield' that it was like something out of the Book of Revelation had happened."

As Brother Beal reached second base, the kids noticed something odd about his base-running:

> He wasn't running bases at all. He was *dancing* them.... There stood our big pious weenie of a Sabbath School teacher on second base, eyes closed, body motatin', zonked face impossibly unembarrassed as his hands mojoed a solo on a sax no more visible than the Holy Ghost. Then he stepped off the bag, swivel-hipped his way toward third, and the second reaction set in: kids started to laugh.... They couldn't help it. Beal's neck was working like a chicken's; and he was sliding his big sneakered feet sometimes forward, sometimes back, and sometimes into such quick, drunken, graceful tangles that you weren't sure whether he'd fall on his face or take off flying.

Up to this point, Kincaid was astonished, puzzled, and mystified. What finally won him over was Brother Beal's butt.

> What finally made it impossible for me not to like the man was how right there on the Adventist basepaths, right in front of eighty or ninety of the kind of pious adult spectators who spent their every Sabbath if not their entire lives trying to forget the existence of things like butts, Beal's buns were trying to light a fire by friction inside his jeans; they were gyrating like a washing machine with its load off balance.

Once Brother Beal's older audience got over being shocked they began to be amused, fascinated, then grateful toward "this writhing reminder that yes, buns did exist, and yes, every one of us owned not one but two of the things, and yes, like the God who created them in His image, they did indeed move in mysterious ways."

— ❖ —

In the New Testament, the Holy Spirit is all over the place but impossible to pin down. In Matthew (1:18) and Luke (1:35), the Holy

Spirit is responsible for the conception of Jesus. In Matthew, John the Baptist declares that Jesus will baptize "with the Holy Spirit and fire" (3:11). Baptized by John, the Holy Spirit descends upon Jesus (3:16). Jesus insists that when the disciples need words to speak, the Spirit of the Father will "speak through" them (10:20). "Blasphemy against the Spirit" is the only unforgivable sin (12:31), and the disciples are to baptize "in the name of the Father and of the Son and of the Holy Spirit" (28:19).

In Luke, especially, the Holy Spirit is a source of joy (e.g., 10:21), and in the Acts of the Apostles the Holy Spirit gives the disciples the courage to proclaim the Gospel and causes them to behave like they are on a toot (2:1–13). In John's Gospel, Jesus says that "the Holy Spirit, whom the Father will send in my name, will teach you everything, and remind you of all that I have said to you" (14:26). For St. Paul, "the kingdom of God is ... righteousness and peace and joy in the Holy Spirit" (Rom. 14:17). The Letter to the Hebrews explains that God distributes "gifts of the Holy Spirit ... according to his will" (2:4).

Traditionally, the gifts of the Holy Spirit are: wisdom, understanding, counsel, fortitude, knowledge, piety, and fear of the Lord. Traditionally, the "fruits," or results, of these gifts are: charity, joy, peace, patience, benignity (being kindly or gracious), goodness, long-suffering, mildness, faith, modesty, continency (self-restraint), and chastity.

"And that we might live no longer for ourselves but for him, [Jesus] sent the Holy Spirit from you, Father, as his first gift to those who believe, to complete his work on earth and bring us the fullness of grace" (Eucharistic Prayer IV).

The constant inclination is to try to build a fence around the Holy Spirit: this far and no farther. The Holy Spirit does this and this, and that's all. Trouble is, history shows that the Holy Spirit not infrequently has other ideas. The Holy Spirit delivers a pope like John XXIII, for example, who upset a good many apple carts, caused the whole world to love him, and launched the Second Vatican Council, after which the Church will never be the same.

Vatican II taught that the Holy Spirit is busy indeed — as the source of biblical inspiration, guiding the bishops, and inspiring all who live a Christian life, among other things. Christ is now "at work" in people's hearts "through the strength of his Spirit" (Pastoral Constitution on the Church in the Modern World, no. 38). With many non-Catholics "there is a true bond in the holy Spirit" (Dogmatic Constitution on the Church, no. 15).

Count on the Holy Spirit to both hold things together and throw a wrench into the works. On the one hand, the Holy Spirit gives people courage and inspiration. On the other hand, the Holy Spirit moves people to behave in wild, crazy, and wonderful ways. When you least expect it....

Questions for Reflection and Discussion

1. What are some ways that you see that Spirit at work around you, in others, in yourself, in the Church, stirring things up and keeping life from being stale?

2. How would you explain who and what the Holy Spirit is and how it has been a part of your life?

Faith in Action

How could you be more aware of how the Spirit is a part of your days and how could you ask for the Holy Spirit's help and presence? One of the Spirit's functions is to inspire. When have you felt inspired to do or say the right thing?

Prayer

St. Paul reminds us in the Letter to the Romans, "the Spirit helps us in our weakness; for we do not know how to pray as we ought, but that very Spirit intercedes with sighs too deep for words. And God, who searches the heart, knows what is the mind of the Spirit, because the Spirit intercedes for [us] according to the will of God" (8:26–27). Put yourself in God's presence and give thanks for the Spirit in your life and in your prayer.

20

The Church: One, Holy, Catholic, and Apostolic

After his suffering [Jesus] presented himself alive to [his disciples] by many convincing proofs, appearing to them during forty days and speaking about the kingdom of God. While staying with them, he ordered them not to leave Jerusalem, but to wait there for the promise of the Father. "This," he said, "is what you have heard from me; for John baptized with water, but you will be baptized with the Holy Spirit not many days from now."

So when they had come together, they asked him, "Lord, is this the time when you will restore the kingdom to Israel?" He replied, "It is not for you to know the times or periods that the Father has set by his own authority. But you will receive power when the Holy Spirit has come upon you; and you will be my witnesses in Jerusalem, in all Judea and Samaria, and to the ends of the earth." (ACTS 1:3–8)

Trese and Tom, and Alice and Tim were a little nervous, but they were happy too. This was a big day. Both couples were the proud parents of identical twins born just a few weeks ago, and today the babies would be baptized. Trese and Tom had boys named Justin and Ryan. Alice and Tim had girls, Jenny and Mia. They sat attentively in the front pew on the left side of the church, surrounded by diaper bags, other baby paraphernalia, and beaming grandparents, aunts, uncles, cousins, and godparents. Each father and mother held a baby, and for the time being the babies were all peaceful and quiet.

When it came time for the homily, Father John stood at the lectern. "Today we will baptize two sets of identical twins at the same time," the young priest said with a grin. "This is a first for me, and I think it's probably a first for everyone here this morning!" The church filled with joyful smiles and quiet laughter.

His gaze fixed on the proud parents, Father John spoke directly to them. "Tim and Alice, Tom and Trese, you bring your babies to the assembly of faith this morning, before the table of the Lord, and on their behalf you seek the sacrament of Baptism. You want Jenny and

Mia, Ryan and Justin, to be received into Christ's Church. In a few minutes, I will ask you if you promise to bring your children up in the Catholic faith, and I will ask the entire community of faith gathered here this morning if they will support you in that commitment. I know that you are determined to do this because you want your children to receive the blessings that come with growing up Catholic."

Father John paused for a moment, then continued. "Here this morning, we will baptize these tiny new girls and boys, and we will do so with joy. We will welcome them into the Church. But I want to emphasize to you parents — and godparents, too — that the first and most important church these babies are baptized into is what we call the 'domestic church' or 'church of the home.' So much depends on the experiences these new little people will have in the day-to-day life of your family. This is where they will have their most basic and most formative spiritual experiences."

The priest paused again for emphasis. "We, your parish community, will support you with our prayers and with whatever practical support we can give. We will be here as your wider faith community and the place where the sacraments of the Church are celebrated. But you parents, as the 'pastors' of your church in the home, are now called by Christ to make of your family a little faith community, a little community of faith, hope, and love, a little community of prayer and service. You are to be what the Church is, but in ways appropriate to family life. If you do your best at this, these little children will grow up knowing what authentic faith is and what it means to belong to the Church."

The Second Vatican Council declared that the Church is a mystery (Dogmatic Constitution on the Church, chap. 1), which means that the Church manifests God's love in ways we can never fully understand. The council also said that in virtue of its relationship with Christ the Church is "a kind of sacrament or sign of intimate union with God, and of the unity of all [humankind]," as well as "an instrument for the achievement of such union and unity" (no. 1). The Church is meant to be a sign that there can be unity among people, and the Church is to work for that unity.

After the council elaborated on the Church as mystery and sacrament, it turned immediately to the words of St. Cyprian, in the fifth century. Cyprian called "the Church *a people* made one with the unity of the Father, the Son, and the Holy Spirit" (emphasis added). Drawing heavily on biblical tradition, Vatican II devoted an entire chapter of its Dogmatic Constitution on the Church to a discussion of the Church as "the new People of God" (no. 9).

The council declared that in the Church laity and ordained clergy have much in common, thus breaking down artificial barriers. Although "they differ in essence and not simply in degree, [they] are nevertheless interrelated: each in its own particular way shares in the one priesthood of Christ" (no. 10). In fact, the faithful "by virtue of their royal priesthood, join in the offering of the eucharist, and they exercise their priesthood in receiving the sacraments, in prayer and thanksgiving, through the witness of a holy life, by self-denial and by active charity" (no. 10).

We, the Church, are called to be for the world what Christ is for the world, teaching, serving, healing, and forgiving. In particular, the council said, married couples are a special sign of the loving intimacy between Christ and his Church (no. 11). From marriage comes the family, the council continued, "to carry on his people through the centuries" (no. 11). In other words, we depend upon families for our continued existence as the Church. Therefore, the nourishment and support of family life in its various forms — two-parent families, single-parent families, childless couples, and single and widowed persons in their extended family networks — should be basic to the life of the Church.

This is so especially in parishes, in particular during an era when there are so many pressures on and challenges to the stability of families. The family, not the parish, is the most basic unit of the Church, "the domestic church" (no. 11); families "form the very substance of parish life" (John Paul II, September 13, 1987, during a visit to the United States).

The Nicene Creed states: "We believe in one holy catholic and apostolic church." These traditional "marks of the Church" are not only gifts given by God to the Church, they are also tasks which we, the Church, must constantly strive to bring about as God's people.

We believe in a Church that is "one." This means that we strive for Christian unity, a unity that even among Catholics need not require uniformity but may be unity-in-diversity. It may be possible to have unity among various Christian churches without requiring all to have exactly the same traditions, customs, structures, forms of worship, or way of life and thought.

We believe in a Church that is "holy." By this we do not mean that the Church has attained a human or moral perfection. Rather, we mean that the Church is an effective means of human holiness and wholeness. The sacraments nourish holiness, for example, even if the human beings who celebrate the sacraments are far from perfect. We believe in a Church that is both holy and sinful. We are imperfect, and we are the Church, so the Church is imperfect, always in need of repentance and reform.

We believe in a Church that is "catholic." Note that is "catholic" with a lower case "c," meaning "universal" or "all-inclusive." To believe in such a Church is to believe that anything good, true, or beautiful is welcome in this Church that we are. Our doors are wide open to all people, and as God's people we go into the world to bring the message of God's love to all people.

We believe in a Church that is "apostolic," which means that we trace our origins directly back to the apostles of Jesus. Also, the word "apostle" means "one who is sent." So we, the Church, are sent into the world to bring the Gospel, the good news of God's love, to all people, first of all by the ordinary ways we live our everyday lives. This is what it means to be the Church.

Questions for Reflection and Discussion

1. When have you experienced the Church to be the people of God?

2. What is your experience of the family — in its various forms — as the church of the home?

3. How is your faith built upon what you experienced growing up?

4. What other important individuals (saints, heroes, people of faith) have influenced your own faith?

Faith in Action

How do you experience yourself as being an active part of the Church as the people of God, instead of the Church being "them" or the institution? What does it mean for you to be called to help the Church be one, holy, catholic, and apostolic? Mention at least two specific implications for your life.

Prayer

Whenever we pray, we pray as part of the Church and we pray for the Church, even if we don't remember to do so explicitly. The Church tells us that even the most isolated hermit prays as part of the whole body of Christ. Mindful of that, choose one of the following readings or prayers about the Church:

- "Go therefore and make disciples of all nations" (Matt. 28:16–20).
- Paul to the Church in Rome: "one body with many members" (Rom. 12:4–12).
- *Prayer for Christian Unity:*

  Lord Jesus Christ, at your Last Supper
  you prayed to the Father that all should be one.
  Send your Holy Spirit upon all who bear your name
  and seek to serve you.
  Strengthen our faith in you
  and lead us to love one another in humility.
  May we who have been reborn in one baptism
  be united in one faith under one Shepherd. Amen.

Part Three

Celebrating the Faith: The Sacraments

Kathleen Hughes, R.S.C.J.,
and Barbara Quinn, R.S.C.J.

21

The Sacramental Principle: God's Initiative

In the beginning was the Word, and the Word was with God, and the Word was God. He was in the beginning with God. All things came into being through him, and without him not one thing came into being. What has come into being in him was life, and the life was the light of all people. The light shines in the darkness, and the darkness did not overcome it.

There was a man sent from God, whose name was John. He came as a witness to testify to the light, so that all might believe through him. He himself was not the light, but he came to testify to the light. The true light, which enlightens everyone, was coming into the world.

He was in the world, and the world came into being through him; yet the world did not know him. He came to what was his own, and his own people did not accept him. But to all who received him, who believed in his name, he gave power to become children of God, who were born, not of blood or of the will of the flesh or of the will of man, but of God.

And the Word became flesh and lived among us, and we have seen his glory, the glory as of a father's only son, full of grace and truth. (John testified to him and cried out, "This was he of whom I said, 'He who comes after me ranks ahead of me because he was before me.'") From his fullness we have all received, grace upon grace. The law indeed was given through Moses; grace and truth came through Jesus Christ. No one has ever seen God. It is God the only Son, who is close to the Father's heart, who has made him known. (JOHN 1:1–18)

Some years ago a friend wrote about her growing-up years. Her letter provides a moving illustration of the sacramental principle. These are her words:

"My father died of cancer in 1947 leaving five young children and a widow consumed with grief. But there is no question in my mind that my father was present, especially to my mother, throughout my growing up. His memory drove her days and consoled her nights. His nearness filled our home. Even inconsequential things like his preferences for food continued to dictate what would be served at dinner. I never tasted spaghetti until I left home fifteen years after his death because my father disliked tomato sauce.

"While all of our experience seemed somehow colored by his proximity, there were certain symbols which were more charged with his closeness to us: his picture on the piano, my parents' bedroom where he spent his last days and where we gathered — uncomprehending — to pray when he died, my brother's uncanny resemblance to my father, mother's wedding band which, especially in the days just after his death, she touched as she wept silently.

"As an adult I was predisposed to understand the power of sacraments because I had grown up surrounded by them, by words, people, objects, even anniversaries, which were revelatory of a reality beyond themselves, which made the invisible visible, which disclosed the continuing presence and activity of my father in our lives."

At the very heart of the Catholic Christian experience is the principle of sacramentality. That means that we view people, events, the world around us, and the whole of the created universe as vehicles for the communication of the divine. We recognize all visible created reality as a potential mediation of the invisible God. We believe that God is all in all and that God, the creator of all, is disclosed in every creature, great and small.

The whole of reality is a "divine milieu," as Pierre Teilhard de Chardin named the cosmos; Gerard Manley Hopkins discovered that earth was "charged with the grandeur of God"; the Psalmist used this hymn to proclaim God's revelation:

> The heavens are telling the glory of God
>   and the firmament proclaims his handiwork.
> Day to day pours forth speech,
>   and night to night declares knowledge.
> There is no speech nor are there words;
>   their voice is not heard;
> yet their voice goes out through all the earth,
> and their words to the end of the world.
>   (Ps. 19:1–4)

Truly through the wonders of creation God has spoken to us in many and various ways.

But it was not enough. God remained invisible. John begins his Gospel with that proclamation: No one has ever seen God. Only the Son, closest to the Father's heart, has made God visible.

What a mystery that the Word took flesh! Was it the longing of God to be in relationship with us that necessitated the Incarnation? Was it God's desire to be known and loved by those made in the divine image that demanded that the true light come into the world? Was it God's yearning to shower us with grace and truth that led to God's perfect self-revelation in Jesus?

It was not until the Word of God leapt down to earth that we encountered God-with-us in Jesus Christ. Jesus said to the community of disciples gathered around him that those who looked upon him saw the one who sent him. They became aware, however dimly, that Jesus witnessed to a new way to relate to God — not distant or other but as close to us as a tender and loving parent — as he told stories that disclosed more and more of the God he called *Abba*.

After Jesus' death and rising the community continued to experience his presence in the power of the Spirit. They *knew* with their whole beings that Jesus was alive and that he continued to invite them into intimate divine-human relationship; his very presence continued to transform their human experience and give it new meaning.

Just as Jesus is the perfect expression of God, the sacrament of God with us, so his followers recognized that to the extent that they lived in his love and as they allowed the Spirit to form them into a body of believers, their lives, too, were sacrament of Christ. This rag-tag band, formed by the Spirit into Church, continues Jesus' saving and reconciling presence in the world.

As members of Christ's body and baptized into his death we, too, are revelation and disclosure of the divine. We are the continuing embodied mediation of Jesus in our world. The whole of our lives and all of our activity have been transformed by Jesus' death and rising. Everything that is most human in us is also most holy. Our experiences of life and death, of birth and maturation, of sickness of body and spirit, of love and friendship and forgiveness — all of it is sacrament for all of it is human and thus all of it is holy.

Only against this backdrop can we understand what it means to talk about the Church's sacraments, for sacraments are the means by which our encounter with God in Christ is brought to public visible expression both for God's glory and our salvation.

The definition of a sacrament that has been traditional for Catholic Christians of the last several generations is found in the old Baltimore catechism: "a sacrament is an outward sign, instituted by Christ, to give grace." That definition, while technically adequate, must be expanded and enriched by contemporary phenomenological and liturgical insights developed during and since the Second Vatican Council.

A more adequate and nuanced definition of sacrament is the following: A sacrament is an event, at decisive moments in the life of the community, that celebrates in symbolic language the experience of encounter with God in Christ dead and risen, in the life of the community and its members. The celebration of sacrament brings to expression and deepens faith-filled human response to God's initiative and commits us to live what, through the event, has been proclaimed in word and ritual action.

Perhaps taking the same definition in slow-motion might make it less cryptic. A sacrament is an *event,* not a thing or an object but a vital action of the Church, at *decisive moments* in the life of the community and its members, moments that are at the very heart of what it means to be most fully human. Birth, passage to adulthood, marriage, physical suffering and serious illness, starting over again after failure, and so on are grace-filled moments, times of divine-human encounter, because in each of these moments Christ reaches to the deepest level of human life, transforming it in the power of the Spirit and directing it toward God.

Sacraments are *celebrations,* which means that they give public, ritual expression to our human religious experience through patterned activity and *symbolic language* (words, gestures, objects, music, space, and time). Moreover, sacraments effect the *encounter* of the community with God in Christ dead and risen. All sacraments are celebrations of the paschal mystery of Jesus' life, death, and rising, but particular sacraments highlight now one facet of that mystery, now another, as they are being experienced and embraced *in the life of the community and its members.*

The celebration of a sacrament does two things: it brings to public ritual *expression* what is already happening and the very expression *deepens* that experience. A couple, for example, are ready for the sacrament of marriage when they have come to the point of total self-giving love to the other in Christ. And the celebration of that experience in sacrament deepens, enlarges, expands their capacity to love one another in Christ.

All sacraments are human *responses to God's initiative,* something we proclaim beautifully about the Eucharist in one of our prefaces: "Our desire to thank you is itself your gift. Our prayer of thanksgiving adds nothing to your glory but helps us grow in your love" (Preface IV Weekdays). All is gift. Ultimately, sacraments are celebrations of *conversion* that *commit* us to a sacramental way of life. With every "Amen" we promise to live what we have just proclaimed.

In the following chapters, many of the elements of this definition will be further developed. First we will turn to the role of liturgical prayer as the community's response to God's self-disclosure in Jesus Christ and God's initiative in our lives.

Questions for Reflection and Discussion

1. In these pages a definition of sacrament has been offered. Do you find it satisfying? What is *your* definition of sacrament?

2. Have you ever had an experience of someone's presence through the mediation of another person, event, or thing? What was it like?

3. When and how is the Church a sacrament? Does that make any difference to the way you want to live your life?

4. What can we learn about sacraments from everyday rituals?

5. What are some obstacles in this culture and age that make the celebration of sacraments more challenging?

Faith in Action

An original eucharistic prayer prepared a few years ago by the International Commission on English in the Liturgy includes these lines: "Blessed are you, strong and faithful God. All your works, the height and the depth, echo the silent music of your praise." As you reflect on these lines, try to become a little more attentive to the silent music that fills your world. Ask God to make you part of the chorus.

Prayer

Read over the suggested passage from the Epistle to the Hebrews slowly and prayerfully, allowing the Spirit to teach you more about Jesus Christ as the perfect sacrament of God.

 • "The exact imprint of God's very being" (Heb. 1:1–4).

22

Liturgical Prayer: Human Response

When you are praying, do not heap up empty phrases as the Gentiles do; for they think that they will be heard because of their many words. Do not be like them, for your Father knows what you need before you ask him. Pray then in this way:

> *Our Father in heaven*
> *hallowed be your name.*
> *Your kingdom come.*
> *Your will be done,*
> *on earth as it is in heaven.*
> *Give us this day our daily bread.*
> *And forgive us our debts,*
> *as we also have forgiven our debtors.*
> *And do not bring us to the time of trial,*
> *but rescue us from the evil one.*

For if you forgive others their trespasses, your heavenly Father will also forgive you; but if you do not forgive others, neither will your Father forgive your trespasses. (MATTHEW 6:7–15)

Though many may conjure up images of quiet, solitary prayer away from the fray when we think of worship, this passage from Matthew's Gospel highlights a remarkable choice that God has made: each life is intimately bound up with the lives of others. No selfish seeking for bread is allowed here. Jesus spoke only in terms of "our." And the requirement for the forgiveness of debts has everything to do with how one forgives others. Likewise, one's life with God is intrinsically linked to one's relationships in the human family. It was as though Jesus were saying, "Practice what you pray for or else I cannot hear you. If you will not forgive your brothers and sisters, how can I forgive you?" This basic prayer to our God was the way Jesus taught his disciples — and us — to pray. Clearly Jesus' prayer reflects God's desire that we become sisters and brothers in one family.

It is no wonder that Cyprian of Carthage, one of the great wisdom figures of the early Church, wrote a beautiful commentary on this central Christian prayer, the Our Father, as foundational for the unity of the Church. In *De Oratione* he states: "Above all, the Teacher of Peace and the Master of Unity did not want prayer to be viewed as something individualistic and self-centered" (22). No, Cyprian notes: "For us, prayer is public and communal; and when we pray, we do so, not for one, but for the whole People because we, the whole People, are one" (23).

This shift from an "I" to a "we" is no easy transition. Our life in the United States is so programmed to focus on the individual that the merit of caring for the common good often needs to be experienced before it can be believed.

The film *Shadowlands* poignantly illustrates this reality. C. S. Lewis, or "Jack," as he preferred to be called, had all the answers to life's most important questions. And people came from far and wide to hear him. Oh, his answers were "right," all right, but he stood strangely distant from the realities about which he spoke. Until he met Joy, that is. His love for her opened him to feelings beyond his imaginings. His pain, as he watched cancer ravage Joy's body, was almost more than he could bear. In an idyllic moment when the consciousness of Joy's disease receded temporarily, his desire to retreat into his old world of control by standing above the reality of what was happening was quickly rebuked by the wife he loved so. "We've got to talk about this now, Jack, if you're going to be with me when the time comes. Don't you see? The pain then is part of the joy now. That's the deal." Yes, he learned through the pain of experience what love was. He could no longer stand on the outside looking in at reality. No, he had thrown in his lot with another. Now he "knew" joy and pain in a very different way. There were no magic solutions for the anguish of grief that he suffered at Joy's death. But he could say sincerely, "The pain now is part of the joy later."

Entering into the life of another or others is not for the faint of heart. The demands are great, as are the rewards. This is the life to which we are called as Christians. This life of relationships is what the God of the Christians has revealed in the Trinity. We worship a community of persons who work together for us that we might have life to the full. But that life has been won at no small price. Our creator God continually offers us life and leaves us free to accept it or not. Jesus, our Redeemer, suffered our pain and offered his life that all of us might live in freedom and in love. The Holy Spirit of God labors now to teach us to understand the heart of God and to draw us into the very life of this community of persons.

It is at the liturgy, the public work of the Church, that we meet this community of persons in a preeminent way. It is at the liturgy that the Spirit of God gathers us unmistakably as sisters and brothers of one God, a holy community, and teaches us to live in the same manner.

Everyone who has lived in a family or in a community of any kind knows the tensions that are inherent in sharing life in common. Everyone has a different view of the way things should be — and (at least secretly) knows that his or her way is best! Our common life of prayer in the liturgy is no different. The tensions over the how, what, when, who, where, and even why of our celebrations are endless even though our desires to pray as a community of faith are just as real.

How can we reconcile such differences in our preferences and needs for prayer? Reflection on several key areas of tension in our public prayer might help us to negotiate a way of coming together in liturgy that leads us to its core value — meeting in worship the community of persons we call the Trinity and responding there to their invitation to share and live out their life in our own time and place.

Mary is overheard saying, "It's the only time during the week that I can be quiet and get my thoughts together. I don't want to participate. All this music and singing distracts me from praying!" And right next to her in the pew is Harry, who stews with frustration over the seemingly lethargic, uninterested presence of this group of people gathered for this Eucharist which was, he believed, the source and summit of the Church's liturgical life and needed to be celebrated as such. He had just finished a training class for the new liturgy committee in his parish, and he was sold on the value of the principle in Vatican II's document on the liturgy: "Full and active participation by all the people is the aim to be considered above all else" (Constitution on the Sacred Liturgy, no. 14). What to do?

The starting point for change is most often the need to help people understand why another way is worthy of consideration. Much education still needs to be done in parishes and in other faith communities about the nature of our sacramental prayer. Habit is on the side of those who prefer a more private, non-participatory celebration of liturgical prayer where the action of the priest is central and above all other actions. But the insights of Vatican II about the central role of the community in sacramental celebration need to be understood, strengthened, and practiced for the community to grasp the wisdom of this development in the Church's self-understanding. Moreover, a rhythm needs to be found that honors both the vocal, participatory prayer of the assembly and the silent, reflective moments of communal prayer. Finally, communal prayer never substitutes for those moments of personal communion with God in one's own private prayer. The balance between the two is key. Personal prayer corrects liturgical prayer from becoming simply a performance; communal worship challenges one's prayer against becoming self-absorbed and self-serving.

Ralph finds that he is becoming more and more disgruntled as he comes to Church every Sunday. "Why does everything keep changing?" he laments. "Every week there is a procession, or a new song, or occasionally even a baptism in the middle of Mass. We never did things this way before!" Sally, on the other hand, finds that she comes to church less and less frequently. "It's so boring! The prayers seem 'canned'; they're always the same. Why can't there be more variety?"

Understanding and balance are the antidotes for such common complaints. Repetition and variation in prayer each have their values. However, those values need to be understood and integrated in a balanced way in liturgical celebrations if our celebrations are going to reflect the genuine life of the community.

Ritual is not unique to Church. Ask someone how she or he celebrated birthdays while growing up and some of the most elaborate of rituals will be revealed: "Oh, I was always awakened to the tune of Happy Birthday. Then, I found a birthday card at my breakfast place. We always had presents at dinner. And, of course, I got to choose the menu. The best treat though was that I never had to do any chores on that day."

Ritual has a way of facilitating communication within a group. Everyone knows the drill, so to speak, and this routine actually frees each one to enter into the heart of the celebration — showering the guest of honor with attention and love. The repetition of gesture and symbol, word and song, from year to year or week to week, subtly recalls feasts of past years and conjures up memories of a people. And so it is with the liturgy of the Church. It is here particularly that the universality of the Church shines. The sacramental prayer of the Church that was celebrated centuries ago is in essence the same celebration that one can pray today in Brazil or Berlin, in Sydney, Seoul, or Seattle. This bonds us as a people and roots us in the family from which we've come, a family united around the same God who has made this communion possible.

But ritual needs to be balanced by spontaneity and variety in prayer, too. As the Constitution on the Sacred Liturgy states: "In matters that do not affect the faith or the well-being of the whole community, the Church has no desire, not even in the liturgy, to impose a rigid monolithic structure. Rather, on the contrary, it cultivates and encourages the gifts and endowments of mind and heart possessed by various races and peoples" (no. 37). This variety in worship — whether in song or symbol — enlivens interest and facilitates engagement by planners and participants alike. It reveals the richness of catholicity: the wonderful array of cultural and geographic diversity, the differences between the sexes and among ages. The newly recovered role of the assembly makes sense in this light. Each one brings to the liturgy his or her unique gifts. It is essential to the catholicity of the Church that these gifts be reflected and shared. Always, the key lies in balance and in understanding.

One of the most prized dimensions of liturgy is the use of symbol. However, as the Church grew in size and liturgical celebrations became more distant from the people, the lavish use of symbol gradually disappeared. It is common fare in many churches to use hosts that look and taste more like paper than bread. The baptismal rite is often reduced to the dribbling of a few drops of water rather than an abundant outpouring that enacts the wonderful mystery of cleansing and rebirth. Words often enough overshadow gestures and fail to draw the assembly into the action of the liturgical event. The full and generous use of symbols serves to invite the assembly into the depth of liturgical prayer. Indeed, the use of symbol can be one of the most powerful ways to communicate to the assembly the mystery that is being prayed.

Over the past number of years, the theme of "passages" or "seasons" has become prominent in popular self-knowledge literature. It is with good cause since anyone who has lived at all knows the ups and downs, the seasons and cycles of life. The liturgical rhythm of the Church embodies this wisdom on multiple levels.

First, the central mystery that lies at the heart of all liturgical prayer is the paschal mystery. Jesus' passage through his passion and death to resurrected life was actually the culmination — though singular and unique — of the lifelong cycle of life and death and new life in God to which all Christians witness. "The fire and the rose are one," said T. S.

Eliot. It is all of a piece. It is only as we revisit this central mystery again and again that we gradually grasp its depth.

This is the wisdom of the Liturgical Year. As a faith community, we travel through the seasons of Christ's life: Advent and Christmas — the waiting of pregnancy and the birth of Jesus; Ordinary Time — the years of growing up when God schooled Jesus about God's desires for all people and for the world; Lent — the moment of radical surrender as Jesus offered his life that all might live; Easter — the central moment of truth that proclaimed the ultimate victory of life over death; Pentecost — the outpouring of the Spirit of God so that all would continue the work of Christ throughout time. So, too, are commemorated in this Church Year those faithful friends of God, the saints and martyrs, who by their lives professed the power of God's love.

Seasons and cycles. Predictable and ever new. Rehearsed and yet surprising when we experience them as our own. This is the profound simplicity of our life as a worshiping community. As we enter into the rhythms of these seasons, we will inevitably find ourselves in the in-between times of learning and growing; in the deaths of dreams shattered and life given for others; in the births and risings of new freedom and stronger purpose that outweigh death. Each one will travel these seasons at different speeds and at different times. How splendid it is that, as a community, we can carry the burden when the other has no energy or little hope. How magnificent it is that the good news of another can be the cause for all rejoicing.

Like Jack in *Shadowlands,* however, the "deal" is that we jump into the action. We will not "know" the wisdom of the mystery — God's, our own, our community's — until we become active participants. And, like Jack, we will know greater pain and deeper joy. Is it worth the price?

Questions for Reflection and Discussion

1. What could be done in your parish or place of worship to draw others into the celebration in a more active and meaningful way? What could you do to help?

2. Describe a time in your life that helped you "know" the meaning of the paschal mystery — the dying and rising of Christ. Did it help you to relate to others in the community in a more sensitive, understanding way? How does this help you appreciate more the richness of the community of faith?

Faith in Action

Join your liturgy committee in the parish so that you can take an active part in enhancing the life of worship in your faith community. If time and energies do not permit this, promise to take the time once in awhile to reflect on the liturgical life of your community. Be concrete and positive in your suggestions and questions as you present them to the pastoral team or to the liturgy committee.

Prayer

Reflect prayerfully on this vision of *all* people coming together at the end of time, praising the one who gathers the children scattered over the face of the earth:

♦ "There was a great multitude that no one could count" (Rev. 7: 9–12)

23

Finding One's Place in the Church's Sacramental Life

Now there are varieties of gifts, but the same Spirit; and there are varieties of services, but the same Lord; and there are varieties of activities, but it is the same God who activates all of them in everyone. To each is given the manifestation of the Spirit for the common good. To one is given through the Spirit the utterance of wisdom, and to another the utterance of knowledge according to the same Spirit, to another faith by the same Spirit, to another gifts of healing by the one Spirit, to another the working of miracles, to another prophecy, to another the discernment of spirits, to another various kinds of tongues, to another the interpretation of tongues. All these are activated by one and the same Spirit, who allots to each one individually just as the Spirit chooses.

(1 CORINTHIANS 12:4–11)

Oskar Schindler was a man of many gifts. He was tenacious in his desire to amass a fortune and shrewd in his ability to exploit the resources at hand, however few. People were pawns in his plan and he played them with a charming though steely astuteness. It was from this posture that Schindler entered the world of the Holocaust. Ah, here was an opportunity to capitalize on the desperate plight of the Jewish people who would do any work to escape the atrocities of the war. His entrepreneurial gifts stood him in good stead. He reigned with confidence over his thriving business. He knew what he could do and he did it well. But what he didn't know and didn't expect was that these same gifts would lead him into the very lives, no, the very hearts of the Jewish people. He did not count on growing to love them. Gradually he came to care about the injustices and indignities they suffered. Now, he turned his gifts to saving them instead of exploiting them. He leveled deals with the authorities that provided more and more jobs and safety for the Jewish community and less and less profit for him. Amazing. The very same gifts and his generous use of them ushered Schindler into worlds entirely beyond his own where he learned what success meant in wholly different ways.

Though life is multi-faceted — personal, professional, familial, civic, religious — ultimately, it is not compartmentalized. It is one world and one life. Oskar Schindler could not avoid running into the spiritual and community hungers of the Jewish people as he wrung labor from them in the establishment of an arms factory. And though each of us wears different hats, it is only one person wearing them. Schindler's genius was that he recognized his ability to transfer his gifts from one setting to another, from one motive to another. Now he made money and protected this people from death.

There is an inherent unity as well between our everyday life and our life of faith, but it is a connection we struggle to make. Perhaps one of the reasons we find sacramental worship so dry and unconnected to our lives is because it is! How can we find our places and recognize our gifts not only in our family, work, and social settings but also within the faith community? Strangely, many adults do not seem to transfer the confident use of their gifts, so evident day by day, to the world of the Church.

Perhaps it would be helpful to think of the sacramental life of the

Church in terms of the life rhythms we follow every day. What the sacraments signal to us in their simplest form is that God hears and cares about our human needs and knows about them before we ever say a word. The sacraments mirror the joy of belonging, the longing for forgiveness, the hungers of our hearts and bodies, the desire to participate in Jesus' vision for the world, the hope for healing, the attraction to giving our lives in commitment. But we will recognize what the sacraments mirror only to the extent that we identify those same dynamics in our everyday life.

For example, the gift of giving birth to a new child, the claiming of a child as one's own in adoption, the welcome extended to a new member of the family through marriage, the mentoring of a person into his or her profession, the offering of citizenship to one who has fled economic and political danger — aren't these expressions of the welcoming we celebrate in Baptism?

When a person confesses a struggle to a friend, when a teacher forgives a child for lying about homework, when a government "forgives" the debt of a country unable to pay, when a labor relations board successfully negotiates a company strike — aren't these expressions of reconciliation?

And isn't Eucharist celebrated each time a family welcomes relatives at holiday time, when a maitre d' creates an atmosphere of gracious dining that invites graciousness from those who gather, when a person goes without in order to send money to a relief fund for a famine-stricken people? When a nurse tends to a dying patient, when a therapist skillfully and compassionately leads a patient through the resolution of a psychological dilemma, when a team of reforestation workers nurses the earth back to life, when an administrator crafts a style that reclaims and nurtures the feminine — aren't these expressions mirrored in the sacrament of healing?

Schindler plunged into his world in an attempt to master it and discovered unwittingly the hidden values that lay therein. So it is with us. As we make use of our gifts in the building up of our world, we can better grasp the deep values that lie hidden beneath their surface. We begin to understand that life is truly holy. We need to plunge into the world of our Church as well. It is only by consciously and actively using the variety of gifts given to each of us in the faith community that we will gradually grasp the unfathomable mystery that God needs and wants us to help build the reign of God. It is in the exercise of these gifts that we will meet the God who is the Giver of all gifts. We will begin to see that God is active in every part of our lives. We will begin to see the connections between what we live and how we celebrate as a Church.

But why is it so difficult for us to see this connection between what we live and how we celebrate in faith? Why do we struggle to accept that the very gifts that propel us through life are the same ones that reveal our unique spiritual direction in the faith community of the Church? Why don't we, some of us at least, experience the same at-homeness and confidence in the Church as we do elsewhere? The struggle is not without foundation.

First, our image of God can undermine any conviction that God, indeed, needs us. Conventional wisdom provides some very concrete images that can help us identify the God to whom we relate. There is the image of God as a "watchmaker." Surely, the watchmaker has carefully crafted the watch and it bears the marks of its creator. Once finished, however, it is offered for sale and the watchmaker has nothing more to do with it. Such a distant God has no interest in how women and men made in the image and likeness of God express their lives or use their gifts. Certainly, there is no expectation of an ongoing relationship between creator and creature.

Then there is the image of God as a "divine puppeteer in the sky." This God, like any puppeteer, acts as an arbitrary and controlling dictator who simply pulls the strings of a person's life at whim. There is no question of collaboration here. And why, in fact, would a self-respecting adult even entertain the notion of putting his or her gifts at this God's disposal?!

On the other hand, there is the image of God as a "parent of adult children." There is no greater pleasure for this God than to see the children grow, mature, and develop their gifts and talents for the service of others. In fact, one of the delights of such a parent is when a daughter or son becomes a friend, and parent and adult offspring share the joys and struggles of each other's lives. This image of God not only makes room for the use of one's gifts but invites their exercise as an essential element in God's design for ushering in the reign.

A second reason why the transference of gifts from our everyday life to the life of the Church might be difficult is that the history of the Church works against it. There was a very long period in the Church when the laity, the people of God, were expected to "pay, pray, and obey." This tradition of being passive members makes it more difficult for us to embrace and use our gifts in the Church with any sort of confidence. It is not uncommon to hear perfectly competent adults respond: "Who me? Read in church? I couldn't; I'm not the holy type!"

Or, "You want me to teach other new parents about Baptism? No way; I don't talk about my faith in public." Or, "Prepare and lead the prayer at the beginning of our next parish council meeting? Ask someone else; I've never done that before." Again, "Welcome new parishioners, explain what our parish is all about, and ask if they have any questions? That's the priest's job!" Or, "I'm not going to a Lenten prayer led by a woman. Are you kidding? I wish women would stop trying to take over the Church!" So many of these reactions come from our inability to recognize the gifts we've been given for others... or at least to recognize that the gifts we have can be used in the Church too.

Whatever the reason for our reluctance to enter fully into the life of the Church, it must be difficult for the One who pours out such a variety of gifts to have them pushed aside or denied. The fact is that God needs each one to find his or her own place in the faith community so that the work of building up the body of Christ can continue with vigor for the life of the world.

Questions for Reflection and Discussion

Reflection on two areas, gifts and needs, will provide some clues about finding one's place in the faith community. The following questions might serve as a guide for finding one's place:

Self-Knowledge about One's Gifts

1. What energizes and attracts you as you think about getting involved in the Church?
2. What are the things that you admire most in others and wish to emulate?
3. What do others point out as your gifts?
4. How do they ask you to help: to organize a function? lead prayer? speak for a group? proclaim the Word? mediate in difficult situations? Listen? help mend fences? help soften hurts? expect you to offer and implement new ideas? stir up excitement for a new project? teach? offer wisdom? sing? preach? welcome?
5. What is so worthwhile that you are willing to sacrifice or even suffer for it?

Knowledge about the Needs of the Community

1. How have you learned about the needs of the community?
2. Has your knowledge come from hearsay or because you have participated in the life of the community?

3. Do you experience a sufficient degree of openness to hear what others really need, whether or not they are your needs?

4. What do people complain about?

5. What do people "wish" for?

6. What will serve the common good?

7. Are there signs that something new needs to happen?

When reflection on both of these areas has been done, how do you match your own gifts with the needs of the community? It may be that there already exists an area of service begging for people to help. It may be that you have both the ability and the desire to create a new response to a need heretofore unmet. Whichever it may be, there have been rare reports indeed of communities that have done all the growth and development necessary for a lifetime.

Faith in Action

Most of us learn by doing. We need to find our way by trial and error and by reflecting with other committed people about whether our efforts are enlivening our community (Church, neighborhood, world, family) or not. We need to reflect periodically on whether our efforts are strengthening or weakening our own spirits. And, always, we need to be ready to do the same for others.

Prayer

Though the exclusive male references might be distracting to some, the spirit of the following prayer by Gerard Manley Hopkins is profound:

The just man justices;
Keeps grace: that keeps
all his goings graces;
Acts in God's eye
what in God's eye he is —
Christ — for Christ plays
in ten thousand places,
lovely in limbs, and lovely
in eyes not his
To the Father through
the features of men's faces.

24

Conversion: Heart of the
Sacramental Life

Saul, still breathing threats and murder against the disciples of the Lord, went to the high priest and asked him for letters to the synagogues at Damascus, so that if he found any who belonged to the Way, men or women, he might bring them bound to Jerusalem. Now as he was going along and approaching Damascus, suddenly a light from heaven flashed around him. He fell to the ground and heard a voice saying to him, "Saul, Saul, why do you persecute me?" He asked, "Who are you, Lord?" The reply came, "I am Jesus, whom you are persecuting. But get up and enter the city, and you will be told what you are to do." The men who were traveling with him stood speechless because they heard the voice but saw no one. Saul got up from the ground, and though his eyes were open, he could see nothing; so they led him by the hand and brought him into Damascus. For three days he was without sight, and neither ate nor drank.

Now there was a disciple in Damascus named Ananias. The Lord said to him in a vision, "Ananias." He answered, "Here I am, Lord." The Lord said to him, "Get up and go to the street called Straight, and at the house of Judas look for a man of Tarsus named Saul. At this moment he is praying, and he has seen in a vision a man named Ananias come in and lay his hands on him so that he might regain his sight." But Ananias answered, "Lord, I have heard from many about this man, how much evil he has done to your saints in Jerusalem; and here he has authority from the chief priests to bind all who invoke your name." But the Lord said to him, "Go, for he is an instrument whom I have chosen to bring my name before Gentiles and kings and before the people of Israel; I myself will show him how much he must suffer for the sake of my name." So Ananias went and entered the house. He laid his hands on Saul and said, "Brother Saul, the Lord Jesus, who appeared to you on your way here, has sent me so that you may regain your sight and be filled with the Holy Spirit." And immediately something like scales fell from his eyes, and his sight was restored. Then he got up and was baptized, and after taking some food, he regained his strength.

For several days he was with the disciples in Damascus, and immediately he began to proclaim Jesus in the synagogues, saying, "He is the Son of God." (ACTS 9:1–22)

The parents of a five-year-old decided one day at the beginning of Lent that it might be time to talk to their son, Benjamin, about conscience. Ben already knew a little bit about the season of Lent, but this year his parents suggested that he try to become more attentive to the voice of God in his own heart. They explained that they would not always be present to him to say, "Good, Ben," or "No, Ben, that's not appropriate behavior." Nevertheless, they promised, there is a little voice inside each of us, a voice that would help Ben sort out right from wrong. Lent, they suggested, was a particularly good time to learn to listen to that inner voice.

Ben took this all in and went off to play. But he was back within the hour to report: "Mom, Dad, there isn't any voice! I think my batteries are dead."

Conversion, it would appear has something to do with voices and maybe even batteries.

The story of Saul is a dramatic account of his journey to Damascus — really his life journey — interrupted by a miraculous divine intervention. In a moment of blinding insight Saul heard the voice of God calling him to account for the patterns of his life, a voice inviting Saul to a new relationship and a new way of life.

Have you ever been a little jealous of St. Paul and other saints like him? Have you ever thought that this kind of dramatic, knock-me-to-the-ground divine intervention seems pretty painless compared to the fits and starts, the falls and recoveries, of most of our lives before God? Have you ever wished for such a radical, instantaneous, and life-changing experience? Well, that's not actually how conversion happens either in the saints' lives or in our own. Paul, for example, spent about three years after his roadside incident wandering the desert of Arabia, perhaps in the process pondering the question he himself had posed: "Who are you, Lord?"

Conversion typically follows a classic pattern and most conversion experiences have some elements in common. In the following pages we'll look first to the pattern and some features of the conversion process and then explore the relationship of conversion and sacrament.

It seems to be characteristic of conversion that it begins in ordinary time. Think of some of the classic scriptural accounts of conversion. The stories regularly begin in the midst of the mundane: Saul encountered the Lord in the course of a journey; the Samaritan woman was drawing water at a well in midday; the prodigal son was in the midst of his farm chores; Matthew was going about the business of collecting taxes; Simon Peter, James, and John were washing their nets after a failed fishing expedition; Martha and Mary were mourning the death of their brother, Lazarus. Examples could be multiplied to demonstrate that an invitation to conversion comes in the midst of the ordinary.

In the process of conversion, something or someone or some event disturbs our complacency or rattles our cage. Sometimes we experience some vague dis-ease with our lives; sometimes there is some restless stirring in our hearts. Sometimes a friend says a word that we find disturbing — a word that we may have heard a hundred times but finally *really* heard for the first time. Sometimes the process of conversion begins because we have experienced death, or fallen in love, or begun a new job, or become seriously ill. Sometimes the process begins in far less dramatic ways: we read something that touches our hearts, we admire the goodness of another, we become aware of our sinfulness, we find we can't live any longer with the duplicity of our lives, or we just long for something more in our relationships. However we hear God's invitation or experience God's love, it is mediated by the people and the circumstances of our lives and it somehow invites us — really, impels us — to a new way of being, to a new or deeper relationship with God.

But experience teaches that we're not always delighted by God's mediated invitations. Sometimes they are inconvenient; sometimes they are too demanding. We should not be surprised at such resistance. Conversion, ultimately, is about dying and rising, and thus all of the stages of the dying process may be operative in our experience: denial, anger, bargaining, depression, and acceptance. We may choose to tune out the invitation altogether, or refuse to deal with it, or try to buy time, or enter into a prolonged and sometimes despondent struggle within ourselves.

But if we finally move to acceptance, if we make the choice to "hear God's voice and harden not our hearts" then that choice leads inevitably to changes. Such was Paul's experience when, years after those moments on the road to Damascus, he reflected on how radically changed were his ambitions: "I want to know Christ and the power of his resurrection and the sharing of his sufferings by becoming like him in his death, if somehow I may attain the resurrection from the dead" (Phil. 3:10–11).

Is conversion instantaneous and dramatic? Rarely; perhaps never. It is rather played out over a lifetime of big and small moments — the tiny daily fidelities, the occasional significant choices, the weighing of goods, the ups and downs. It is the slow and imperceptible putting on of the mind and heart of Christ; it is the gradual embracing of God's desires for us; it is becoming more attentive to the Spirit of God and attuned to God's plans for us.

And there's the crux of it: *God's* plans. Conversion is not about poking around in the sinful debris of our lives. It is not about sin and self and past at all but rather about God and grace and future. Conversion is an invitation to a new or a deeper relationship (grace) with God who draws each one of us into a new future of hope and rich possibilities.

Conversion, finally, is an experience of liberation for the sake of mission. It frees us from the past and energizes us for the work of the Gospel, "forgetting what lies behind and straining forward to what lies ahead." That was Paul's experience, and he continued in the same vein: "I press on toward the goal for the prize of the heavenly call of God in Christ Jesus" (Phil. 3:13b–14).

What, you may wonder, does any of this have to do with sacrament? Conversion is clearly a focus of the Rite of Christian Initiation, but doesn't that just about sum it up? Not at all! Certainly initiation is a celebration of conversion, of coming to faith, of discovery of the person of Jesus Christ as Lord of my life with all the upheaval and change that coming to faith entails. But initiation simply marks a threshold in our journey of conversion — our journey into God — that is the work of a lifetime.

Each of the sacraments celebrates a new threshold of the conversion journey; each of the sacraments invites us to die and rise with Jesus, whether that death is to unbelief, selfishness, self-seeking, hopelessness, isolation, prejudice, pride, or whatever. Particular sacraments highlight critical moments and life choices; the Eucharist recapitulates them all.

The Eucharist is the repeatable sacrament of initiation, the primary sacrament of reconciliation and healing, the recurring sacramental repetition of our promises and vows. Eucharist, for Christians, is the place where we bring our daily experiences, our struggles to remain faithful, our constant daily deaths, both large and small, and where we hand over our lives again and again to be transformed, through Christ and with Christ and in Christ. Eucharist is the place where we bring our simple selves together with bread and wine and beg that the power of the Spirit will come upon us just as truly as we believe the Spirit changes the elements into Christ's body. Eucharist is the place where we know most surely that all is gift, where we experience that God draws us together and makes of us a community, enabling our human response of praise and thanks.

Conversion begins with a personal, internal experience, a grace-full invitation to a new or deeper life with God. The invitation may take the form of forgiveness, healing, service of others, self-donation in love, or countless others. Sacraments are celebrated when we are ready to embrace that divine invitation to become more deeply human and holy. Sacraments are the public, ritual celebrations of our "yes" to conversion. They give visible expression to these invisible realities, and in the process they commit us to live, in deed, what we have proclaimed in word and ritual action.

Questions for Reflection and Discussion

1. Identify a conversion experience in your own life and think of key words or phrases that describe your experience before and after the conversion, the continuities and discontinuities.

2. Has this conversion experience changed your perception of yourself? your world (others, objects)? God? How?

3. Has the experience issued in decisions concerning your priorities, your style of life, your relationship to family, friends, and professional colleagues?

4. Can you see the intimate connection of conversion and sacramental celebration?

Faith in Action

Eucharist celebrates our daily experiences of dying and rising with Jesus, of trying to put on the mind and heart of Christ. Before you participate again in Eucharist, try to become conscious of the particular struggles, the "deaths" you are joining to that of Christ, for the sake of new life.

Prayer

Use the psalmists words — "If today you hear God's voice, harden not your heart" — as a beginning of a prayerful conversation with God.

--------------------------- *25* ---------------------------

Origins of the Church's Sacraments

Awe came upon everyone, because many wonders and signs were being done by the apostles. All who believed were together and had all things in common; they would sell their possessions and goods and distribute the proceeds to all, as any had need. Day by day, as they spent much time together in the temple, they broke bread at home and ate their food with glad and generous hearts, praising God and having the goodwill of all the people. And day by day the Lord added to their number those who were being saved.

The whole group of those who believed were of one heart and soul. . . . With great power the apostles gave their testimony to the resurrection of the Lord Jesus, and great grace was upon them all.

(ACTS 2:43–47; 4:32A, 33)

Have you ever wondered where the sacraments came from? Have you ever stopped to question how our various rituals developed over the centuries? The story of the rabbi and his disciples with which Elie Wiesel prefaced his novel *The Gates of the Forest* suggests the vicissitudes of such evolution as well as the enduring core of our liturgical prayer.

When the great Rabbi Israel Baal Shem-Tov saw misfortune threatening the Jews, it was his custom to go into a certain part of the forest to meditate. There he would light a fire and say a special prayer; a miracle would be accomplished and the misfortune averted.

Later, when his disciple, the celebrated Magid of Mezritch, had occasion to intercede with heaven for the same reason, he would go to the same place in the forest and say: "Master of the Universe, listen! I do not know how to light the fire, but I am still able to say the prayer." And again the miracle would be accomplished.

Still later, Rabbi Moshe-Leib of Sasov, in order to save his people once more, would go into the forest and say: "I do not know how to light the fire, I do not know the prayer, but I know the place and this must be sufficient." It was sufficient, and the miracle was accomplished.

Then it fell to Rabbi Israel of Rizhyn to overcome misfortune. Sitting in his armchair, his head in his hands, he spoke to God: "I am unable to light the fire and I do not know the prayer; I cannot even find the place in the forest. All I can do is tell the story, and this must be sufficient." And it was sufficient.

God loves the telling of stories.

The Acts of the Apostles presents a compelling picture of the early Christian community sorting itself out after Jesus' death, gradually creating a new story with which to delight God. On the one hand, there was no immediate or radical break with the past. Most of the early Christian community were *Jewish Christians,* men and women who continued daily in attendance at the morning and evening services of the temple. As observant Jews, they had patterns of prayer, ways of ritualizing key moments of birth and death, marriage and priestly ministry. They had ways of caring for those who were ill and rituals for restoring those who were alienated. There were feasts and seasons and a rhythm of weekly celebrations among them. Life went on.

On the other hand, everything was new! Even as they continued worship at the temple and even as they persevered in living according to the familiar rhythms of Jewish ritual celebrations, these first-generation Christians began to meet in one another's homes for the teaching of the apostles and for table fellowship with one another. Only very gradually did the early community break with these familiar patterns and establish themselves as a community set apart.

One can imagine their conversations following the apostles' teachings: What difference did it make that they had been captivated by the life and ministry, the teaching and the desert prayer of the Lord Jesus Christ? Who had he become for them? What had he taught them of the One he called *Abba?* What vision of life did he offer? What ways of being in the world did he ask of his followers? How could they continue his saving mission?

These were not idle questions. For a community captivated by the person and work of Jesus and seized by his very Spirit, these were urgent concerns. How, concretely, were they to continue Jesus' mission? How were they to be his presence in a world so in need of healing and hope? What habits of heart had Jesus embodied that his followers must emulate if they were to be recognized as Christian?

EUCHARIST. The Acts of the Apostles describes the community meeting regularly for the breaking of bread. Surely one of their earliest realizations was of the presence of the Risen One among them as they kept his memorial in praise and thanksgiving. Table fellowship had been such a central aspect of Jesus' life and ministry. Throughout his ministry Jesus had gathered people at table — both rich and poor, outcasts and those with social standing, some dubious characters, a few whom their culture had marginalized, even disreputable sinners. In the sharing of food there was a sharing of life, an experience of universal reconciliation — everyone was welcome at the table! And when Jesus was not at table he was using the imagery of banquets to give the same message; sharing food is sharing life. By his actions Jesus was saying: "I long to share life with you, with all of you, no exceptions."

The last supper was precisely that, *last* in a whole series of meals during the earthly life of Christ. The last supper was a recapitulation and reinterpretation of all the others: "This is my body for the life of the world; this is my blood poured out for the forgiveness of sins; do this to keep my memorial."

With hearts filled with thanksgiving, literally, with Eucharist, the early community — reflecting the words of Jesus, "Do this in remembrance of me" (Luke 22:19) — celebrated the supper of the Lord. The breaking of bread joined to a prayer of praise and thanksgiving became the heart of Christian sacramental life. As Christians gradually differentiated themselves from others, the pattern of reading, preaching, and prayers in the synagogue was joined to the breaking of bread. Our two-part eucharistic structure of word and table was set by the end of the first century.

INITIATION. By that time, too, other sacraments were also evolving. Initiation, for example, was forged as the community tried to address the growing numbers attracted to membership. Day by day, as the

Acts of the Apostles has described, "the Lord added to their number
those who were being saved." Under these circumstances, several questions would have had to preoccupy the leadership of the community
simultaneously, questions about faith, conversion, signs of readiness
for membership, even ritual patterns.

In the first century there were a number of initiation patterns to
choose from: Jewish proselyte baptism, the initiation process of strict
sects like the Essenes, patterns of the mystery religions, and various
rituals of purification. Borrowing from these patterns and reinterpret-
ing them, the early community, following Jesus' instruction to baptize
in the name of the Father, the Son, and the Holy Spirit (cf. Matt.
28:19), chose a rite of water and word, of immersion, dipping, or
sprinkling depending on circumstances, joined to the believer's confession of faith in the triune God (Matt. 28) or in Jesus as Lord (Acts
22:16). And the ritual prayer as it developed, in turn, deepened the
community's understanding of the meaning of what it was doing: going
down to death with Christ, being buried with Christ, washing, sancti-
fication, justification in the bath of regeneration, "our hearts sprinkled
clean from an evil conscience and our bodies washed with pure water"
(Heb. 10:22).

PENANCE. From the beginning, Christians understood that in Baptism
sin was forgiven. But what happened when people lost their first fer-
vor, when they fell into patterns of sin once again? Baptism did not
free Christians once and for all from the struggle with evil. Then, as
now, members of the community experienced the inner conflict articu-
lated so well by Paul: "I do not understand my own actions. For I do
not do what I want, but I do the very thing I hate" (Rom. 7:15).

The early community was clearly conscious of the possibility of sin
and of forgiveness of sinful members. Christians were urged to prevent
sin by fortifying each other with example and exhortation. Penitential
practices included prayer, fasting, works of mercy, and fraternal and
sororal correction. In addition, when a sin was particularly grave and
scandalous, sometimes the community exiled a sinner lest that person
corrupt the community (Matt. 18:15–17).

After Baptism a Christian is saved yet still sinful, liberated yet ever
in need of conversion. This paradox was the origin of the community's penitential disciplines that evolved over time into the sacrament
of Reconciliation as we know it today, but not before it had passed
through a very strict and unrepeatable public canonical form, a model

more like spiritual direction, and a pattern from Ireland sometimes called "tariff" penance (confessors actually had lists of sins together with their appropriate "tariffs," or penances) from which private auricular penance was derived. Reconciliation, a history of changing structures, most clearly demonstrates that the Church's sacramental life is a living reality, changing, sometimes declining, eventually renewing itself, shaped in part by different cultures and changing religious experience.

Other questions and other needs gradually gave rise to other sacraments. The impetus in this evolution was the Church's desire to remain faithful to the life and ministry of Jesus as it attempted to continue his saving presence in the crossroads moments of the community's lives: birth, sickness, death, vocational choice.

Always there was the question: What would Jesus do? What did he teach about this experience, this threshold moment, this life choice? How would he care for those who were sick? What way of life did he enjoin on those who would serve the community? How would he prepare those who were pledging their lives to one another in marriage? And how, today, shall we celebrate these basic human threshold moments? How shall we give public ritual expression to the presence and power of the Risen One so palpably present to the community?

Traditionally in reflecting on the origin of the sacraments we have spoken of the sacraments as "instituted by Christ." That does not mean that we can trace each of the seven sacraments to a particular word of Jesus or pinpoint a founding experience during his ministry. "Instituted by Christ" simply means that the Church has evolved a pattern of sacramental activity over the centuries as it attempts to remain faithful to Jesus' life and ministry and to replicate his saving presence in word and ritual activity.

Sacraments are so many ways of telling the story of God's love affair with humankind, God's longing to be in relationship with us, God's gift of presence and power that touches the very core of what it is to be most human and holy. The patterns change from time to time; the basic story remains the same. And God must delight in our prayer, for God loves the telling of stories.

Questions for Reflection and Discussion

1. How would you explain the institution of the sacraments by Christ?

2. Does it make sense to you that sacraments evolved very gradually as the community continued to plumb the depths of who Jesus was and how they (and we) are to continue his saving presence?

3. Many of our patterns of prayer changed after the Second Vatican Council. Think of one change that stands out for you and ask yourself whether, even in the change, the story we enact remains the same?

Faith in Action

History can be both enlightening and freeing. Read about the origins and development of one of the sacraments and imagine how it might continue to evolve in light of contemporary experience and need.

Prayer

In the course of strategic planning, the archdiocese of Seattle invited members of the Church of Western Washington to say a "Prayer for the Church in Transition." In union with that local Church and in the name of all who struggle with inevitable change in these turbulent times, we pray:

O faithful God,
As your people we cherish our memories
and our history as a sacred gift.
We also ask you to guide us in our time of transition.
We need your wisdom that we might be receptive
to change, conversion, and growth.
We need your grace to redirect our hearts
that we may be willing to offer ourselves in joyful service.
Do not allow fear, ignorance, or pride
to limit the work of your spirit,
nor custom to prevent the creativity within us from bearing fruit.
Open our hearts to the call of the Gospel.
Give us courage and renewed hope
that we may meet the challenges
of being the Church of our time. Amen.

26

Sacraments of Initiation

An angel of the Lord said to Philip, "Get up and go toward the south to the road that goes down from Jerusalem to Gaza. (This is a wilderness road.) So he got up and went. Now there was an Ethiopian eunuch, a court official of Candace, queen of the Ethiopians, in charge of her entire treasury. He had come to Jerusalem to worship and was returning home; seated in his chariot, he was reading the prophet Isaiah. Then the Spirit said to Philip, "Go over to this chariot and join it." So Philip ran up to it and heard him reading the prophet Isaiah. He asked, "Do you understand what you are reading?" He replied, "How can I, unless someone guides me?" And he invited Philip to get in and sit beside him. Now the passage of the scripture that he was reading was this:

> *Like a sheep he was led to the slaughter,*
> *and like a lamb silent before its shearer,*
> *so he does not open his mouth.*
> *In his humiliation justice was denied him.*
> *Who can describe his generation?*
> *For his life is taken away from the earth.*

The eunuch asked Philip, "About whom, may I ask you, does the prophet say this, about himself or about someone else?" Then Philip began to speak, and starting with this scripture, he proclaimed to him the good news about Jesus. As they were going along the road, they came to some water; and the eunuch said, "Look, here is water! What is to prevent me from being baptized?" He commanded the chariot to stop, and both of them, Philip and the eunuch, went down into the water, and Philip baptized him. When they came up out of the water, the Spirit of the Lord snatched Philip away; the eunuch saw him no more, and went on his way rejoicing. (ACTS 8:26–34)

Maureen, a single professional woman in her mid-forties, is a modern-day Philip. Maureen was asked to be a sponsor in our local parish, "to proclaim the good news about Jesus" to a catechumen, a young graduate student from the University of Chicago. This is what it was like for her in her own words:

"I remember being a little startled when I got the call asking me to be a sponsor in the RCIA program. The initial explanatory meetings reassured me that sponsors did not have to be models of the official Church; instead, we represent the 'ordinary face' of our extraordinary parish and as such serve as companions, wise friends, sounding boards to the truly amazing individuals who seek to join our Catholic community as adults.

"I was the sponsor (and later godparent) to a wonderfully vibrant, intelligent young woman. Our initial meetings quickly grew into wide-ranging conversations about Scripture, ethics, doctrine, the Gulf war, history, and even bread-making. I needed to run pretty fast at times to keep up.

"I had expected that watching and listening to her process of conversion would be interesting and absorbing. What I did not expect was the effect it had on me. I found that being a sponsor uncovered my own middle-age hunger for spiritual enrichment. It challenged me to re-examine, question, and ultimately recommit myself as an adult to the beliefs that are at the core of my being. It was very awkward at first to get over some shyness in speaking deeply about God and matters of the soul. But once over that hurdle, I found many kindred spirits in the other sponsors, catechumens, and the RCIA team members.

"The experience still reverberates. I probably have more questions now than I did a year ago. But being a sponsor has opened up avenues of further growth and study, brought new friendships, and enriched the depth and my appreciation of my friendships and family."

How do we join people to ourselves? The same questions that preoccupied the early Christian community are questions to be asked of every age: What does it take to hear and believe the good news? What is the substance of ecclesial faith? What evidence of conversion should we look for? And, once people are ready to throw in their lot with us, what ritual should mark their initiation into Christ Jesus? Answers to these questions have varied over the centuries, influenced in great measure by the relationship of the Church to its environs, the age of the candidates, the addition of preparatory and explanatory rites to the core ritual of water and word, and, in the West, the availability of the bishop to oversee the process.

It was Tertullian (d. 225) who coined the phrase: "Christians are made, not born." In these words he captured the simple truth that conversion to Jesus Christ, and to the community that bears his name, is a fairly arduous event that takes time and the nurture of candidates by faith-filled members of the community. Tertullian witnessed to a time in the post-apostolic period of the Church when Christians were a threatened minority in a pagan culture. Robust faith had to be developed in candidates in order for them to withstand the pressures of their culture. A catechumenal process emerged in the early centuries of the Church that, over three or four years and through hefty teaching, serious examinations, and frequent prayer, prepared catechumens to join the community.

The actual ritual of initiation included, among other elements, renunciation of sin, confession of faith, a water bath, anointing, and reception of the Eucharist. Since candidates were nude, the first part of the ceremony, under the direction of presbyters and deacons, was done apart from the community. When they had dressed they were led into the assembly, where the bishop had remained with the community, and there he anointed them with the laying on of hands and prayer and, after an exchange of peace, brought them to the eucharistic table. Candidates were generally adults, although when whole households approached the community, children were included. Note that Baptism, Anointing, and Eucharist were in these early days celebrated as a combined rite of initiation under the presidency of the bishop.

After the Peace of Constantine and the recognition of Christianity as a state religion, it became positively advantageous to be a Christian. Large numbers approached the community for membership, some with defective motivation. The lengthy and arduous process of preparation gave way to a much-shortened catechumenate of a few months and sometimes only a few weeks, and some who were enrolled as catechumens and who found that such status was sufficient to get the good jobs never proceeded to Baptism.

Numbers also played havoc with the sacrament itself. When the community became too large for the bishop to preside over all initiations, presbyters became ordinary ministers of the sacrament. In the East, presbyters baptized, confirmed with the holy oil blessed by the bishop, and welcomed the candidate to communion. In the West, on the other hand, bishops remained the ministers of the "anointing" or "sealing" of the sacrament. When a bishop was not present, either because of numbers or emergency baptism, the candidate was baptized and received communion and only later was presented to the bishop for the ritual anointing. Over time, "Confirmation," once simply a ritual moment in a larger complex of rites, drifted further and further away from Baptism. Eventually Confirmation was understood as a separate sacrament, often linked with adolescence, and a theological rationale for its existence had to be developed.

Infant baptism gradually became the norm not simply because parents wanted for their children what they themselves already possessed, but because of the high rate of infant mortality and the growing understanding of the doctrine of original sin. St. Paul taught in his letters that sin entered the world from the beginning and salvation came through Christ. The problem was that no ritual was designed especially for babies. Many of the rites and prayers designed for adults, including the prayers of scrutiny and exorcism, were collapsed into a single rite for babies. While scrutiny and exorcism made sense when used with adults who had committed personal sin, the use of these prayers in the rite over babies reminded them that, although babies were not guilty of personal sin, as members of the human race they share in the human condition, for from the dawn of human history people have turned away from God.

The separation of the three sacraments of initiation was complete with the postponement of First Eucharist until the age of reason, an age in adolescence according to medieval reasoning. Finally the order of the three sacraments of initiation was rearranged: Baptism, Confirmation, Eucharist became Baptism, First Eucharist, Confirmation. In our day, the insertion of First Penance in this process has further complicated an already confused development.

This short history simply indicates the major mutations of the sacrament of initiation over time. After Vatican II, and with the help of serious historical, theological, and pastoral investigation, the reform of the rites of initiation has been undertaken. The catechumenate has been restored. A rite of infant baptism, designed for babies, is being developed. The age of Confirmation is under discussion, with many leaning to a restoration of its modest relationship to Baptism. And the ancient order and unity of the three sacraments of initiation is informing both theological debate and pastoral practice.

What does it take, in our day, to hear and believe the good news of Jesus dead and risen? How are we to help people on their journey of conversion? How do we assure that they come to know Jesus, not just about him? that they come to *ecclesial* faith, needing to repent and celebrate with other members of Christ's body? that they discover that the Church of Jesus Christ is a missionary Church committed to completing Christ's work on earth? That's the content of the catechumenate now: we teach less a body of doctrine than a way of life, and we do so, not in isolation, but in the midst of the community with friends, sponsors, godparents, priests, deacons, the bishop, and the entire community, each having an indispensable role. The Rite of Christian Initiation of Adults tells us: "The initiation of catechumens is a gradual process that takes place within the community of the faithful. By joining the catechumens in reflecting on the value of the paschal mystery and by renewing their own conversion, the faithful provide an example that will help the catechumens to obey the Holy Spirit more generously" (par. 4).

The potential for the spiritual renewal of the whole Church as new members join us cannot be underestimated.

Questions for Reflection and Discussion

1. Some think of the Eucharist as our regular dip in the baptismal font. What does this mean to you?
2. Does it make a difference to you that there are catechumens and candidates in your Sunday assembly? Do they challenge you in any way to a more faithful discipleship?
3. What qualities would you look for in a sponsor?

Faith in Action

Why not consider becoming part of the RCIA team in your parish, perhaps by becoming a sponsor yourself?

Prayer

When someone is ready to become a catechumen, the community celebrates the "Rite of Becoming a Catechumen" with them. During the celebration, their sponsor signs their senses and other parts of their body with a cross, thus opening their whole being to God's action. Ask another person to pray this prayer with you and to sign your body with the cross.

Signing of the Senses

Receive the cross on your forehead.
It is Christ himself who now strengthens you
with this sign of his love.

Learn to know him and follow him.
Receive the sign of the cross on your ears,
that you may hear the voice of the Lord.
Receive the sign of the cross on your eyes,
that you may see the glory of God.
Receive the sign of the cross on your lips
that you may respond to the word of God.
Receive the sign of the cross over your heart
that Christ may dwell there by faith.
Receive the sign of the cross on your shoulders,
that you may bear the gentle yoke of Christ.
Receive the sign of the cross on your hands,
that Christ may be known in the work which you do.
Receive the sign of the cross on your feet
that you may walk in the way of Christ.
I sign you with the sign of eternal life
in the name of the Father, and of the Son,
and of the Holy Spirit. Amen.

Almighty God,
by the cross and resurrection of your Son
you have given life to your people.
Your servants have received the sign of the cross;
make them living proof of its saving power
and help them to persevere in the footsteps of Christ.
We ask this through Christ our Lord. Amen.

27

God's Family Gathered: The Eucharist

Have you ever wondered how you might spend your time if you were
told that you had only one more night to live? The nature of such
"prime time" has a way of pushing to center stage the best and the
most valued of our priorities. Amazing, isn't it, that the way Jesus
chose to spend his last hours was to share a meal with his friends?

When the hour came, he took his place at table, and the apostles with him. He said to them, "I have eagerly desired to eat this Passover with you before I suffer; for I tell you, I will not eat it until it is fulfilled in the kingdom of God." Then he took a cup, and after giving thanks he said, "Take this and divide it among yourselves;, for I tell you that from now on I will not drink of the fruit of the vine until the kingdom of God comes." Then he took a loaf of bread, and when he had given thanks, he broke it and gave it to them, saying, "This is my body, which is given for you. Do this in remembrance of me." And he did the same with the cup after supper, saying, "This cup that is poured out for you is the new covenant in my blood." (LUKE 22:14–20)

"Do this in memory of me." Could Jesus really have intended to leave us a last will and testament based on such an ordinary and necessary human activity? Could the way to God and the way to holiness truly be as close to us as sharing a meal with friends? What did Jesus want us to understand about God's reign by giving such primacy of place to the eucharistic meal? How does Jesus become present to us in this simple celebration?

Perhaps we need to follow Jesus' lead in our effort to grapple with these questions. If Jesus offered us the meal as the privileged way to God, what is it about the meal that uncovers and reveals God's deepest desires for us as a family of God?

An excerpt from *Simon's Night,* a novel by Jon Hassler, offers some insight into this. Simon, a retired professor of English, had left one too many burning pots on the stove of his little cabin. His absent-minded ways finally confronted him with the fact that he could no longer live alone. Reluctantly, though courageously, he sought refuge in a nearby nursing home where he found himself the companion of women and men with whom he otherwise may not have associated. This new world ushered Simon into a motley collection of people and experiences:

Simon nodded his agreement. For several days now Simon, as a matter of principle, had been forcing himself to be attentive in the dining room, to listen, to say *yes, no, perhaps, indeed,* and *you don't say.* The talk was deadening, to be sure, but was it not his inescapable calling as a human being to endure the speech of his companions? He believed it was. No matter how clogged the ideas, no matter how asinine the assumptions, no matter how stale the platitudes and the breath that uttered them, Simon would listen. He thought of it as a vocation. By a trick of fate or the grace of God, age had led him to the Norman Home, where these six people were summing up their long years at the end of that longness. They mused and shook their heads and gave mumbling voice to countless memories, and he would listen like a brother. (p. 8)

It was in this unfamiliar though common place that Simon heard what was universal to the human heart: the need to rehearse the joys and sorrows of the past; the acceptance of this very unremarkable but providential present; the small but persistent longings for a future full of hope. This was Simon's "vocation": to count himself as one among these others who were no longer strangers but sisters and brothers. It was here, in this very ordinary setting, that he was graciously served and was called on to serve.

And so it was with Jesus. In those fateful hours before his death, he remained true to the vocation he had been given. His call from God was to meet people in the ordinary and necessary moments of their lives. For the Gospel writer Luke, the place par excellence where Jesus did this was at table. It was there that he listened to them, shared food and drink and presence with them. It was there that he revealed his own worries and joys, his pain over the pain of others, his hope for what could be. It was by gathering friend and foe alike at the table that Jesus revealed God's desire for God's family gathered: that all be included, that all be fed, that all remain alive in the hope that God promises to fill the deepest hungers of humanity during the final banquet at the end of all time.

It is this that the Church celebrates in the Eucharist. At Jesus' command to "do this in memory of me," the family of God gathers at the table to remember and rehearse as a community that for which Jesus lived and died. By participating in this meal, the community professes its hope that God's vision of life will win in the end in the same way that God secured the victory of life over death in Jesus.

But what happens when we gather? Does anything in our world change by coming together to this table? Is the Risen Jesus really present to us and in us as we celebrate this meal? Are we changed by participating in the celebration? Does this meal have anything to do with all the other times we gather to eat?

The Catholic Church has professed from the beginning that when the family of God gathers around the eucharistic table in memory of the One who lived, died, and was raised for us, that the same Risen Christ is truly present in the consecrated bread and wine. Moreover, the Christian community is actually formed as it partakes in this sacred meal: "The cup of blessing that we bless, is it not a sharing in the blood of Christ? The bread that we break, is it not a sharing in the body of Christ? Because there is one bread, we who are many are one body, for we all partake of the one bread" (1 Cor. 10:16–17). The belief that the bread and wine are mysteriously changed into Christ's body and blood has been reiterated throughout the history of the Church and even as recently as the Second Vatican Council. But the Church, like any person, grows in its understanding of the Eucharist only step by step and over a very long time. A simple review of the history of the Eucharist in the Catholic Church will illustrate this development and also offer rich insights into the depth of this central mystery of our faith.

The supper on that last night before he died has to be seen in light of all the other meals in which Jesus participated during his life. The Gospel of Luke is particularly helpful in revealing what the meal meant to Jesus. He ate with tax collectors and sinners and insisted that he had come not for the well but for those who needed his healing (5:29–32). The meal was a place where Jesus could teach the priority of love over etiquette and correctness. Yes, the Pharisees knew all the proper ways of doing things, but Jesus was drawn more by the sinner woman who showed great love by anointing his feet with ointment (7:36–50). The meal was a time when Jesus acknowledged that it bothered him when people got hungry, in body and in spirit, and that he wanted to fill them (9:10–17). Jesus seemed to know that real-life issues have a way of surfacing during a meal. For example, what does it mean to be "clean" — to use the proper rituals and silverware or to be gracious and proper in one's living (11:37–54)? Does competition motivate us as we vie for the best seats at the table, or is our motive collaboration as we concern ourselves that everyone has a place to sit (14:7–11)? And who gets invited to our tables: Do we invite only those who can repay us or do we sometimes include the poor and the outcast, the lonely and the burdened (14:12–14)? Jesus illuminated the meaning of salvation through a gesture of acceptance as he shared a simple meal with his friend Zacchaeus, an unpopular senior tax collector. Jesus' unconditional love for him inspired Zacchaeus to give to the poor and make amends for any wrong he had done (19:1–10). The meal was the resting place along the road of life where Jesus continued to talk with his disciples about all that he had taught (24:13–35). The meal was the way Jesus revealed a God who washes our feet and waits on us. It was the best example Jesus could find to explain to us how he wanted us to live (John 13:1–15).

It was in the style of this simple meal that the early Christians, called together by the host or hostess, gathered around in each other's homes for the eucharistic meal. They recalled the *mirabilia Dei,* the wonderful saving ways of God in Jesus, and reminded God to continue working such power in their lives now. The familiar setting of the Jewish meal with blessing and the sharing of the bread and wine, now surrounded by the spontaneous prayer of the Christian community, became the privileged place where the Christians grew in their understanding of who they were and how they should live.

However, the tides of history often obscure the original simplicity of something, and this is the case with the Eucharist as well. As members in the Christian community increased, it was necessary to move the place of celebration from the house churches to larger churches or basilicas. The ordinary time of the Eucharist changed to the morning so as to accommodate the work day (including Sunday), and thus the association with the evening meal was lost. Stronger emphasis was placed on the Eucharist as the unbloody sacrifice of Calvary. The spontaneous nature of the prayers was replaced by a collection of prayers written out in full, establishing a certain uniformity in the celebration. By the early Middle Ages, there was a growing emphasis on the priest as the central figure. Only the priest and a server were allowed in the sanctuary and, in fact, the central part of the Eucharist, the consecration, was prayed in inaudible tones. He turned his back to the people and prayed in Latin. Preaching became the tool for explaining simple truths of the faith, but it often had little to do with Scripture, failing to challenge those gathered to a more adult faith. The role of the laity became simply attending rather than participating. As the integrity of the shared action of the priest and assembly faded, a stronger focus developed on the question of the Real Presence of Jesus in the Eucharist. The debates centered not on the *if* and the *why* of Jesus' presence but on *how* and *when* Jesus became present in the Eucharist.

The understanding of the Eucharist as a paradigm for living gradually but seriously became lost. The people sought with greater frequency to satisfy their need to worship the Eucharist in devotions outside of the Mass. The practice of reserving the Blessed Sacrament developed as a result.

Martin Luther, an Augustinian priest, realized the serious implications of this discrepancy between the way the practice of the Eucharist had evolved and the way it was prayed in the early Church. He called for a renewal of the practice of the Eucharist; thus was launched the sixteenth-century Reformation. Among other things, Luther submitted that the people's own languages should be used in the eucharistic prayer and that participatory singing be reinstated. He proposed that the priest face the people during the celebration, that the homily take on more substantive teaching, that communion be received in the hand and that the cup be offered as it would be at a meal.

The Council of Trent responded rather defensively to Luther's efforts at reform and mandated that our eucharistic practice remain the same. It was not until the Second Vatican Council that Luther's insights received a hearing.

The council incorporated many of Luther's recommendations as well as clearly reiterating the longstanding doctrine that the Mass is both meal and sacrifice. A better balance was reached between the repetitive prayers of the sacred ritual that keep alive the age-old tradition of the Church and the more spontaneous expressions of the contemporary Church. Likewise, the council reaffirmed the doctrine of transubstantiation: Christ is truly present in the consecrated bread and wine. However, the bishops of the council went beyond traditional teaching and stated that Christ is also present in the *community* that has assembled for worship, in the person of the *presider,* who leads the Eucharist prayer in the name of the assembly, in the *Word of Scripture* as it is proclaimed, and in the *consecrated elements* of bread and wine.

The heightened role of the laity as co-pray-ers has opened the way to many avenues of participation that the laity can take to become actively involved in the eucharistic celebration: greeters, proclaimers of the Word, eucharistic ministers, leaders of song, servers, etc. Above all, the entire assembly has a ministerial role as a priestly people. This shift to greater participation is difficult for those who have experienced the way the Eucharist was celebrated for years, i.e., in a more private and uninvolved manner. Nonetheless, if we recall what Jesus tried to say through his ministry at the table, it becomes clear that he wanted to gather God's family in such a way that we practice there what we want

The Eucharistic Celebration

Homily

"What word in
Scripture speaks
to you today?"
"What 'word'
echoes in your
heart as you come
to the eucharist?"
(joy, hope, fear?)

Word

"How does the
Scripture challenge
and support your
life this week?"

Penitential
Rite

"How might you be
resistant to new life?"

WORD
SACRAMENT
ASSEMBLY
PRIEST

"Who are you aware of
as you enter the church
for the eucharist?"

Greeting

Peace

Mission

"To what do you
say *Amen* and how
do you do it?

Communion

"How do you experience
communion with God,
yourself and others?"

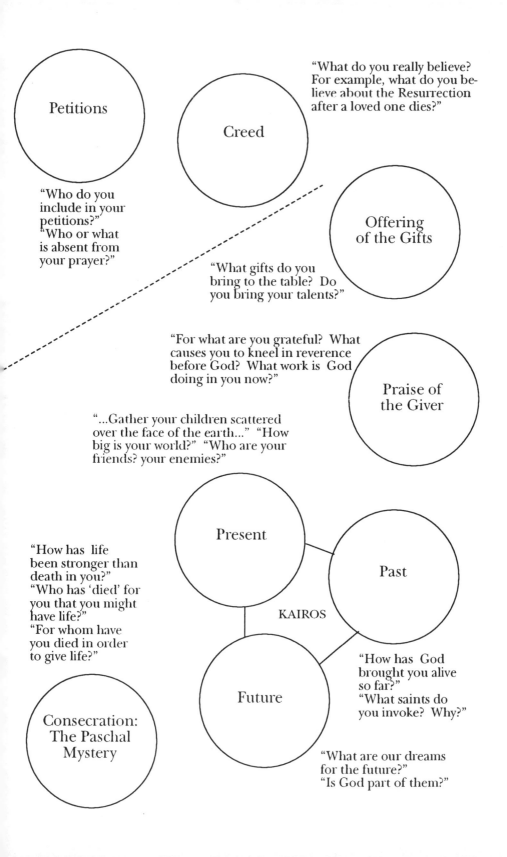

Petitions

"Who do you
include in your
petitions?"
"Who or what
is absent from
your prayer?"

Creed

"What do you really believe?
For example, what do you believe about the Resurrection
after a loved one dies?"

Offering
of the Gifts

"What gifts do you
bring to the table? Do
you bring your talents?"

"For what are you grateful? What
causes you to kneel in reverence
before God? What work is God
doing in you now?"

Praise of
the Giver

"...Gather your children scattered
over the face of the earth..." "How
big is your world?" "Who are your
friends? your enemies?"

Present

Past

KAIROS

"How has life
been stronger than
death in you?"
"Who has 'died' for
you that you might
have life?"
"For whom have
you died in order
to give life?"

Future

"How has God
brought you alive
so far?"
"What saints do
you invoke? Why?"

Consecration:
The Paschal
Mystery

"What are our dreams
for the future?"
"Is God part of them?"

to preach and live. It is as ordinary as Simon in *Simon's Night* listening to the mutterings and mumblings of his companions at the Norman Home. It is as extraordinary as realizing that we have become sisters and brothers of the one family that God has gathered in Jesus' name. This mystery requires participation of us as it demanded it of Simon. Each has the choice to be a bystander. Each of us has the choice to live our vocation and thereby experience in an entirely different way what it means to be "God's family gathered."

Questions for Reflection and Discussion

1. How could the celebration of the Eucharist more clearly call to mind our daily vocation of sharing life and meals with family, friends, and foes?

2. What would need to change if you were to share meals and life more in harmony with the spirit of the Eucharist?

Faith in Action

It is a noble challenge for each of us to bring our lives to our prayer and to see in our prayer the stuff of our everyday experiences. This is especially true of the Eucharist. Sometimes all we need are a few suggestions about how to let our prayer and our lives dialogue with one another before we understand the inherent connection between the two. When we do see the relationship, we no longer have to exert energy trying to live in two separate worlds. In fact, we discover the rich wisdom and guidance that the Eucharist can offer to us in our everyday life. And we find that the reality of our daily living keeps us honest in our prayer. The following "walk" through the several parts of the Mass might offer some help for praying the Eucharist in a new way.

Prayer

Prepare for next Sunday's Mass by reading over the Scripture for that day. Become familiar enough with the texts that you can ponder them at different times through the week. What word or image or person gets your attention? Why? Ask what the reading might be saying to you about your life right now. Chances are it is holding out a word of hope or challenge or consolation for you.

28

Sacraments of Healing: Reconciliation and Anointing of the Sick

Are any among you sick? They should call for the elders of the church, and have them pray over them, anointing them with oil in the name of the Lord. The prayer of faith will save the sick, and the Lord will raise them up; anyone who has committed sins will be forgiven. Therefore, confess your sins to one another, and pray for one another, so that you may be healed. (JAMES 5:14–16)

A couple of months before the great event, Corky's solicitous aunt inquired about his forthcoming First Eucharist. "So, are you excited, Corky?" she asked. "Uh huh," replied Corky. "There's something else that goes with it but I can't remember the name of it." "Hmm," he pondered, snapping his fingers. "I think it's called 'first relaxation!' "

Ah, the wisdom of children who grasp with simplicity and an uncomplicated intuition the compassionate heart of God. They just *know* that God's instinct is to salve the wounds of body and soul, effecting ease and peace in all who ask. For, always, God is a God of life. In the face of alienation and unease especially, Jesus reveals that God desires to lead us to deeper and deeper life, even to life beyond death.

The Letter of James places this healing and reconciling ministry squarely in the forefront of the Church's life. People are to see in Christians the same desire as is God's: to support and sustain us in trials of mind, body, and spirit. The Church is called to reveal the compassionate heart of God. It is upon this foundation that the sacraments of Reconciliation and the Anointing of the Sick are based.

THE SACRAMENT OF RECONCILIATION. Perhaps you remember going to confession on a Saturday afternoon, expecting that your soul would become as spotless as you were after your parents put you in a bathtub and scrubbed you clean. Trepidation lurked as you memorized the laundry list of sins that you drew up, insuring that you had made a "good confession." And by an odd kind of logic some thought that the worse the sin, the better the confession. Imagine the self-restraining response of the confessor as an eight-year-old admitted to three counts of adultery.

Jesus demonstrated no interest in lists of offenses. Nor did he define a person by what he or she failed to do. Peter was overwhelmed as he encountered the power of Jesus in the miraculous catch of fish. "Leave me, Lord, I am a sinful man," he cried as he experienced the tremendous discrepancy between the greatness of Jesus and his own human frailty. But Jesus seemed to say, "I know what you are like, Peter. But that's not the point. Concentrate on your friendship with me and the rest will right itself. Now come help me gather in other people" (see Luke 5:20–26). Luke recounts one story after another of God's desire to be in relationship to us. "What gives me joy?" Jesus inquires rhetorically. "The rejoicing that goes on in heaven over one sinner who repents is greater than the ninety-nine who have no need of repentance!" "To what lengths will I go for you?" Jesus persists. "I am like a poor woman who turns her house upside down to find one lost coin." "Do I know you are prone to wander off and squander the gifts I have given you? Of course I do, and it saddens me. But I will throw the biggest party you have ever experienced when you come back home to me!" (see Luke 15). Jesus came to save the world, not to condemn it (John 3:16).

The Church is gradually discovering the meaning of this profound mystery of God's forgiveness. The process has predictably included emphases, sometimes on one aspect of reconciliation, sometimes on another. Vatican II attempted to wed the various elements in a balanced whole, for each aspect lends something to our understanding of what eventually has come to be known as the sacrament of Reconciliation. A brief overview of its development will illustrate this.

Adult baptism, the norm in the nascent Christian Church, required such a total reorientation of one's life that any radical departure from this new commitment was considered serious. For the early Christians, post-baptismal forgiveness was a once-in-a-lifetime event (prompting a "get it all in before you have to reform" mentality for some!).

As the Church took its place on the world stage, cohesiveness became all-important. Heresy, murder, adultery, and apostasy so threatened the very existence of the community that they warranted excommunication. Those seeking reconciliation presented themselves to the bishop, who assigned a public penance like wearing a hairshirt for a lengthy period. Finally they were readmitted publicly to the worshiping assembly on Holy Thursday. This process was called public canonical penance because it took place in the midst of the community, it was guided or directed by rules made by various church councils, and its emphasis was on the doing of penance.

Eventually there was a shift from the doing of penances to the telling of sins. The practice of private auricular confession grew and with it a moral manual that listed every sin under the sun, giving in each case an appropriate penance. This highly moralistic and rather scrupulous approach to wrongdoing was interestingly complemented by the practice of spiritual direction and lay confessions. The custom of talking over one's experience of alienation with a wise guide in order to get to the heart of the wrong is a rich element in the life of the Church.

But, predictably, the pendulum swung. By the sixteenth century the Council of Trent determined a precise form for confession. Number, kind, and determining circumstances of serious sins should be reported in full to the priest, to whom the role of hearing and absolving sin was reserved.

Vatican II attempted to restore the rich elements that have dotted the history of the sacrament over time. The title "Reconciliation," recaptures its relational character. The laundry list of offenses is not the focus; violation of one's relationship with God and neighbor is. More emphasis has been placed on the *social* dimensions of sin. Hardly private, sin affects the community at large and even pollutes whole systems of life as we witness all too sadly in abuses of the environment. Communal services of Reconciliation underline the essential interrelationship that constitutes the body of Christ. The new rite of Reconciliation highlights the role of the *priest* as the *healer* who listens like the wise guide of old to the underlying patterns in a person's misguided choices. The penance, reflecting the compassionate God of Scripture, suggests ways to restore the person to right relationships and ease and peace with oneself. And always, the grace of the sacrament is offered in an essential way through the kind support and forgiveness of the community as we confess our sinfulness to one another.

Reconciliation, the healing of divisions in one's heart and one's relationships, is the work of a lifetime and indeed a rehearsal of that final surrender at death when all divisions cease. It is a work that can be joyful — and even relaxing, as Corky would say — because it trusts that Jesus wants more than anything to draw us into friendship with the One who is the source of all peace.

— ❖ —

THE ANOINTING OF THE SICK. If you or someone you love has ever suffered a serious illness, perhaps you know the experience of isolation, depression, or anger that can accompany it. Life goes on for others but you find yourself relegated to the fringes, stripped of the normal ways of being involved. You become a reminder to others of the fragility of life, a fact some want to avoid at any cost. The lonely experience of carrying the illness or injury can stir up anger, even at God. The lament "Why me?" cries out to be answered.

Jesus was not indifferent to such cries. To the leper's probing statement, "If you want to, you can cure me," Jesus replied, "Of course I want to! Be cured" (Mark 1:40). The instances when Jesus healed in the Christian Scriptures are numerous and lie at the very center of his ministry. The call to continue this ministry rests at the heart of the Church as well.

The Anointing of the Sick was not designated as a sacrament for several centuries but the practice of healing was existent from the start. The restorative oil, applied externally and even taken internally, was joined with the prayers of the community for the person's physical and spiritual well-being. Although the bishop was the one to bless the oil, it was used by both priests and laity for their personal needs and among their household.

A major mutation in the practice occurred when the association was made between anointing and deathbed confession. As noted in the section on Reconciliation, the customary practice for the early Church was to postpone Reconciliation for grave sins until the end of one's life because the penances were so stringent. In addition, Innocent I established that anointing should not be conferred on those in need of penance. This sequence of penance first and then anointing relegated anointing to the time of death. It became known as the "last rites" or Extreme Unction, obscuring the original focus on the spiritual and physical health of a person at any time. During this same period, a time when the practices and responsibilities of ministry were concentrated more in the clergy, the act of anointing was reserved to the priest and lay anointing was suppressed.

The core of this debate, that is, whether the sacrament was for the sick or for the dying, was addressed at Vatican II. The bishops decreed that the sacrament is properly called the Anointing of the Sick and that the entire people of God share in the ministry of attending to those of its members who are struggling in any way. "If one member suffers, all suffer together," said Paul to the Corinthians (1 Cor. 12:26). By standing with the one who suffers, whether through visiting the sick or by participating in the sacrament, all share in the sufferings of Christ, a particular ministry to which the sick person calls the Church. The attitude of heart that guides this ministry is the hope for new and deeper life. God is a God of the living, and the human instinct for life in body, mind, and spirit is holy. This instinct impels us to seek healing. And, yes, the day will come when one faces the limits of life as we know them. On that day we can relax in the faith that Jesus the Christ, the one who broke the bondage of death, will lead us to our eternal home where there will be no more weeping and where the Giver of all life will welcome us with open arms.

Questions for Reflection and Discussion

1. What deters people from celebrating the sacrament of Reconciliation?

2. How has the sacrament of the Anointing of the Sick brought you or someone you know healing and peace?

Faith in Action

Look for a way this week to offer forgiveness or provide a compassionate atmosphere for an alienated or suffering person in the community.

Prayer

When the early Christians wanted assurance that the Spirit of Jesus was alive and well in them, Paul pointed to the fruits of the Spirit as the surest guide. Pray Galatians 5:22–23 and ask God to restore whatever of these gifts you need in mind, body, and spirit:

"The fruit of the Spirit is love, joy, peace, patience, kindness,
generosity, faithfulness, gentleness, and self-control.
There is no law against such things" (Gal. 5:21–23).

29

Sacraments of Vocation

Mary stood weeping outside the tomb. As she wept, she bent over to look into the tomb; and she saw two angels in white, sitting where the body of Jesus had been lying, one at the head and the other at the feet. They said to her, "Woman, why are you weeping?" She said to them, "They have taken away my Lord, and I do not know where they have laid him." When she had said this, she turned around and saw Jesus standing there, but she did not know that it was Jesus. Jesus said to her, "Woman, why are you weeping? Whom are you looking for?" Supposing him to be the gardener, she said to him, "Sir, if you have carried him away, tell me where you have laid him, and I will take him away." Jesus said to her, "Mary!" She turned and said to him in Hebrew, "Rabbouni!" (which means Teacher). Jesus said to her, "Do not hold on to me, because I have not yet ascended to the Father. But go to my brothers and say to them, 'I am ascending to my Father and your Father, to my God and your God.'" Mary Magdalene went and announced to the disciples, "I have seen the Lord"; and she told them that he had said these things to her. (JOHN 20:11–18)

It has been said that the most beautiful sound in the whole world is being called by name by someone you love. No story could illustrate that truth more beautifully than the story of Mary in the garden, weeping and desolate, her world shattered by the death of the one she loved. At least she could go to the tomb, care for his body, perform all the delicate rituals of burial, touch and hold him one last time and say her good-byes. But she reached the tomb and he was not there. One can only imagine what happened to her heart at that moment. Then a man she barely noticed, the one she thought to be a gardener, called her by her name: "Mary!" There was, for Mary, no more beautiful sound in all the world.

Odd, perhaps you have already thought, that a reflection on the sacraments of vocation would be prefaced by the account of Jesus' apparition to Mary of Madgala. Her reputation — largely apocryphal — makes her a curious witness to marriage and orders. Perhaps. But this

Scripture passage illustrates the underpinning in any discussion of vocation, namely, that vocation involves being called by name, being attuned and attentive to the voice of God, mediated to be sure by the people and events of our lives, in order to discover and "grow into" the name God has for each one of us.

The basic Christian vocation, celebrated in Baptism, is what the Second Vatican Council called the universal call to holiness. The word "holiness," once reserved to saints, is a word being rehabilitated and welcomed back into religious vocabulary as we make the connection between holiness and wholeness. Holiness, the Christian's lifelong task, is becoming whole because holiness means to become more and more fully human. Holiness includes delighting in this world rather than fleeing it, recognizing that God, the creator and sustainer of all things, is revealed at the very heart of the world and of human experience. Holiness involves *becoming* the person whom God calls us to be in the very midst of the world, allowing the action of God and the life of God to invade and transform our lives. Holiness is coming to be more and more Godlike by putting on the mind and heart of Christ, for Christ is the perfect sacrament of God.

While we share a call to holiness, each of us is truly unique in God's eyes and each of us has a singular vocation and mission. The Book of Revelation uses an intriguing metaphor to communicate both the universality and distinctiveness of our vocations: "To everyone...I will give a white stone, and on that stone is written a new name that no one knows except the one who receives it" (Rev. 2:17).

Discovering and becoming that new name written on the stone involves discipleship in order to learn a way from Jesus to be human and holy. At the same time, being faithful to the "white stone" takes us down different paths of discipleship. Marriage, the single life, the religious life, and the priesthood all represent ways of discipleship. We may discover, falling in love with another person, that we will become most fully human and holy by following Jesus in total self-giving love to another; we may be drawn to the single life and imitate the solitary Jesus, rootless and restless about the reign of God, going about doing good; we may realize that we need to throw in our lot with others of like vision in order to follow Jesus, poor, chaste, and obedient, in a community of life and mission; or we may be drawn to the imitation of Jesus whose ministry was that of word, unity, and charity.

Only two of these vocational choices are numbered among the seven sacraments. Single life has never been designated a sacrament, strictly speaking, because historically and culturally it was not considered a suitable choice, or a choice at all! That religious life is not included among the seven sacraments is largely an accident of history and too narrow an interpretation of "institution by Christ." Both of these ways of life are obviously open to sacramentality although only the vocational choice of religious life is blessed by a liturgical rite.

MARRIAGE. One of the prefaces of the rite of marriage captures well our contemporary understanding of this sacrament: God created man and woman in love to share God's own divine life, a high destiny mirrored in the love of husband and wife. Love is our origin, our constant call, our fulfillment in heaven. The love of man and woman, bearing the imprint of God's own divine love, is made holy in the sacrament of marriage and becomes a mirror of everlasting life. This understanding, however, was not always thus.

Marriage as a social institution obviously preceded the advent of Christianity. Many of the elements of our present marriage rite, for example, veiling, giving of a ring, processions, witnesses, consent, and so on, are found in pagan and Jewish domestic ritual practice. The early community followed cultural models, continuing to marry and give in marriage but eliminating any obviously idolatrous practices. They understood that Christians were joined in Christ and that their marriage embodied God's love (see Eph. 5:23–32). Early frescoes even depict Christ as presiding at the marriage.

A decided ambivalence about marriage soon developed, however, thanks mostly to Augustine, who suggested that sexual desires were one of the regrettable side-effects of original sin. Marriage became understood as a remedy against desire; while there was disapproval of sexual relations, the rationale for marriage was the procreation of children. Despite such vague disapproval, liturgical rites gradually replaced domestic and civil practices and eventually the Church acquired exclusive authority in matrimonial affairs. Medieval scholastic debates and canonical rulings finally made of marriage a juridical abstraction.

The teachings of Vatican II have rescued marriage both theologically and liturgically. Marriage is recognized as a lifelong process through which a couple grows in holiness both in their life together and in raising their children. The family is called a little church, a community of love, a covenant of irrevocable personal consent. In bringing their love to public ritual expression in the sacramental celebration, the couple welcomes Christ into their common life, the ups and downs, the good times and bad, the daily routine. Trusting that Christ will stay with them and help them remain faithful to one another, they attempt to give visible expression to God's steadfast love over a whole lifetime. While marriage does not exhaust the witness of faithful relationships, it is a sacrament of the power of transforming love.

HOLY ORDERS. Ordained ministry has a complex history in the Church. Jesus himself, while a prophet, healer, and servant, was *not* a priest, at least he was not a member of the Levitical priesthood. He did not offer sacrifice nor preside at public prayer. Nor did he leave behind him an organizational chart to assist the community in matters of structure, maintenance, and mission. The early community appeared to explore a number of models of leadership and to recognize that there are a multitude of gifts lavished on women and men alike. Leadership of the Eucharist appears to have been entrusted to a variety of people. The rule appears to have been: let's not stifle the Spirit.

Organization, of course, was not a pressing concern in a Church that believed that Jesus' second coming was imminent and that that would signal the end time. But as time elapsed, the hope of a second coming was replaced by the need to structure the community for the long haul. The role of leadership was recognized to have several key elements: leaders were to keep the Gospel alive, unite the community in love, and exercise vigilance that the community remain faithful to the life and ministry of Jesus.

Gradually a tripartite structure of ministry (including bishop, priest, and deacon, to use their modern designations) replaced the earlier, more charismatic models of local churches, and with it came certain ritual developments. To prayer and a laying on of hands were added the giving of insignias of office, anointing, investiture, and fairly elaborate consecratory prayers through which it is possible to trace the Church's developing self-understanding of office and ministry over the centuries.

What remains important is a recognition that now, as in the Church of every age, the community is in need of authoritative leadership for the service of word, unity, and charity. God inspires service in the heart of individuals and bestows gifts on those whom *God chooses*. Ministry is always a function of need. It is the role of the community to determine its need for particular service, to recognize that some of its members possess God-given gifts, and to publicly ordain those it recognizes to the service of the community.

Questions for Reflection and Discussion

1. Do you believe that to be holy is to be human? What shape does "holiness" take in your life?

2. What would you look for in a couple to determine if they were ready to sacramentalize their union?

3. What would you look for in a candidate for Orders or Religious Profession?

Faith in Action

Each of us has promises to keep, because of both our basic Christian calling and the specific way of life we have entered as adults. Reflect on the promises you have made; ask God to keep you faithful; renew your vows or recommit yourself to the promises you have made.

Prayer

One day Jesus asked his disciples, "Who do you say that I am?" Spend some time in prayer, asking the same question: "Who do you say that I am? What is my name that is written on the white stone?" Hear yourself called by name, the most beautiful sound in the world.

30

Sacraments and Mission

With what shall I come before the Lord,
and bow myself before God on high?
Shall I come before him with burnt offerings,
with calves a year old?
Will the Lord be pleased with thousands of rams,
with ten thousands of rivers of oil?
Shall I give my firstborn for my transgression,
the fruit of my body for the sin of my soul?"

He has told you, O mortal, what is good;
and what does the Lord require of you
but to do justice, and to love kindness,
and to walk humbly with your God?

(MICAH 6:6–8)

An old Hasidic story included in Martin Buber's *Tales of the Hasidim* is called "At the Pond." It goes something like this: In the days following the death of a beloved rabbi, his disciples came together to talk about the things he had done. When it was the turn of the oldest among them, she asked: "Do you know why our master went to the pond every day at dawn and stayed there for a little while before coming home again?" They did not know why. The wise woman continued: "He was learning the song with which the frogs praise God. It takes a very long time to learn that song."

Day after day the rabbi had spent time by the side of the pond. Day after day, in the stillness of the early morning, the rabbi had listened to the tone, the nuance, the timing of the song. Day after day the rabbi had rehearsed the song of praise. But maybe — because only one of his followers was aware of what he was doing — maybe he never perfected the whole song so that he could say to his followers: "Listen to me; I've learned the frog's song of praise. I've got it down pat. Let me teach it to you." Maybe, in an entire lifetime, all he had learned were a few of the words, a phrase here or there, perhaps one verse and the chorus. But he never grew weary of rehearsal, possibly content in the recognition that it takes a very long time to learn that song, especially if he had hoped to sing it by heart.

What do *we* go to the pond to learn? Why do we gather, week after week, at the table of word and sacrament? Why do we mark our bodies with the sign of Christ's cross, or try to still our gathered selves? Why do we beg the Lord for mercy or open our hearts to words of consolation and challenge? Why do we try to join ourselves to Jesus' one great sacrifice of praise? Why do we say prayers, or recount our history, or confess our needs? Why do we embrace one another, break bread and share a cup of wine? Why, at the pond, do we welcome, unite, mend, heal, bless, bury, pray, praise, and promise — all of it in one another's company? Don't we gather together to rehearse a song, a song that takes a very long time to learn by heart? Don't we come, week after week, as well as in times of special need, in the hope that one day we will get it right?

Prayer, Aquinas once wrote, is not for the sake of God but rather for the sake of the community, to bring us to reverence. We say we are "heartily sorry" not because it is already true but because we hope the very saying of the words will make us just a little bit more repentant. We say of our hearts that they are "lifted to the Lord," and we hope to shake the torpor that so often weighs them down. We pray "thy kingdom come," barely comprehending the implications of our words, here, now, in very concrete ways as we walk out of church, yet acknowledging in our recital that God's longings for us — God's reign — *must* be played out in our everyday lives. That's the whole point of returning often to the pond. What we do there makes a difference. Our "choir practice" shapes our lives in attitudes, desires, and virtues.

Micah, whose words began this reflection, tells us something about the relationship of liturgy and life. Liturgy, he discovered in his conversation with Yahweh, is a rehearsal of values of the reign of God or it is worse than worthless. Micah muses about what authentic worship ought to look like: Should we celebrate with burnt offerings? oil? a sacrifice of rams? (A contemporary Micah might ponder: new vestments? matching communion cups? women altar servers? real bread?) The question of the prophet is the perennial question: What patterns of worship will please God? Yahweh responds to Micah — and to us — not with a pattern of pleasing worship but with a way of life. "This is what I ask, only this: act justly, love tenderly, walk humbly in my sight." "Only this" can make it sound so easy — as if the song might be mastered overnight — until we actually try it. What do all those sacraments do for us? Two things: they form in us habits of heart such as justice, love, and humility, *and* they commit us, individually and as a community, to live what we proclaim. "Amen" is a word that commits us to a mission. "Amen" commits us to complete Christ's work on earth. It's as simple as that.

In an interview with Robert Coles, Dorothy Day talked about her mornings at the pond. She said that she didn't go to church to be calmed down, as some people say they get when they are at Mass. No, she said, "I'm worked up. I'm excited by being so close to Jesus, but the closer I get, the more I worry about what he wants of us, what he would have us do before we die."

Clearly, liturgy isn't meant to be an escape from the realities of life, nor should it provide insulation from the crying social needs of our time or the violence and mayhem of our present world. We bring our world with us. We bring our preoccupations, our fears, our own complicity in the racism and sexism and struggle for power being played out on a global scale. We bring, too, our powerlessness before the sufferings of our brothers and sisters and the crushing weight of social structures that seem to ensure no end to their pain. And, in spite of all this — perhaps even because of all this — we try to learn a song of perfect praise.

When we gather for the Eucharist or for the celebration of any of the other sacraments, the song we rehearse is a vision, God's vision for us, and a set of values, the values of God's reign. We confess our sinfulness and fragility before the One who calls us to holiness. We name our unworthiness but beg, nevertheless, for the healing, forgiveness, and transformation that Christ's saving presence will effect. We make promises and bind ourselves, with every "Amen" that we utter, to keep those promises — and we try to mean the words we say, for the very rehearsal of God's vision and God's values commits us to a mission. When we leave the pond we have pledged to bring good news to the poor; to prisoners, freedom; and to those in sorrow, joy — at least in our tiny corner of the globe.

The song with which we praise God is the song we sing with our lives. We need time at the pond, prolonged time, but we don't stay there. We go to listen and to try to learn. We go to join our voices with others who may have learned different verses, or sing in different parts, or help us stay on key when we find it hard to sing at all. We go in the hope that one day we will get it right, together, finally reproducing the song perfectly. And when we do, we will discover that all of our liturgies are simply one dress rehearsal after another for the great end-time banquet when God will be all in all.

Questions for Reflection and Discussion

1. The rabbi took a lifetime to learn (and live) the song of the frog. What do you hope to learn at the pond to help you in your mission?

2. What attitudes characterized Jesus' mission?

3. Which of those same attitudes do you wish to characterize your own life and mission as you leave the pond?

Faith in Action

Ponder the following reflection on the word "Amen" by Barbara Schmich Searle. Try to mean it when next you say the word "Amen."

Amen

Be careful of simple words said often.
"Amen" makes demands
like an unrelenting schoolmaster:
fierce attention to all that is said;
no apathy, no preoccupation,
no prejudice permitted.
"Amen": We are present. We are open.
We hearken. We understand
Here we are; we are listening to your word.
"Amen" makes demands
like a signature on a dotted line:
sober bond to all that goes before;
no hesitation, no half-heartedness,
no mental reservation allowed.
"Amen": We support. We approve.
We are of one mind. We promise.
May this word come to pass. So be it.
Be careful when you say "Amen."

Prayer

The following is a contemporary rendering of the morning offering, a prayer that asks Jesus to bless our words and works and unite them to his own offering for the salvation of the world. Ask the Lord for a deeper commitment both to prayer and to mission.

O Jesus, I come before you at the beginning of this day.
I gaze at your face, I look upon your side pierced by the lance.
Your wounded heart speaks to me of God's love poured out for us.
Take, Lord, and receive my heart; the words of faith that I speak,
the works of justice I would do, my joys and sufferings.
When I come to the eucharistic table,
gather my offerings to your own for the life of the world.
At the end of the day, place me with Mary, your mother,
and for her sake take me to your Heart. Amen.

31

Sacraments: From Holy Things to a Way of Living

Jesus' time to depart from the earth and from his friends was close at hand. What could he say to them to put them on course for the long journey of living what he had tried to teach them during his life?

> *When they had finished breakfast, Jesus said to Simon Peter, "Simon son of John, do you love me more than these?" He said to him, "Yes, Lord; you know that I love you." Jesus said to him, "Feed my lambs." A second time he said to him, "Simon son of John, do you love me?" He said to him, "Yes, Lord; you know that I love you." Jesus said to him, "Tend my sheep." He said to him the third time, "Simon son of John, do you love me?" Peter felt hurt because he said to him the third time, "Do you love me?" And he said to him, "Lord, you know everything; you know that I love you. Jesus said to him, "Feed my sheep. Very truly, I tell you, when you were younger, you used to fasten your own belt and to go wherever you wished. But when you grow old, you will stretch out your hands, and someone else will fasten a belt around you and take you where you do not wish to go." (He said this to indicate the kind of death by which he would glorify God.) After this he said to him, "Follow me."*
>
> (JOHN 21:15–19)

Peter, the one chosen to lead this new community of disciples, had come to love deeply his friend Jesus, the Holy One of God. But Peter, like the rest of us, had to learn day by day and over a lifetime what loving Jesus meant. It was far more demanding yet more within reach than he had imagined. Peter learned that loving Jesus required his whole life.

Love is the "work" of liturgy. Love is the "work" of living. God, the one whose best name is Love, wants more than anything to share friendship with us. But we, like Peter, must be ready for the surrender and change that love requires.

Flannery O'Connor, in her short story entitled "Revelation," tells a wonderful and all too true tale of a woman who reluctantly confesses this struggle to love. Mrs. Turpin was a good woman who wanted to be good. She helped others in need and frequented church services. Her prayer was often one of gratitude for all she had been given but mostly, if the truth be told, for not being like other people. She prayed her litany of grateful righteousness in a doctor's office one afternoon to the curious and impressed glances of the other waiting patients. All but one, that is. An adolescent glared icy indignation across the room as she heard Mrs. Turpin register her virtues and criticisms. And all at once, as though she could no longer contain her hateful feelings for this pompous preacher, she hurled her novel at Mrs. Turpin with the acclamation, "Go back to hell where you came from, you old wart hog." That odd and humiliating gesture stunned Mrs. Turpin into a reverie that changed her life. She "saw" for the first time a vision of heaven:

> She saw a streak as a vast swinging bridge extending upward from the earth through a field of living fire. Upon it a vast horde of souls were rumbling toward heaven. There were whole companies of white-trash, clean for the first time in their lives, and bands of black niggers in white robes, and battalions of freaks and lunatics shouting and clapping and leaping like frogs. And bringing up the end of the procession was a tribe of people whom she recognized at once as those who, like herself and Claud, had always had a little of everything and the God-given wit to use it right.... They were marching behind the others with great dignity, accountable as they had always been for good order and common sense and respectable behavior. They alone were on key. Yet she could see by their shocked and altered faces that even their virtues were being burned away.

Somehow, perhaps imperceptibly, Mrs. Turpin had separated Jesus' message from the reality of her life. Though she prayed the Gospel, the radical acceptance and love that Jesus offers to all escaped her and rested on top of the crust of her daily living. Her "revelation" was that Jesus meant what he said about all being sisters and brothers, about all being sinners and saved, about her need for redemption too. The "crust" crumbled at the hand of God's mercy and grace and she was faced with the truth of herself, of others, and of a whole new way of living.

This transformation is the hope of our liturgy: that we may hold fast in our lives to what we have grasped by our faith (Prayer for the Monday after Easter). How astonishing that God not only asks us to live what we believe but that God, in Christ and through the power of the Spirit, gradually but concretely forms and strengthens us in God's own image. Then we become living sacrifices of love to God. As St. Augustine said in one of his sermons: If you are the body and members of Christ, then what is laid on the Lord's table is the sacrament of what you yourselves are, and it is the sacrament of what you are that you receive. It is to what you yourselves are that you answer "Amen," and this is your affidavit. Be a member of Christ's body, so that your "Amen" may be authentic (Sermon 272). Yes, sacraments signify what they effect and they need to effect in our living what they signify.

But how does this transformation happen? In a certain way, it is such common-sense that it alludes us. If we take the prayer of our liturgy as the starting point for change, we can examine the process. First, our language of prayer creates new images. In the third eucharistic prayer we petition: "Father, hear the prayers of the family you have gathered here before you. In mercy and love unite all your children wherever they may be." If we listen closely as we utter that prayer, words like "family," "all your children," "wherever they may be" begin to echo in our hearts and bounce against the reality of our world. What if we did look on each other as children of the same family, wherever and with whomever we find ourselves? How different this image is from our notions of isolated nationalism or "we against them" or "get ahead at all costs."

Second, new images prompt us into new ways of thinking, feeling, and believing. We begin to see and interpret the world through different lenses. God's vision of our world and our human family frame our everyday life from a different perspective. We become uncomfortable with the status quo of each one for oneself. The refugees in Africa *are* our concern and the poor in our neighborhoods become more than nuisances or real estate liabilities. They become — not without the strength of grace — our sisters and brothers.

Third, as we see rightly so we do rightly. The human instinct for harmony and integrity goads us to practice what we preach. Of course, we can always refuse to act on what we have been given to see, but not without the loss of peace and a certain congruity at the very heart of who we are. Even if we refuse to act on the "revelations" given to us, others will surely remind us of our hypocrisies, whether by hurling a novel across the room or simply failing to give credence to our words. "Your actions speak so loudly, I cannot hear what you say."

Fourth, as we live differently our worlds grow. We become aware of other "children" in places before unknown. We humbly admit how difficult it is to live as "family" and how skilled we have become at building up our own protected worlds. We taste the joy of barriers breaking and relationships formed and we wonder how we could have been so blind to the goodness of others. And our very living sends us to our knees all over again in cries for strength and love, in whispers of gratitude for pretenses of superiority and isolation crumbled, in awesome worship for a God who counts us as members of God's own family. The catalyst for our change will vary. Sometimes our point of entry will be prayer, at other times new images on the news at night or an innocent word spoken by an unsuspecting person. What matters is that more and more our words and actions, our prayer and our lives, become one. If transformation leads to such peace and integrity, why do we find it so difficult? Why, in fact, do we seem to resist it? People do what they do for good reasons even if those reasons aren't reasonable to anyone else. And there is a certain logic about why we defy transformation. What might be some of the elements of this "logic"?

Change is difficult for most. We would rather suffer "the fleshpots of Egypt" than venture out into the unknown. It takes faith to enter into a process of transformation, an uncommon virtue in a world where mediocrity is all too common and hard evidence about the "returns" on our human investments is expected.

Sometimes people have faulty expectations about what can be anticipated from each other. Rosemary Haughton expresses the danger of this in an essay about marriage. She believes that couples often approach marriage against the backdrop of the "romantic myth" where each expects the other to provide all that is needed for happiness. If each is lucky enough to have found the "knight in shining armor" or the "fair maiden," surely they will live happily ever after. In reality, this idyllic marriage never happens. That expectation simply sets one up for failure, and the energy needed to negotiate differences and invitations to grow are spent in facing disappointment and disillusionment. Haughton suggests that a more helpful context is the "heroic myth," where each expects struggle in living but accepts the process of change and growth together. Then the commitment to surrender to each other for the sake of a common vision of life becomes meaningful and even joyful.

God, too, never asked for perfection. "Be ye perfect..." is more about the willingness to love and forgive as God does than about avoiding all mistakes. Why would people open themselves to transformation if they felt that it was beyond reach? God asks us to keep changing because there is deeper life yet to be enjoyed. Yes, sometimes it means letting go of idols or preconceived notions about the way life ought to be. But the promise of God is that when the Spirit of God transforms us as disciples and friends, it leads always to peace, freedom, and joy.

If we could admit it, perhaps we are scandalized at the way God works for change in our lives. It is not ordinarily dramatic. Jesus resisted the temptations in the desert to be a "showy" magician God. He chose instead to work through the everyday events of people's lives in ways unspectacular, though no less profound. Maybe the greatest challenge that we face is to develop fine-tuned sensitivity to the way we are called to change ourselves and our world and then to trust that God will give us what we need to respond.

And that is perhaps another resistance to transformation. Each of us might admit that we can hardly believe God counts on us to help with the transformation of our lives and world. "Why would God ask me?" we protest. "There are others around stronger, more talented than I am. They'd do a better job at improving things. These prayers and calls to conversion aren't for me." How do we respond to Paul's prayer that professes "God's power working in us can do infinitely more than we can ask or imagine!" (Eph. 3:14).

Finally, our culture can make it difficult for us to engage in the work of transformation. Television and radio barrage us with so many needs that we hardly know where to begin to respond. We are tempted to pull down the shades of our minds and hearts, simply trying to keep our own bodies and souls together. Our U.S. way of life is founded on the bedrock of individual rights, sometimes sadly to the neglect of others' rights. It takes genuine asceticism to go against the grain of an individualistic and privatistic view of the world and assume instead the posture of a disciple who professes union with the other children of God's family, scattered over the face of the earth.

Praying, as individuals and as a community, is not for the faint of heart. Those who pray must know what they are choosing — a willingness to let the vision of God for each of us and for our world have the first and strongest word. Love, the "work" of God, shows itself in concrete deeds. And what are the clues that our prayers are authentic and "on course" with God's ways? The results will be unmistakable:

"Love is patient; love is kind; love is not envious or boastful or arrogant or rude. It does not insist on its own way; it is not irritable or resentful; it does not rejoice in wrongdoing, but rejoices in the truth. It bears all things, believes all things, hopes all things, endures all things" (1 Cor. 13:4–7). Who of us fails to recognize and rejoice in these gifts when they are in evidence? But there is nothing magic about them. They are gracious gifts of God that are there for our choosing with the help of God's grace. Love is the work of our prayer. Love is the work of our living. "Peter, do you love me? Then feed my sheep." Will we?

Questions for Reflection and Discussion

1. When you have been offered an invitation to change, why were you willing to pay the price of such change? Why might you have resisted?

2. What makes it difficult for you to connect your prayer with your living? Do you think this is so for others, too?

Faith in Action

Take time to reflect on a news event or a conversation or an incident that has remained in your memory during the week. Does it give you hope about the way life can be? Does it "haunt" you about what needs to be changed? Bring the experience to the liturgy this week. What does the prayer of the Church say about your experience and what it might be calling you to do?

Pay attention to the words of the liturgy this week. Is there anything that particularly gets your attention? How and why? Can you recognize a connection between what the prayer focuses on and what is going on in your life right now?

Prayer

Take time to reflect on some person(s) you greatly admire. How did (do) they live what they preach? If they have died, pray for the virtue that they so exemplified. If they are living, tell them how affected you are by the integrity and transforming power of their life.

Part Four

The Moral Life

Timothy E. O'Connell

32

Morality: Responsibility for Creation

Then the king will say to those on his right hand, "Come, you that are blessed by my Father, inherit the kingdom prepared for you from the foundation of the world; for I was hungry and you gave me food, I was thirsty and you gave me something to drink, I was a stranger and you welcomed me, I was naked and you gave me clothing, I was sick and you took care of me, I was in prison and you visited me." (MATTHEW 25:34–36)

One of the most popular movies of summer 1994 was *The Lion King.* Simba, the son of the great King Mufasa, thinks he is guilty of his father's death. And so in shame he flees his homeland. Eventually he comes to a new place, where he makes new friends from whom he learns a new philosophy of life: "No Worries," a carefree, uncommitted lifestyle.

But then his childhood friend, the lioness Nala, arrives on the scene. She tells Simba of the terrible situation in his homeland, where evil rules and all the animals suffer. She challenges him to return, to take up his role as king.

In responding to her challenge, then, Simba faces the two great questions of life. Is he responsible? Can he be respons-able? Is it his responsibility to do something? And does he have the ability, the skill and strength, to make a difference? Simba's questions are our own.

When God entered into a covenant with the People of Israel, its terms were clear: "I will be your God, and you shall be my people."* That was the promise that sent Abraham out from Ur of the Chaldees. It was the gift, expressed in the Passover of the Lord, that sent the Egyptian captives free. It was the compact that carried the people through forty years of wandering in the desert — and through several other experiences of exile. And it was the stirring proclamation that launched the faithful into the promised land.

---

*The general shape of the covenant is described in Genesis 17:7f; Exodus 6:2–9; and especially Exodus 19. This classic formulation of the covenant is, however, a later development, found in the prophets: Jeremiah 31:33 and 32:38; Ezekiel 11:20 and 36:28 and 37:27.

But the covenant is not only gift; it is also command. And so the question arises: What does it mean to be God's people? The Jews wrestled with this question for centuries, ultimately concluding that it means two things: love God and love neighbor. Jesus ratified their wisdom when he quoted their Scriptures and declared that the whole moral life comes down to these two commandments (see Matt. 22:37–40; also Mark 12:29–31 and Luke 10:27).

Of course, that answer does not resolve all our doubts. What does love of neighbor entail? In the inspired words of the Jewish Scriptures we find the honored formulation that we know as the Ten Commandments (Exod. 20:1–17). In the Christian Scriptures we find the summary of Jesus' teaching known as the Sermon on the Mount (Matt. 5–7). And throughout the pages of the Bible we find discussions of what love of neighbor entails. These discussions give us three things.

First, they give us resources, a library of wise answers that spoke to the writers' circumstances and may speak to ours. Second, they give us humility, an appreciation of how difficult it is sometimes to identify what love demands. Third, and most important, they give us affirmation, confirming the importance of the question. Morality is a faith-challenge that no true follower of Jesus can avoid.

In *Othello*, the title character says of himself: "Speak of me as I am. . . . Of one that lov'd not wisely, but too well" (Act V, Scene 2). Catholic teaching agrees. Love of neighbor is not just a matter of warm feeling. It is also — perhaps more importantly — a matter of wise behavior, of actions that are truly, genuinely helpful to our neighbors. In the movie *Oh, God!,* when John Denver, the reluctant prophet, asks what message God wishes him to bring to the world, George Burns, speaking as God, responds with words to the effect of: "Tell them I went to a fair amount of trouble to make this world, and I wish they'd take a little better care of it!"

In the Catholic tradition this has been called a "natural law morality," a morality built into the very structure of the created world. Many of the details of this natural law morality can be, and are, debated. But its core affirmation, rooted in our tradition, is accepted by all. That core affirmation of the natural law morality is this: human persons, all the more so followers of Jesus, are called to "take good care" of the world into which God has placed us. And toward that end, we are to use our intellect and will, our body and spirit, our individuality and our community, for the project of loving the world *both* wisely and well.

And so we conclude: actions are *moral* to the extent that they are worthy of the one who performs them, appropriate to those who experience them, helpful to those affected by them. And actions are *immoral,* to the extent that they are not.

These words present the abiding Catholic commitment to an *objective* morality. And it is an important commitment for us to understand, especially those of us who are Americans. For we live in a land of pluralism, and we have learned to live together by leaving one another as much room for freedom as possible. But that strategy can lead us to say: "You do your thing, and I'll do mine. And as long as you are doing what you think is right, I won't complain." That is, we can too easily reduce morality to good intentions, nothing more, as if personal sincerity were the only thing that counts.

Of course, sincerity is a critical component. After all, the doorway to good behavior is the desire for it. But sincerity is not the only component. Sincere people hurt one another all the time, despite their good intentions. Indeed, "mistaken sincerity" is practically a definition for auto accidents! So, while recognizing the importance of our personal intentions, the Catholic tradition has sought to avoid a "relativism" or "subjectivism" that would reduce morality to it. A moral discussion is not concluded when someone declares: "That's my sincere opinion." Rather, only the first moment in the discussion is concluded. The second moment, in which we inquire whether the opinion is in fact accurate in its assessment of what behaviors really help human persons, has yet to begin. That second moment, in which objective morality is affirmed and relativism is rejected, is integral to the Catholic vision of the moral life.

But if our vision of morality goes beyond relativism, it also goes beyond "legalism," an approach that reduces morality to arbitrary rules. Once again, it is not that rules are unimportant. Rules are very important to children; they help train young people in habits of right behavior, making clear to them the importance of moral living and providing them with standards against which to measure themselves. Rules are also important to adults, inasmuch as they provide pithy summaries of the wisdom of a community, its judgments about what behaviors really help and what behaviors really hurt. When a community says "Don't cheat!" or "Respect life!" it is really attempting to spotlight harmful or helpful behaviors and to challenge us to love our neighbors well.

So in the Catholic vision, rules do not make behaviors wrong; rather, they summarize and proclaim the fact that behaviors are already wrong. And the reason for the wrongness is that the behaviors are irresponsible, doing harm when help is possible. Thus, if we speak of the "moral law," it is not a law that commands so much as a law that teaches. And the adult responds to this law not so much with obedience as with docility (a willingness to learn).

So morality is a matter of accepting responsibility for our world, of "taking good care," of behaving in a way that is not only sincere but also actually helpful. And that is not a simple thing.

First of all, we live in a complicated world, a world of alternatives, of competing values. Often we are confronted with the painful truth: "I can do this or that, but I cannot do both. I can avoid this or that bad result, but I cannot avoid both." Because we humans are *finite,* our efforts to do what is helpful and to avoid what is harmful are burdened by the limits of what is concretely possible. That is why many of the wise teachers in the Catholic tradition have declared that the skill most needed for living the moral life is *prudence,* not a mealy-mouthed cowardice, but a down-to-earth ability to sort through life's complexity in order to discover how best to be responsible.

Even with prudence, though, there is a second problem: we live in a world where things change. In our individual lives things change as we grow older, enter commitments, gain opportunities, move to new locations, and so on. So a concrete behavior that was helpful in one setting may not be so elsewhere. It might be morally upright for a young single person to spend money for a vacation that would be morally wrong for a person with family obligations. And sexual behavior that is positively virtuous in the context of marital commitments is destructive and therefore wrong in the absence of that bond of love.

And the same is true of the world as a whole. As we have conquered the atom, developed new medical technologies, united the world through electronics, come up against the finiteness of our resources — as all this has happened, our moral challenges have changed. We are not only finite, we are also *historical,* changeable beings in a changeable world.

This does not mean that everything changes. That view presents a silly — and destructive — trendiness. But it does mean that some things change and that change in our moral universe cannot be altogether avoided. And thus, there is no substitute for courage: a strong stance in the presence of our ambiguous historical world, a willingness to trust in past wisdom while also remaining open to new insights, to do the best we can now while hoping for more clarity in the future. As followers of Jesus, we are challenged to reject a simplistic fundamentalism that trades truth for easy clarity. Instead, we are challenged to remain faithful to the call of the real, to be responsible, to love one another and our world both wisely and well.

In sum, then, the Catholic tradition proposes a view of morality rooted in our call to responsibility. This view embraces morality as objective, not just subjective. It understands morality as transcending rules, though using rules as tools for education and inspiration. It accepts the anxiety-provoking truths that we live in a finite world, where options compete, and a historical world, where new issues cannot be avoided. And it challenges us, as Nala challenged Simba, to accept the responsibility that is ours.

But is all this possible for you and me? Simba had two questions. The first was: Must I do it? But the second, equally important, was: Am I able to do it? And Catholics throughout the ages have struggled also with these questions.

In *The Lion King*, Simba is urged to look to himself, to his own heart, and to the memory of his father in order to discover his ability to respond. The Judaeo-Christian tradition offers a different prescription. We are told to look to God.

Our tradition teaches that we do not *earn* God's love by our good behavior, so that right behavior comes first and God's gifts only later. Quite the contrary, we are taught that God loves us first, even in our unworthiness. Indeed, it is that very love which comes from God that empowers us for our good deeds. When Christians speak of "grace," they are referring to the presence of God that touches us, transforms us, strengthens us, illuminates us, and empowers us for the moral life to which we are called.

Of course, this grace does not immediately conquer all that gets in the way of our good living. Every one of us has plenty of experience to the contrary. But it does support us in our efforts to live into our future, and it provides the promise that our efforts will not be in vain.

It is because God is present to us that we can speak of our moral skills not just as human accomplishments but also as God-given virtues. Thus, in these pages we have talked of humility and courage, prudence and docility, faith and hope. And all these terms refer to facets of the abiding, loving, transforming presence of God within us, accompanying us in the moral life we seek to live.

Questions for Reflection and Discussion

1. This chapter contrasts "objective morality" with a "morality of good intentions." What do you think of this distinction? Do you think most people believe in objective morality? Should they?

2. The chapter rejects a "legalism" that reduces morality to rules. Were you raised to have a positive view of rules or to be suspicious of them? What do you think is the proper place of rules today?

3. A true view of objective morality takes seriously how complicated the world is. Do you find it complicated? Are most of your moral dilemmas really difficult, or rather simple? Can you give examples?

4. People say: "Well, things change. Old views don't work any more." Do you agree? Why or why not? Can you give examples?

5. What do you think is the greater danger: that we will impose "certitudes" that do not really exist or that we will ignore certitudes that are real? What prompts your answer?

Faith in Action

Look in the newspapers for examples of moral issues, moral virtues, moral failures. Imagine what Jesus has to say about each. Share your reflections with those you trust.

Prayer

God of creation,
I give you thanks for your love for me,
revealed in your gifts to me, within me, around me.
In gratitude I seek to love my neighbor, near and far.
Give me the courage and wisdom to love them well. Amen.

33

Conscience: Personal Responsibility

*If an unbeliever invites you to a meal and you are disposed to go,
eat whatever is set before you without raising any question on
the ground of conscience. But if someone says to you, "This has
been offered in sacrifice," then do not eat it, out of consideration
for the one who informed you and for the sake of conscience — I
mean the other's conscience, not your own.*

(1 CORINTHIANS 10:27–29)

Christians are called to be women and men of conscience: this idea
is as ancient as the faith itself. Since scholars tell us that the letters
of St. Paul were written even before the four Gospels achieved their
final, written form, it could be that the text quoted above is the oldest
written assertion of the primacy of conscience that we have. It is also
one of the most pointed.

The case discussed by Paul makes a wonderful story. He is writing
to the Christians in Corinth, a city known for its many pagan temples.
Some of these groups practiced animal sacrifice. Rather than "waste"
these carcasses, they were sold on the open market. And that created
a moral problem for the Christians.

"My heavens, Henrietta. That sure is good-looking filet mignon in
the butcher's window."

"Beware, Gladys. The meat came from that temple yonder. It was
slaughtered in their religious sacrifice. If you serve it for dinner, you'll
be participating in their worship!"

What's a Christian to do? St. Paul answers: "Oh, Henrietta, relax!
Gladys isn't intending pagan worship. She just wants to serve a nice
dinner. There's no problem with that — at least if no one in the family
has high cholesterol!"

But then Paul continues, in an amazing vein. "Still, you'd better be
alert to your neighbor, Gladys. It could be that some of them, like
Henrietta, think it's wrong to serve that filet. If they see you serving
it and get the impression that you are knowingly doing what's wrong,
they might be inclined to do it too. But if they do, truly (though erro-

The Moral Life

neously) thinking it's wrong, they'll commit a sin. And you sure don't want that.

"So, be attentive to your neighbors. For their sake, you may need to skip that filet mignon. Or you may need to be discreet about serving it or to explain yourself to them so they don't get the wrong impression. But at least be attentive to how your actions impact others. For at the last judgment, before the throne of God, we won't be judged for guessing right. We'll be judged on whether we acted in accord with what we *believed* to be right."

— ❖ —

"Conscience" is not a thing, as if we could locate it in some particular part of our body. Rather it is an aspect of human personhood, our *conscientiousness.* (The Hebrew Scriptures use the word "heart" to point to the reality we call conscience.) The word refers to the fact that we humans are responsible for our lives and our behavior, that we know ourselves as responsible, and that we consequently experience ourselves as innocent or guilty depending on whether we are faithful to what responsibility seems to dictate.

This simple idea, that God will judge us for our fidelity to our best wisdom — whether or not it turns out that our wisdom is correct — has often been reaffirmed in Catholic tradition. We can hear it in the challenging words of Jesus:

> Do you not see that whatever goes into a person from outside cannot defile, since it enters not the heart but the stomach, and goes out into the sewer?...It is what comes out of a person that defiles. For it is from within, from the human heart, that evil intentions come. (Mark 7:18–20; note: "heart" = "conscience")

And we can hear it in the famous words of St. Augustine (d. 430), "Love and do what you will."

In the middle ages, St. Thomas Aquinas (d. 1274) raised the painful question of what one should do if one thought one had only two options, to violate one's conscientious judgment or to be evicted from the Church. He responds that one should accept eviction, since our eternal salvation does not utterly depend on being in the Church, whereas it absolutely depends on our doing what we believe (correctly or not) to be right. And in the nineteenth century, the English convert John Henry Newman summarized his understanding of the faith in his famous after-dinner toast, "To the Pope to be sure, but to conscience first, and to the Pope afterward."

This vision of conscience, then, is a deep Catholic tradition — and a beautiful one. Imagine that this Church were to talk to people considering membership, to women and men thinking about being Catholics. Here is what the Church would say:

> We believe deeply in the gift that our Church is. We believe we are blessed to share in this community of faith. We believe one can find Jesus here — and life and hope. So with joy we invite you to share with us the life of this Church.
>
> But, on the grounds of our faith itself, we believe even more deeply in you. So, if you do not find our community to be for you a path to God and a fountain of strength for service to the world, then do not join us. Far more important than membership in the Church is fidelity to the path God seems to be showing you. Paradoxically, the faith of the Church to which you are invited is this: that faith in you and your conscience takes precedence. So the love that is in the Church will even set you free from the Church, if that is what your reflections say must be.

Yes, a deep and beautiful tradition. But for such a simple idea, conscience has often become terribly controversial. Some will shout about the supremacy of conscience — and use that argument to silence those who criticize their behavior, whether the behavior is abortion or firing a large group of employees. Others will insist that "the only true conscience is a rightly formed conscience" — and use that argument to criticize those whose judgment differs from theirs, whether they are military officers with an understanding of the need for national defense or married people seeking to limit the size of their families. What are we to make of these comments, and of the controversy they point to? Two things, perhaps. For one, they reveal how easy it is to misunderstand the Christian vision of conscience. And second, they remind us of the importance of balance in these matters.

As understood in the Catholic tradition, conscience does not stand over *against* objective morality; rather it is the way we achieve contact *with* objective morality. That is, it is not the judgment of conscience that makes something objectively right or wrong. No, as we saw in the previous chapter, things are right or wrong depending on how they actually serve the true fulfillment of human persons and the world.

Rather, conscience is the human capacity to discover the already-true rightness or wrongness of the behaviors we consider.

On the other hand, it is true that, at the moment of personal judgment, we have no access to that objective morality other than our consciences. That is, there is no way to circumvent the judgment of conscience by some *other* judgment of morality; rather the word "conscience" is the word we use to name the very *personal* judgment of *objective* morality that we have. So, as the tradition sometimes put it, the *ultimate* measure of morality is objective truth. But the *immediate* measure of morality is the personal judgment of conscience.

An analogy may help. People who drive cars use their eyes to guide themselves along the road. Their eyes don't *make* a particular road go north or south; the road either does or doesn't. But there is no way for them to *discover* the objective direction of the road except through the medium of their eyes. On the one hand, it makes no sense to say: "Just follow your eyes and don't worry about objective truth." But it also makes no sense to say: "Ignore your eyes, and follow objective truth." Blithely following one's eyes without worrying about the quality of one's eyesight doesn't make one liberal; it makes one dangerous! And without one's eyes, one doesn't become more "loyal"; one becomes a menace!

So a balanced view of conscience stands between these two extremes. And this balance was always sought, though described in many different ways, within our Catholic tradition. One helpful description emphasized three "moments" in the living out of our conscience — not actual moments of time, but elements or aspects of the one integrated reality.

The first "moment" is really a permanent *quality:* our deep-down sense of responsibility for our behavior. If children are properly raised, they come to understand that human persons are responsible for their behavior. That's why they should tell the truth, pay their debts, keep their promises. That's why human persons sometimes feel it necessary to apologize, to admit fault and make amends. We humans are "conscientious beings," beings characterized by an abiding awareness that can be called conscience.

The second "moment" is a *process* that takes place within us: the process of searching for right and wrong. Precisely because we experience ourselves as responsible (the first moment), we feel obliged to try to "figure things out." We wonder if a particular action is right or wrong, and we try to find the answer to our wondering. In this moment we are intensely aware of our ignorance. Indeed, the very reason this moment happens within us is that we are not born knowing what is right and what is wrong. We have to figure that out by looking, thinking, talking, learning.

In this second moment, then, we would not speak of the *rights* of conscience; rather we would speak of the *duty* of conscience, a duty to be open to the truth wherever it may be found. And in this moment, whether it lasts ten seconds or ten years, we are acutely aware that primacy goes to reality. We humans are called to be learners.

But humans are also called to act. There comes a moment when one must do something; indeed even the decision not to act is an action of a sort. So eventually, one must face the question: What is the right thing for me to do? And in answer to that question, a judgment must be made. That *judgment* is the third moment of conscience.

Inasmuch as this judgment really is just the summation of what the process of learning has achieved, it is always susceptible to error. After all, I may have missed some important data; I may have been deceived by what I think I learned. So, as often as we make these personal judgments, concluding that we should do this or should not do that, it is probably the case that we are never absolutely certain of their correctness.

But inasmuch as this judgment of conscience is, for better or worse, my best attempt to make contact with objective truth (second moment), and inasmuch as we humans are, in the end, conscientious beings who cannot evade responsibility for their behavior (first moment), I have no choice. At this moment, no matter what I may learn later, this judgment of conscience is the voice of God for me, the demand that I must follow. If I choose to act in accord with this judgment, I am acting virtuously; if I choose to violate this judgment, I am committing sin. For in these cases I am either doing or refusing to do that which (correctly or not) I truly believe to be the will of God for me. As Pope John Paul II put it, "in the practical judgment of conscience, which imposes on the person the obligation to perform a given act, the link between freedom and truth is made manifest. Precisely for this reason conscience expresses itself in acts of 'judgment' which reflect the truth about the good and not in arbitrary 'decisions' " (*Veritatis Spendor*, no. 61).

And that, of course, is precisely what St. Paul was saying to the Corinthians.

Questions for Reflection and Discussion

1. Is the understanding of conscience that is presented here something you were already familiar with? Do you associate it with the Catholic Church? Is it one of the things that makes the Catholic Church attractive to you? Why or why not?

2. Some people think we're easily led to forget the important role of conscience and to slip into fundamentalism, where we blindly follow the judgments of others. Have you seen this? Do you have experiences where the rights of conscience seem to be overlooked?

3. Some people think we're easily led to abuse conscience, using its claims as justification for selfishness. Have you seen this? Do you have experiences where the duties of conscience seem to be overlooked?

4. In your situation, in your community, in our country today, which do you think is the greater danger: to overlook conscience or to abuse it? Have you had any particular experiences that have shaped your view?

5. Granted that children need special attention and different emphases for their growth to moral maturity, how would you express to them this twin truth about the rights and the duties of conscience?

Faith in Action

As you go through your day, try to notice the three "moments" of conscience in action: the sense of responsibility, the process of discernment, and the act of judgment. Try to find an opportunity to encourage the responsible enactment of conscience in someone you meet.

Prayer

God of Faithfulness,
in the Spirit of Christ help me to be a conscientious person,
responding generously to your will as I perceive it.
And help me to live out my decisions in courage and trust. Amen.

Discernment: Learning in Community

I truly tell you, if two of you agree on earth about anything you ask, it will be done for you by my Father in heaven. For where two or three are gathered in my name, I am there among them.
(MATTHEW 18:19–20)

Fred and Sylvia had a problem. The opening of school approached, and they hadn't yet decided where to send little Freddy Junior. The Catholic school taught the sorts of values they believed in, but it was so expensive. The public school worked at serving the community, and deserved being supported, but was so "loose." What to do?

They couldn't quite tell you how it happened. They'd simply walked out of Church that Sunday, planning to head for home. The next thing they knew, they were chatting with Agnes and Carl. Then they were at the local diner sharing breakfast. They talked about their own growing-up experiences. They talked about their dreams for family life. They even talked about the homily they'd heard that morning. Rarely had they talked so deeply, so candidly about what they believed in. It was a wonderful meal — and they could hardly remember what they ate!

By the time they got home, they knew what they were going to do.

In the last chapter we reflected on our personal responsibility for the conduct of our lives. We saw that we are each challenged to use the eyes of our conscience, in the attempt to discern how best to live, and then to obey the insights that those eyes discover. At the same time, we recalled the conclusion of the chapter before that moral rightness is not simply a matter of personal opinion, that sincerity is not enough. Sincerity must be harnessed to correctness, to the extent that we are able.

How is that to be done? How does the process of discernment that was conscience's second moment take place? How can we make it more successful in finding the truth about how we should live? These questions — and the answers given by the Catholic tradition — will occupy us now.

—❖—

When people make a judgment about how they ought to act, they are doing something intensely personal. If they judge, for example, that a lifestyle of consumerism is contrary to the Gospel, their judgment will cost them! They will need to change, to make sacrifices and accept consequences. So they are not likely to be indifferent in moving to these judgments.

And because they are so personal, these judgments are also highly emotional. They are rooted in one's feelings, instincts, sensitivities. They come out of one's "gut," not one's head. The activity of moral discernment looks less like an operation of a computer, logically moving from premises to conclusions, and more like a Geiger counter, responding sympathetically to what is discovered "out there."

Probably your own experience confirms this. There are probably values about which you feel deeply, out of which you live. And you measure concrete behaviors against those deeply felt values; you react to the fact that they either conform to or diverge from those values. And on the basis of those gut reactions, you act.

As we've noted, this does not mean that moral values are a "mere matter of feelings." Rather it means that, to the extent that we live out of our feelings, it is the function of our feelings to put us in immediate touch with the moral values that objectively exist in the world.

But feelings do not automatically fulfill that function. Our moral sensibilities are shaped and honed by life experiences, so they are as accurate or as distorted as these experiences. Racism and sexism continue to exist less because people really set out to be mean and more because people's experience allows them to live with moral "blind spots." Our tolerance for grave social evils — such as the abuse of migrant workers, the lack of medical support for indigent mothers and children, or the absence of an effective food distribution network to prevent widespread starvation despite the fact that the human family grows enough food for everyone — is less a matter of cold indifference and more a matter of learning to live without noticing.

At the other extreme, the moral sensibilities that we developed during our years of growing up can be excessively tender in some matters. Some older persons claim they were raised to experience automatic guilt about sexual urges and acts, no matter how proper they may be. Others, particularly in some forms of dysfunctional families, can feel personally responsible for any conflict or disturbance, with a consequent obligation to "make it all right at any cost."

Finally, we should note that even when our moral sensibilities are neither callous nor neurotic, they remain diverse. Different ways of behaving have priority in different families, nations, cultures. For example, some Americans live in a cultural setting that gives priority to values such as promptness, precision, duty, and self-reliance. Others live in cultural contexts that see hospitality, the cultivation of relationships, and warmth as more important. The first group accuses the second of laziness. The second responds with an accusation of cold disregard for persons.

Still, whether these feelings fully succeed in touching objective moral values, they are real. And in our moments of personal decision, we tend to live out of them. So our moral sensibilities must be given their due.

Giving these feelings their due means accepting them as real. But it also means recognizing them as imperfect, perhaps deeply flawed, and certainly in need of correction, completion, or cultivation. And that is the function of reasoned reflection in our process of moral discernment. Even though it is an illusion to believe that people actually live out of their more rational side, that doesn't mean moral living can be a simple matter of uncritical feeling. No, reasoned reflection allows us to step back from the intensity of our life decisions and to inquire about their character.

We can check ourselves for consistency. Do our decisions mesh with one another, or do they contradict each other? We can measure our "felt judgments" against recognized universal standards. Do they exhibit fairness, treating similars similarly, or are they arbitrary, playing favorites? Do they reveal respect for others, or is a selfish narcissism evident? And we can measure our judgments against the standards of those we trust. No one lives life utterly alone. We all depend on the wisdom of others. We call these trusted others "authorities." So we wonder: Do our judgments coincide with those of our families? Our Church? Special experts in one field or another? And if not, what does that mean?

And what shall we do? Here is a very important question. If reasoned reflection finds discrepancies between our moral sensibilities and what it appears ought to be, that conclusion does not change the sensibilities. Only experience can shape moral feelings. So rationally discovered discrepancies are a call for new experiences.

If I find a pattern of racism in myself, the solution is not self-flagellation. It is initiatives to encounter persons of other races. If I judge that my behavior is driven by neurotic guilt, I cannot just command change in those feelings. I may need counseling or participation in a Twelve Step group. If I find that moments of intensity lead me to act out of competitive or aggressive urges, perhaps only a regimen of quiet prayer will bring about the needed transformation.

Thus far, we've been looking at the process of our moral discernment, describing how the exploration that is the second moment of conscience takes place. We've noted that, when we're in the midst of such exploration, we tend to operate out of our "gut instincts." And we've noted that these "instincts," these moral sensibilities, are shaped by our life experience. Now, let's notice a simple but profound truth: in living our lives we are never alone. We always exist as a member of various groups. Human persons, at base, are communal animals.

So our personal values, the priorities about which we feel deeply, come from the experiences we have in groups. Indeed, for all practical purposes we can say that all our values come from the groups in which we live. We might even say that these value commitments abide more in groups than in the individuals who comprise the groups. If each of us were to list things about which we feel deeply, we could probably also list next to each item a group in which we've been involved that has shared that deep conviction. We might even be able to identify quite clearly how and when the group led us to appropriate that value.

This insight has powerful implications for our lives. It reminds us how pivotal is family life. Each of us is inescapably shaped by the family in which we were raised. As we move into adulthood many of us start families of our own, to continue the process. And all of us know the power for good or ill that family experience can wield.

The insight also helps us appreciate the importance of all the other groups in our lives: the friends with whom a young person spends time, the military unit with which a young adult faces some of life's most frightening experiences, one's work associates, and, indeed, the underlying climate of one's work situation. We are shaped by our groups, and so the process of moral growth is a process of weaving individuals into groups that stand for the positive values we espouse.

So communities play a key role in the formation of our deeply felt values. Communities also have a role in the process of reasoned reflection we discussed earlier. If we are to assess the quality of our felt values, a central place in that assessment is occupied by those around us. They give us "feedback"; they support or challenge us in our moral decisions. By their own behavior they offer us an alternative with which we can compare our behavior. In all this, communities serve as places of moral discernment, of reinforcement and critique.

All of the comments made thus far lead us to reflect on the wonderful role of the Church in moral living, a role cherished by Catholics as one of God's most gracious gifts.

First of all, the Church is our community of moral living. It is the group from which we absorb a set of value commitments out of which we try to live. Here we are focusing not on the intellectual teaching that takes place in the Church, but on the even more fundamental and more important "chemistry" that takes place by being together. Catholics find strength for moral living in their common presence in worship on Sunday. They find support in the example of sacrificial love and faithful justice lived by their sisters and brothers in community. By observing the generosity and love of other married couples, they are deepened in their commitment to the vocation of marriage and the cultivation of family. By sharing one another's struggles to behave with honor and integrity in places of work, in civil communities, in the ordinary commerce of every day, they are confirmed in the values of their heart to do likewise. In a word, by "being Church," by sharing in the life of faith and faithfulness, the Catholic's skill of accurate and empathetic moral discernment is progressively developed.

But the Church also plays a role in the process of reasoned reflection. Catholics are proud to belong to a "teaching Church," to a community that believes deeply enough in Christ's call to love our neighbor that it speaks boldly about the concrete shape of that love. The community of the Church, speaking especially through the leaders given by God to the Church, articulates its wisdom about what behaviors accord with our vocation and what behaviors do not. And while the challenge of that clearly spoken wisdom can sometimes leave Catholics disturbed, it is nonetheless embraced as a gift. For all of us do indeed want to love our neighbors both well and wisely. And if someone — anyone — can shed light on the suitability of concrete behaviors for that project, that light must surely be welcome.

To the individual considering membership in the Roman Catholic Church, our tradition of strong moral teaching can be both attractive and troubling. On the one hand, in a world of confusion, certitude is most desirable. So some people can be inclined to Catholicism precisely for its aura of certitude, even to the point of falling into a sort of fundamentalism that betrays our vocation as sojourners in this world. Even some long-time Catholics can succumb to this aberration. The truth is that on very few matters does the Church claim absolute certitude. In moral matters, particularly those that attempt to explore very concrete, complex current questions, we do not claim absolute certitude.

Other individuals find the teaching practices of the Church troubling. They note that Church teachings, at least on some questions, seem terribly conservative. It is probably best simply to acknowledge that fact. The Catholic community has a two-thousand-year heritage. And members of that community trust that the abiding aid of God has been present throughout those years. As a result, there is a bias toward the tried-and-true, a tendency to remain faithful to past wisdom until and unless it becomes absolutely clear that change is called for.

There are cases, to be sure, where the Church has come to realize that past teaching was in error. The condemnation of Galileo and Church opposition to scientific study is a classic example. There are other cases where past teaching may have been completely accurate, but circumstances have substantially changed the state of the question. For example, it appears that past teaching about war as a means of resolving international conflict must be modified in light of frightening modern technology. But until such calls for change — and an utterly convincing summary of new wisdom — emerges, one will hear from the Catholic Church traditional value commitments.

So how do Catholics respond to these teachings? They give them high regard. Even those less-than-certain teachings, even teachings that one suspects may someday undergo adjustment. For it is our faith that God abides in this community, and particularly in its leaders, as guide and support for the human process of moral reflection and discernment. And so Catholics offer respect to all the teachings of the Church.

Catholics, like all human persons, must ultimately think for themselves and obey the judgments that their consciences present. But in the process of discernment we have been describing, one sees in Catholics a *docility*, an openness to listen, a willingness to learn. That is what it means to discern — and to grow — in community.

Questions for Reflection and Discussion

1. Can you identify priority values in your life? Can you remember experiences in your life that have shaped and reinforced those values?

2. What do you believe was the finest gift of your family to the shaping of your moral vision?

3. Do you have moral sensitivities that strike you as *not* appropriate, because they are either excessive or deficient? Can you imagine experiences that might help to change those sensitivities?

4. The chapter recommends reflection, to check your moral feelings for consistency and for how they match with universal standards or with the personal standards of those you trust. Can you think of times when you have done this? Do you have suggestions for making this reflection more successful?

5. At this point in your life, do you have a "community of moral discernment"? Are you looking for one? Or to put this another way: Whom do you consult when you have a tough decision to make?

6. Do you look to the Church for moral guidance? In your experience, has the community of the Church, or the words and deeds of its leaders, served as moral guides for you? How do you feel about belonging to a "teaching Church?"

Faith in Action

Some time today have a conversation about an issue of current importance. In other words, create, at least for a moment, a community of moral discernment with someone you trust.

Prayer

God of the People, bring us together.
Teach us to speak with candor, to listen with compassion,
and to share with faith.
Lead us, together, to your truth. Amen.

35

Sin: Facing Limitation and Failure

*Then some people came, bringing to him a paralyzed man. . . .
When Jesus saw their faith, he said to the paralytic, "Son, your
sins are forgiven." Now some of the scribes were sitting there,
questioning in their hearts, "Why does this fellow speak in this
way? . . . " At once Jesus . . . said to them, "Why do you raise such
questions in your hearts? Which is easier, to say to the paralytic,
'Your sins are forgiven,' or to say, 'Stand up and take your mat
and walk'? But so that you may know that the Son of Man has
authority on earth to forgive sins" — he said to the paralytic — "I
say to you, stand up, take your mat and go to your home." And
he stood up, and immediately took the mat and went out before
all of them.* (MARK 2:3, 5–12)

The story is told of the married couple who came to a therapist for
counseling. Their relationship, they freely admitted, was a shambles.
Indeed, they had not spoken a civil word to each other in weeks.

At first, they argued even about the details. He said that she had
begun the war by a nasty complaint about his watching football. She
disagreed completely. It was he who had started it, describing as "slop"
the dinner she had so carefully prepared.

After listening for some time, the therapist asked a question: Was
each of them absolutely sure that their memory of the beginnings of the
conflict was accurate? After some hesitancy each admitted some uncer-
tainty. Indeed, after some more conversation they acknowledged that
the battle of words had gone on so long, its beginning was shrouded in
history. "So let us grant," said the therapist, "that we do not know —
and probably will never know — precisely how the war began!"

The therapist added a second question, "As you consider the period
of your conflict, can either of you claim to be simply and solely a victim? Can you honestly say that at no time have you, by your actions,
made it worse?" They could not. Each admitted, after some prodding,
that they had indeed made things worse. Of course their justification
was the prior attack of the other party. But each still acknowledged
that, having been attacked, they had retaliated in kind.

"So, then," said the therapist, "it may be that the real problem is not that one or the other of you is ultimately to blame for having struck the first blow. Rather the problem may be that both of you are caught in a pattern of reciprocal attack, a pattern you wish had never begun and would like now to bring to an end." The couple agreed that this, indeed, was their situation. And in that agreement began a process of healing and reconciliation that was beautiful to behold.

"Sin" is an ugly word. None of us likes to admit that it's part of our life. And when we come together to explore our faith, many of us would prefer to speak of it as little as possible.

But the truth is that if nothing has gone bad with our world and ourselves — and sin is the believer's word for "bad" — then we have no need for faith. We turn to God when we become aware of the lacks in our lives, when we realize that as human persons we yearn for more than we can accomplish, more than this world can give, where we face the fact that one way or another, we are "out of control." We trust in God when we realize that trusting in ourselves is not enough.

So in exploring the meaning of discipleship and the moral challenge of our faith, we must speak of sin. In Catholic tradition this word is used to point to three realities.

ORIGINAL SIN. First, there is "original sin," sin in its basic fundamental sense. Everyone confronts the painful life-experience of failure and catastrophe. Good persons hurt each other despite their best intentions. Innocent men, women, and children are "caught in the cross fire" and become victims. The most worthy dreams and aspirations come to naught. Forces of nature, so often our friends, go on a rampage, causing destruction almost impossible to imagine. And most profoundly, no matter what our successes in life, our joys and satisfactions, for each one of us the end will be that final failure, that ultimate humiliation, known as death.

What do you make of these experiences? Really there are only three answers: (1) God is evil; (2) there is no God; (3) God is good, but something is out of joint in our world. This last is the answer embraced by the Judaeo-Christian tradition. The reality of evil in our world is a mystery. But when confronted by that mystery, we refuse to blame God, for God, we believe, is good. If blame there must be, we accept that blame ourselves. But since no one of us seems personally responsible for all the evil of life, we project that blame back to the beginning, to the biblical characters, Adam and Eve. And through the imagery of these two we accept the blame corporately.

So the bad news is that, from the beginning, before any one of us can be blamed, we are caught in patterns and experiences of evil. We are subject to this evil — and most of all to its greatest example, death. And this evil is beyond our capacity to fix; there is no escape. As creatures we are subject to captivity.

The good news, however, is that, "where death abounded, grace did more abound" (Rom. 5:15). The liberation of which we are incapable has been accomplished by another, that Jesus of Nazareth who brings divine love, divine life, divine power, divine freedom, divine salvation to our world and to ourselves. Over against the reality of our captivity is the gratuity of God's liberation. Over against the reality of sin is the gratuity of salvation.

This salvation is not yet completed of course. The Catholic tradition declares that while original sin can be conquered by Baptism, its effects still remain. To put this another way, God's love immediately disposes of guilt; but only at the end will it conquer captivity. "The whole earth groans," as Paul's letter to the Romans says. Still, we believe that through faith and fidelity we can become participants in Jesus' journey to freedom, through death to everlasting life in community with God and one another.

ACTUAL SIN. So in the first instance, sin is the fact of captivity; and we are its victims. But that is not all. A moment's candor manifests the truth that, in the conduct of our lives, we have all made it worse. No doubt in many ways we have made it better; but not in all ways. To some extent and in some situations we have also made it worse. So we can speak also of "actual sin," of behavior by which we have freely chosen to contribute to the death-dimension of human life. Some of our sins are acts of "commission" in which we actually do something that makes it worse. Others are sins of "omission" where our failure to act has led to evil results. But the pattern is the same: the use of our human freedom has been aligned with the forces of death and destruction against the loving, liberating forces set in motion by Jesus. Besides the fact of our shared captivity, there is the humbling truth of our personal culpability.

As our tradition put it, actual sin occurs when we knowingly and freely do what we understand to be wrong. Each of these words can be explored, of course. One sometimes wonders how free human persons are. Sometimes one has the experience that our knowledge is clouded by ignorance or our freedom is compromised by emotion. But it wasn't the intention of the tradition to guess in advance how things actually are within any one of us. Rather its intention was simply to hold up in bold relief the challenge: that we should enact in our behavior the faith we espouse. And toward that end, the tradition prophetically proclaimed: to the extent that we knowingly and freely act in ways that make things worse, that action deserves the name of sin.

Again, this experience of our capacity to choose actions that make things worse is "bad news." We are not only victims, innocent if entrapped; we are also perpetrators, guilty of the actions we perform. But again, there is also good news. For Christian faith has as a central conviction that the loving life and death of Jesus brings not only salvation, but also forgiveness. Indeed, this personal forgiveness is the act by which the power of salvation in Jesus is applied to each of us as persons, making us righteous in the eyes of God, transformed by divine love and empowered to live the lives to which we have been called.

STATE OF SIN. Finally, in utilizing the word "sin," the Catholic tradition spoke also of a human way of being, of a "state" that can be taken on by human persons. We can speak of persons being in the "state of sin." Indeed, we can imagine persons so rooted in that state that they are, in reality, dead to the journey of faith; they are in the "state of mortal sin."

These words are sometimes the stuff of controversy. Can a person really do this? Do people actually choose so decisively to stand against Jesus' pilgrimage toward life? The answer of Catholic faith is a profound and sensitive answer, one that holds on to central convictions without trying to guess how things go with particular persons.

First, the tradition decisively affirms that God has set us free, that God calls us to a union formed by love and that love can only be given freely, never extorted. A consequence of this freedom, though, is that human persons are genuinely able to say "No" as well as "Yes"; anything else would contradict our freedom. So as mysterious as it may be, we affirm that persons have the capacity to choose death over life.

In trying to understand this, it is perhaps best not to attempt the road of logical calculation. Look instead to your own experience. Have there been times in your life when you have chosen self-destruction, at least in small ways? In some mysterious, perverse way you knew this choice would not bring genuine happiness, but you chose it anyway. Have you done this? If you have, you know the truth of the Catholic affirmation that God's gift of freedom includes the frightening capacity for self-destruction, perhaps even for that ultimate self-destruction that we call "mortal sin."

Second, though the tradition is careful to say that we can describe the shape of such deadly sin and can even describe concrete behaviors so destructive that, if done with true understanding and genuine freedom, it seems right to call the behaviors themselves "mortal sin," still we judge no person's heart. We do not know if a particular person has turned away from God so decisively. We do not know if anyone, in the whole history of the world, has persisted in such a self-destructive decision. And even if such decisions in the course of life as might be called mortal sins take place, we do not know how often they occur, though one must presume that such radical denials of the human drive to life and love and community must be relatively rare.

Much more common, we presume, is the event of destructive behavior "fallen into" through weakness or passion or ignorance. Such sinful acts are called "venial," an obscure English word that means "daily" or "common." The term also refers to specific acts that, because they are less significant in themselves, are commonly and predictably performed by persons who nonetheless remain committed in their underlying effort to love the neighbor.

Once again, in describing specific behaviors as "venial sins," the tradition is not prejudging what happens in people's hearts. It's not as if action automatically becomes sin: if you did this action, then God is angry with you. No, the word "sin" primarily refers to the event of the human heart, a saying "no" to God. Only secondarily does the word refer to the external action by which the heart's event is made visible.

So whether an external act that we observe is really a sin (in the full, technical sense of actual sin) can be determined only by the one who performs it. Still, the tradition often used the language of sin, saying "X is a sin" or "Y is a mortal sin" or "Z is a venial sin," to highlight the destructiveness of particular behaviors, in the expectation that this information would be helpful as we live our lives. And if we take the information in the spirit with which it is provided, it is helpful indeed.

The point of these reflections is simple. The highest priority is not to know precisely which acts have been sins. Even less is it to be in a position to label the behaviors of others, sinful or otherwise. Rather, the priority, for us as for the paralytic man and the married couple, is to see truly the situation in which each of us abides. First, there is the fact that we are alienated from our own most precious dreams, caught in a reality of sin that only God's loving, liberating salvation in Jesus can overcome. Second, in the course of our lives, we do sometimes make things worse. When that happens nothing but our own sincere repentance, supported by God's generous initiative of forgiveness, can provide new possibilities. And third, the drama of our moral lives, usually focused on our sincere efforts to love our neighbors both well and wisely, has a cosmic dimension as well. For we are called and invited by God into a universe of free, loving communion; but God will not violate the gift of freedom by imposing the gift of communion. So our genuine commitment to the project of daily love, a commitment itself empowered by God's prior love, is the essential key to the ultimate fulfillment of those dreams of ours.

In the coming chapters, then, we will try to develop wisdom about the sorts of behaviors that actually help or hurt human beings. We seek this wisdom, and share it, in the presumption that good persons, truly trying to live this commitment to God and neighbor, will receive it gratefully. But in naming the various behaviors, we will not be "naming sins," as if our wisdom could dare to assert what happens in the hearts of individual persons. This we leave to God and that person.

Trusting in God's mercy and accepting God's challenging invitation, we devote ourselves to the communal effort to discover truths by which we can live.

Questions for Reflection and Discussion

1. Some people ask, "Whatever happened to sin?" How do you react to this question? Have we lost a sense of sin? Has our view of it changed? What of you yourself?

2. This chapter explains how our tradition speaks both of "sin as captivity" and "sin as culpable deeds." Can you locate both of these realities in your personal experience? In our modern world? How do the two realities seem to relate?

3. Do you have experiences like that of the married couple recounted at the beginning of the chapter? How are your experiences similar or dissimilar to those of the couple?

4. Have you ever met anyone who struck you as truly evil? What was that like?

5. What role is played by an "awareness of sin" in the decision to be a Christian or a Roman Catholic?

Faith in Action

Today, as you encounter people you find unpleasant, reflect on the ways their behavior (actual sin) has been shaped by a bruising past (original sin). Like the people who brought the paralytic to Jesus, pray that this person may experience liberation and forgiveness.

Prayer

Jesus, giver of holiness and health, to you we confess our sin.
We are caught in sin and we act with sin.
We need your gifts of new possibilities:
new life, new energy, new mobility, new opportunity.
Give us your gifts.
And help us to make good use of what we receive. Amen.

36

Respectful Living

See, I have set before you today life and prosperity, death and adversity. If you obey the commandments of the Lord your God that I am commanding you today, by loving the Lord your God, walking in his ways, and observing his commandments, decrees, and ordinances, then you shall live and become numerous, and the Lord your God will bless you in the land that you are entering to possess.... I call heaven and earth to witness against you today that I have set before you life and death, blessings and curses. Choose life so that you and your descendants may live.

(DEUTERONOMY 30:15–16, 19)

— ❖ —

The expert in liturgy was asked a question: "What do you think is the perfect prayer?" His response was immediate: "I don't know if this is the perfect prayer, but it comes close. In the morning, when you wake up, face the east, looking at the rising sun. And wordlessly, bow from the waist. Acknowledge all that is implied by that sunrise: the giftedness of life, your dependence. And let your body speak the love, the gratitude, the adoration that follows."

I think it was Abraham Lincoln who said: "I have often fallen to my knees for the simple reason that I could think of no place else to go."

All morality starts with reverence for life. It does not end there, since simple reverence in no way eliminates the complexities and conflicts that confront our daily lives. But it does start there — and therefore so do we. Not surprisingly, the Catholic tradition has spoken often and forcefully about our responsibility to treat life respectfully. Some of the issues often addressed in the tradition will be considered in this chapter.

"Love your neighbor as yourself": no doubt many behaviors can be plausible enactments of that challenge. Perhaps the only behavior that could never be so would be killing. That is why some people feel the fundamental commandment, on which all others are based, is: "Thou shalt not kill."

Of course, in the real world of everyday life, matters are complex. People can threaten us with bodily harm. Enemies can beset us in war. There is no avoiding stories of the perpetrators of heinous crimes. In the face of these experiences, we struggle about what to make of "Thou shalt not kill." And in later chapters we will consider just these sorts of complex cases. For now, however, at least we can say that it is hard to imagine how killing a person who is no threat to me, no threat to you, no threat to society could be justified. "I love you, so I kill you." This contradictory phrase is reminiscent of the declaration associated with the Vietnam War: "We had to destroy the village to save it." It should never be so.

So it is not surprising that, for centuries, spokespersons for the Catholic tradition have held in special esteem the prohibition against "direct killing of the innocent." The contemporary version of this insight speaks of a "consistent ethic of life" that demands that we "respect life" at all times and in all places. Or, as it was expressed in the *Catechism of the Catholic Church,* "human life is sacred because from its beginning it involves the creative action of God and it remains for ever in a special relationship with the creator, who is its sole end. God alone is the Lord of life from its beginning until its end: no one can under any circumstance claim for himself the right directly to destroy an innocent human being" (no. 2258).

These aphorisms do not resolve all the ambiguities of our situation, of course. But they do present in bold relief the foundational conviction of Christian morality. Our God is the God of life. God has called us to life, indeed to life in community with one another and in communion with God's own self. Human persons fulfill themselves by participating in the creating and recreating work of God. Cultivating and protecting life are, then, the objectives of the entire moral enterprise. Therefore, at the least, it is always wrong to end the life of an innocent and non-threatening person.

This abiding Catholic conviction may strike us as beautiful but irrelevant. After all, we are not likely to engage in the wanton killing inflicted by criminals or sociopaths. But several contemporary dilemmas bring the challenge much closer to home: abortion, euthanasia, and suicide. Before we consider each of these, an overall comment is in order.

For the most part Catholic moral teaching on these questions represents straightforward application of the core conviction outlined above. But that fact has not prevented controversy from plaguing discussions of these issues. In some cases there are arguments about the *presumptions* that ground the Church's application of the principle to a particular circumstance. In other cases, the debates are about public social *policies* and whether they should legally enflesh a particular moral conviction. In yet other cases the issue of *autonomy,* of "who should decide" (really a separate question), has held center stage. Readers of these pages will join these discussions as they wish. For the moment, the real question for us is whether we are faithful to the life-commitment that is the heart of the Christian moral vision. Or, in the fury of the current debates, have we lost sight of that vision and become enmeshed, despite good intentions, in a cultural style that is often shamefully death-dealing?

ABORTION. We start, then, with abortion. If the center of our morality involves the prohibition of killing the innocent, that prohibition would seem to apply most particularly to the innocent who are defenseless, unable to fend for themselves. And in this category, we would surely place children, and perhaps most surely those children not yet able to live even a physically autonomous life. In general, the tradition has

held the presumption that pre-born life is human and that we are therefore dealing in this case with human beings. The tradition has taken
this as either obvious or as so probable as to make an alternative presumption unreasonable. And on the strength of that presumption it has
made a simple, earnest application of our core conviction to the case
of unborn life.

It seems likely that most of those who are involved in abortions,
women who receive them, men who share in the decision, medical
personnel who perform them, are not persons of intentional bad will.
And the argument against abortion does not presume so. Rather, the
argument claims simply that those who are involved are, however unwittingly, participating in a grave evil. And the passion of abortion
opponents arises from their conviction that we have a culture that easily ignores the rights and needs of the invisible and that our respect for
life in general is therefore under unparalleled attack in the casual or
routine disposal of unborn life.

EUTHANASIA. It is interesting that a second area of contemporary
controversy focuses on the other end of life, not its beginning but its
conclusion.

Clearly all human persons die. In that sense, one could say that we
are all dying. But in some cases we are in the presence of irreversible
physical and biochemical processes whose conclusion is so obvious
that we can say the person is "dying," using the term in a very focused
sense. In this case, the question arises: How should we, in our desire to
love, be present to the dying? Is our task to attempt to make the person
comfortable and then simply to be present in communal solidarity? Or
could it be that, in this unusual case, the loving act is to facilitate or
expedite the dying process — in a word, to kill the person?

The Catholic tradition has responded in a forthright and consistent
manner: the first choice is the right one. Indeed, however we may ra-
tionalize it, the act of euthanasia really is an act of "getting us off the
hook." We are fleeing our responsibility either to use science to make
the person reasonably comfortable (unlike some doctors, the Catholic
tradition sets no limits on the quantity of permissible pain-alleviating
drugs, so long as the objective is rendering comfort, not ending life,
pain-killing and not person-killing) or to develop the social and organizational arrangements that will provide the sort of community
network and dignified setting in which a person can humanely pass
through the final stages of human life in this world. As Pope John
Paul II trenchantly put it, "the origin and the foundation of the duty of
absolute respect for human life are to be found in the dignity proper to

the person and not simply in the natural inclination to preserve one's own physical life" (*Veritatis Splendor,* no. 50).

Many find these arguments compelling and are challenged to develop technology and social structures to the point that euthanasia becomes obviously inappropriate. Others confess that, at least for the moment and in tragic circumstances, they do not find the arguments convincing. Our challenge is to hold firmly to our core convictions and to remain involved in the community of moral discourse.

SUICIDE. Recent American developments in "assisted suicide" have raised this issue in a new way. Traditional discussions of suicide had focused on two other cases. On the one hand, the act of self-sacrifice, undertaken to protect others, was judged to be admirable but not obligatory. On the other hand, the act of self-killing to escape the human condition was judged to be wrong. But it was also judged to be rare, presuming rather that suicide victims are actually in the grip of a psychologically paralyzing despair and therefore not really culpable.

This new case is different. What shall we say of a life-ending act undertaken in apparent calm, with extensive forethought and, indeed, in the presence of loved ones? The Catholic tradition has been clear in finding such an act to be immoral, a denial of that respect for life, in all its ambiguity, that ought to characterize human persons. But just as in the case of euthanasia, the emphasis should perhaps be not so much on fervent condemnation as on candid questioning. What scientific or interpersonal failure makes such a suicide an attractive alternative? As Marsha Norman, the director of a hospice program, said, "Hospice believes there is no reason for [assisted suicide]. We look at all areas of pain — physical, spiritual and emotional — and we work on them. If we can take care of these, I can't believe anyone would want to end his life prematurely.... With good hospice care, people are going to want to live life to the fullest" (*Chicago Tribune Magazine,* August 21, 1994, 33).

ECOLOGY. The last quotation suggests that many acts can express respect for life. In one sense, all the topics to be considered in coming chapters are really nothing more than applications of this central challenge. Two specific topics, however, because of their intimate connection to a reverence for life, deserve consideration here. The first raises various issues of ecology.

A major twentieth-century development in moral reflection has been our growing appreciation of the challenges of living in this physical world. Advances in mobility, technology, and communication have all led us to become far more aware of two things. One is the limited character of our planet. The other is the impact of our behavior upon that planetary context.

This world is finite. Its resources are finite. The flourishing of our planet, in contrast to the sterility of so many others, is the result of a delicate balance of forces. There is an interdependence of the parts of the world; it is, in the technical term, a "closed system." This means that nothing additional comes into it from the outside. It must find what it needs within itself, cycling its various parts, seeing to their renewal, and carefully modulating their depletion.

There is also a fragility to this home of ours, a vulnerability to our ill-advised actions, that we did not used to know. New scientific knowledge gives frightening evidence of our power for destruction. For example, innocent, well-meaning efforts to make human life more comfortable, using the cooling potential of fluorocarbons in air conditioners, lead to an erosion of the ozone layer and ultimately to increases of suffering in the form of skin cancer. Sincere efforts to clear land for cultivation, to provide housing or food or jobs, have the effect of wasting resources that cannot be renewed, at least in a reasonable time frame. The construction of dams to control flooding and to meet energy needs lowers the water table downstream or mortally disrupts the breeding patterns of fish.

Examples can be multiplied. None of these problems can be successfully addressed by facile solutions. But all of them are worsened by attitudes of denial. In our day, the challenge is to understand that respect for human life inevitably extends to respect for the overarching life of our planet.

In a special way, Americans must wrestle with the troubling truth that, even while our own aspirations remain less than fully met, we already monopolize great portions of the world's resources to the detriment of our sisters and brothers in the human family. The challenge is the same: not facile response, not naive or self-serving denial, but rather deepening commitment to the call to respect life, combined with honest conversation in communities of moral discernment.

WORSHIP. Reverence for life surely implies reverence for the author of life. In one sense, the entire moral enterprise is an expression of our adoring love of God. It is for that reason that many scholars tell us that "love God and love your neighbor" can also be expressed as "love God by loving your neighbor." At the same time, since time immemorial believers have felt that human persons have a specific moral obligation to give explicit worship to God. The Catholic tradition has, not surprisingly, added its words of challenge to this conviction. But what does worship involve?

First, it involves *attitudes*. Wise commentators have claimed that growing up involves a long process wherein we first grasp the mystery of our freedom and then acknowledge the mystery of our dependence. Some have even said that the first half of life is primarily about freedom, an outward, creative journey, and the second is about dependence, an inward, integrating journey. But at every moment of our lives we are called by the truth to affirm that we are not the author of our life, our talents, or our opportunities. Granted our role of responding and of using what comes our way, the center of life remains gift. The response to gift is gratitude, which is why the Judaeo-Christian tradition is radically "eucharistic" (from the Greek word meaning "thanksgiving"). And the response to the source of all gifts is adoration, which is why Catholic life always keeps worship at its center.

Still if worship is an attitude, it must also be an *act*. Indeed, with human persons it is doubtful whether attitudes without acts really exist. If I say I love you but never enact that love, my claim is questionable. Similarly, if I say I believe in God, but never express that belief in acts of worship, I am liable to be kidding myself. The acts can be as simple and primordial as the gesture of adoration described at the beginning of this chapter. Or they may be as elaborate as the recited psalms and prayers known as the Liturgy of the Hours. The important thing is acts that express the attitude.

Third, worship involves *association*. A common question: "Why should I take the trouble to join in common worship when I can adore God as I walk on the mountain or by the seashore or in the forest?" The answer is not the cheap legalism of "God demands it," even less that it is a rule of the Church. The real answer has to do with our social nature as humans. On the one hand, we depend on one another to maintain the strength of our convictions. So the reason I need to join in common worship is not that God needs it, but that *you* do. Only by experiencing the solidarity of shared faith will your faith be reinforced and deepened. On the other hand, when things are really important to us, we usually want to share them. Everything from birthdays to football games goes better with others, and the same is true of adoration. Acts that are really rooted in attitudes tend inevitably to engender association.

And that is why common worship of the God of life seems to flow so organically from the challenge to respect life.

Still, if respect for life provides a core to the Christian ethical vision, it does not exhaust it. In the next three chapters, we will explore various specific areas of living that present us with moral challenges. In each case, benefiting from the wisdom of the Catholic tradition, we will try to inform ourselves and provide ourselves guidance for the struggles we each must face in our daily lives.

Questions for Reflection and Discussion

1. In our society do you think that living in a way that respects life is easy? difficult? impossible? Can you think of examples for your assessment?

2. What do you think are the greatest threats to a life-respecting lifestyle today?

3. What do you think of the current controversies around issues such as abortion and assisted suicide? Are they healthy debates? Are they leading us to the truth?

4. This chapter links issues such as abortion and ecology. Do you think they belong together? Why or why not?

5. Worship is attitude, act, association. Can you locate worship, in all these senses, in your life? Do you find worship valuable? How so?

6. What can religions — and religious people — do to make a positive contribution to the struggle to respect life in all circumstances?

Faith in Action

Respect for life can find a thousand expressions. Today, as you go about your usual tasks, find something specific to do, some modest action that will resist tendencies to cheapen life and, instead, will express an appreciation for its value.

Prayer

God of all life,
we adore you and we praise you,
we thank you for your gifts.
May our treatment of all that lives
reflect your gentle and caring touch. Amen.

37

Interpersonal Living

Just then a lawyer stood up to test Jesus. "Teacher," he said, "what must I do to inherit eternal life?" He said to him, "What is written in the law? What do you read there?" He answered, "You shall love the Lord your God with all your heart, and with all your soul, and with all your strength, and with all your mind; and your neighbor as yourself." And he said to him, "You have given the right answer; do this, and you will live."

But wanting to justify himself, he asked Jesus, "And who is my neighbor?" Jesus replied, "A man was going down from Jerusalem to Jericho, and fell into the hands of robbers, who stripped him, beat him, and went away, leaving him half dead. Now by chance a priest was going down that road; and when he saw him, he passed by on the other side. So likewise a Levite, when he came to the place and saw him, passed by on the other side. But a Samaritan while traveling came near him; and when he saw him he was moved with pity. He went to him and bandaged his wounds, having poured oil and wine on them. Then he put him on his own animal, brought him to an inn, and took care of him. The next day he took out two denarii, gave them to the innkeeper, and said, 'Take care of him; and when I come back, I will repay you whatever more you spend.' Which of these three, do you think, was a neighbor to the man who fell into the hands of the robbers?" He said, "The one who showed him mercy." Jesus said to him, "Go and do likewise." (LUKE 10:25–37)

Jesus said, "Love your neighbor as yourself" (Matt. 22:39). What does that mean in the concrete? What behaviors are truly loving (i.e., helpful) to the neighbor? Over the centuries the Christian community has developed wisdom around these questions. And using the human wits that God gave them, while struggling to remain open to the in-breaking grace that God promised to the community and to its leaders, they have struggled to articulate that wisdom as a service to one another.

In the next three chapters we will summarize some of that accumulated wisdom. Please keep in mind, however, that it is wisdom about how to love the neighbor; that is, it is wisdom about the care and tending of relationships. The Catholic tradition of moral wisdom does not propose the goal of self-perfection. Our objective is not to perfect ourselves, polishing ourselves like marble. Rather than being self-focused, our objective is other-focused. This explains the order of our discussion in these chapters: first, responsibility in our ordinary relationships; next, responsibility in intimate relationships; third, responsibility in our relationships with society.

This is not the only possible arrangement, of course. Some arrange this wisdom by moving sequentially through the Ten Commandments. For example, this is the ordering in the *Catechism of the Catholic Church*. That approach has the advantage of being traditional, in the sense that it has quite commonly been used through the centuries. Its danger, however, is that one may "hear" the conversation as presenting rules to be obeyed rather than wisdom to be utilized. Others have arranged these matters by gathering various topics under a listing of virtues: justice, temperance, fortitude, chastity, and the like. This approach has the advantage of emphasizing the positive nature of our moral wisdom, where the goal is not so much to avoid evil as to do good. Its danger, on the other hand, is that it can make the moral life sound self-centered, as if *you* are simply grist for the mill of *my* growing virtuousness. No, if we want to say that Christians are called to grow in virtue, we must also say that this growth occurs precisely when we forget about ourselves in outreaching love of others.

On balance, then, it seems best to organize this summary of Catholic tradition around the headings of the three arenas of relationship.

What is required in our ordinary relationships? We have known the answer since we were children: "Play fair!" "Leave other people's stuff alone!" "Tell the truth! (Can you keep a secret?)" "Don't snoop!" "Keep your promises!" So true is this, that we are not starting this chapter with a story. Instead, simply listen to the children! Hear what they say! Let their comments be the story that introduces these reflections.

Working all this out in detail is terribly difficult, of course. Over the centuries, Catholics have struggled to discern what these childhood aphorisms mean in various circumstances. They have never fully resolved the ambiguity, for circumstances never cease to change and life forever presents us with conflicts. But they have raised some key questions, highlighted issues that might be overlooked, and helped to structure our reflections so that we see clearly the facets of our situation.

Similarly in our time, to help us in the living of our moral lives, nothing works better than candid, caring discussion with others who understand our circumstances. These few pages cannot replace that exploratory conversation. Rather, they can assist by highlighting a few points that the group will wish to consider, points brought to clarity by our forebears in this conversation of the centuries.

PLAY FAIR. The core of the matter is, of course, fairness. "Justice" is its other name. Given that all human persons are fundamentally equal, our ways of treating one another ought to have a certain quality of consistency. Not that we are not different from each other in a thousand ways; we surely are. And our interactions must reflect those differences, too. But we ought not to "play favorites," take "unfair advantage," or in any other way violate the truth of our basic equality. Even more true is this when we add the Christian conviction of our call to community. How can we relate to one another with intimacy and concern, if we do not first treat one another with respect? So justice is, at one and the same time, the expression of human equality and the prerequisite for human community.

Over the centuries our tradition has distinguished several different sorts of justice. But the first and fundamental one is the justice we owe one another as individuals. The following sections will discuss several specific topics that follow from this call to justice. But here let's think for a moment about a painful question raised from the start: does the competitive way of living that is so common in the modern world get in the way, maybe inevitably, of our living with justice? Justice, after all, calls for us to "play fair" and not "take unfair advantage." But in so many matters that concern us in our daily lives we struggle precisely to get some sort of advantage. One thinks, for example, of the style portrayed in the book and movie *Bonfire of the Vanities,* where the central character sees himself as "master of the universe."

It can be the same with us, even if less obviously. There is plain old cheating, of course: that is surely wrong; but there are a thousand ways of trying to acquire an advantage. Similarly, there is the spreading of lies about a work colleague or a business competitor: that is surely wrong; but there are a thousand ways of trying to acquire an advantage. Again, there is bribery offered to teachers, bosses, business suppliers: that is surely wrong; but there are a thousand ways of trying to acquire an advantage. What does it mean to play fair? We will struggle with this question, in conversation with those we trust, for as long as we live.

LEAVE OTHER PEOPLE'S STUFF ALONE. From our earliest days, we seem to know intuitively that "what's mine is mine." Observing the ways of children leads one to suspect that it takes a little longer to realize that "what's yours is yours!" But eventually the fact that these are two sides of the same coin becomes clear. A key element of a justice lifestyle is recognition of property rights.

It is important to emphasize again the *interpersonal* tone of our moral expectations. Property rights are not simply based in my right to keep what's mine. That is, they are not simply an assertion of individual rights. For, to use an interesting example, Catholic tradition argued that my right to have a possession must yield to your right to live, so that if you are starving, you have the right to pick apples from my tree whether I approve or not. As one text put it, "the seventh commandment forbids theft, that is, usurping another's property against the reasonable will of the owner" (*Catechism of the Catholic Church*, no. 2408). And emphasis was clearly put upon *reasonable* will.

Even more so, in recent centuries the Catholic Church has spoken forcefully about the "social function of private property." (We'll return to this topic in chapter 39 below.) So the justification for property rights is that our success at interpersonal living requires that we have some clarity about what belongs to whom. Otherwise chaos would overtake us.

An interesting example of this focus on *social health* as the basis for property rights is the tradition's strong concern about "restitution," which means giving back what was stolen. If the evil of stealing is simply that I am thereby a bad person, then the only necessary solution would be that I repent my badness. But if the evil is, more precisely, that I have taken what is yours and thereby put a block in the roadway of community-building, then I must also reestablish the conditions for that collaboration. And what are those conditions? Why, that you should have what is yours, of course. Hence, the tradition was clear that an infallible indicator of one's sincere repentance is the willingness to "pay it back." Sometimes, when much money is involved, for example, one may not be in a position to make restitution immediately. But at the least, one should be able to say with sincerity: "If I am ever in a position to give back what I have wrongly taken, I will do so. For it is, and always will be, yours, not mine."

In any case, our vision of justice calls us to respect what belongs to one another. In our day, a thousand complex questions confront us. A simple vision of justice is complicated by inequities in our circumstance. If "the system" has abused me in the past, am I nonetheless obliged to respect the property that system has given to you? The vision is also challenged by the anonymous character of so much private property. One thinks of income taxes, insurance payments, charge-card balances, claims of liability. Who does this money belong to? These pages cannot answer these complex questions. Perhaps with the basic shape of the vision outlined here, discussions with those you trust can help to sort things out.

TELL THE TRUTH (CAN YOU KEEP A SECRET?) Apparently all people have some sense that one ought to tell the truth (although different cultures seem to handle the tension between truth and politeness in different ways). Needless to say, we don't always fulfil that obligation, but we seem to be aware of it. At the same time, it doesn't take much life experience to realize that truth-telling is not a simple matter, because over against this first obligation is another: keep secrets. Perhaps these obligations are not *really* in opposition to each other, but it certainly seems so. The child is asked: "Is your mom home?" and the dilemma arises.

Over the centuries, Catholics have wrestled with this dilemma, but it has never been completely solved. Perhaps as good an effort as any at addressing it can be found in the *Catechism of the Catholic Church:* "To lie is to speak or act against the truth in order to lead into error someone who has the right to know the truth" (no. 2483). Notice the way the statement balances the two aspects: tell the truth and respect privacy.

That balance reflects the *source* of the obligation to tell the truth. It is not rooted in some arbitrary rule, nor in some vision of the isolated person. Rather, as noted above, it is rooted in our social human nature. You and I cohabit the same universe. Our individual human fulfillment can be achieved only in communion with one another, through the painfully slow development of authentic, respectful community. How will we ever be able to trust each other, though, if we do not tell the truth? Truth-telling, then, since it is a critical component of the project of building community, is a fundamental obligation of human persons as social.

A wonderful example of this is found in the text of the Eighth Commandment: "Thou shalt not bear false witness." What this commandment rejects is not lying but perjury, speaking falsely under oath in a formal juridical setting. Now that doesn't mean that the ancient Israelites approved of other lies. Rather, it simply means something like this: "You really ought to tell the truth at all times. But human weakness being what it is, and life being complicated as it is, that may not happen. At the least, if we are going to succeed in being community with one another, we have to be able to trust one another in those key moments in which communal judgments are made. So, if nothing else, you must at least tell the truth in those moments." In other words, the emphasis upon perjury as the greatest violation follows from an appreciation of the fact that the obligation of truth-telling is a facet of the more basic obligation of community-building.

DON'T SNOOP. Justice also seems to require that we affirm one another's rights to privacy not only by keeping quiet, but also by leaving space. For even as we seek community, we remain individuals. Indeed, the two are not in opposition. Just as it is true that only in community can individuals grow and flourish, it is also truth that only an individual can enter authentic community. So recognizing that fact, the Catholic tradition has spoken forcefully of our right to privacy.

An interesting example will highlight this. Not surprisingly, our tradition firmly rejected "slander," the spreading of falsehood about another. But it also rejected "detraction," the spreading of unflattering *truths* until now unknown! For everyone has done something embarrassing in the course of life, and one should have the chance to learn from such mistakes and grow. So even our bad actions do not rob us of our right to a good reputation. Rather they challenge us to change.

If we ever embraced this facet of the Christian vision, imagine how quickly the tabloids would go out of business!

KEEP YOUR PROMISES. The act of making promises is one of the more sacred examples of interpersonal living. Our tradition has taken promises very seriously, perhaps because our entire faith hangs on the fidelity of God to the divine promise. But that does not mean that the matter is simple. What shall we do when keeping a promise will hurt someone else? What do we think of promises that are somehow "extorted" when one is under pressure? What if one later finds out that a promise involves costs that were unforeseen?

There are no simple answers to these questions. The Catholic tradition continually held up the ideal of promise-keeping. The Catholic community continues to struggle to define what this means in complex circumstances of competing values. Nothing more is possible.

— ❖ —

The biblical story of the good Samaritan presents a bold statement of the challenge of loving our neighbor. It rejects escapism, self-centeredness, lack of concern. But one can imagine dialogues with the various characters in the story that might lead us to a bit more sympathy. Could it be that the priest is on his way to minister to his flock? Could it be that the Levite has an important group of colleagues waiting for him? Such considerations can, of course, be an excuse for avoiding our duty. But they can also be honest admissions of the complexity of it all.

This complexity — and our capacity for self-deception, as we have repeatedly noted — is the reason we need a community of moral discourse. So, as we conclude these remarks on the moral challenges of interpersonal living, let the conversation begin.

Questions for Reflection and Discussion

1. Do you think it is possible to live justly in our world? What elements are most encouraging or discouraging?

2. What do you think of all the contemporary emphasis upon competition? Is it inevitable? Good? What effect does it have upon our efforts to live with justice?

3. Some people feel that in our time we have lost a sense of property rights. What do you think? Can you give examples that have shaped your judgment?

4. What has been your experience of the challenge of truth-telling? How do you distinguish between the need for "delicacy" in some matters and the attempt to shade the truth simply to "look good"? Do you find the Catholic tradition's reflections helpful? What would you say in advice to someone trying to sort out moral problems in this area?

5. This chapter emphasizes privacy as important, though as a basis for community rather than in opposition to it. Is it your experience that privacy is properly appreciated nowadays? Is it overemphasized? Easily overlooked? Can you think of experiences that have revealed the difficulty of addressing issues of privacy?

Faith in Action

Where do you spend most of your waking hours: on the job, at school, in the home? In that locale, do something concrete to protect the values of truth, property rights, or privacy.

Prayer

O God of patience,
the long course of our lives,
though it may sometimes feel like a burden,
is really a gracious opportunity to grow as persons
and as members of community.
May we use this opportunity well and grow in your Spirit. Amen.

38

Embodied Living

Some Pharisees came, and to test him they asked, "Is it lawful for a man to divorce his wife?" He answered them, "What did Moses command you?" They said, "Moses allowed a man to write a certificate of dismissal and to divorce her." But Jesus said to them, "Because of your hardness of heart he wrote this commandment for you. But from the beginning of creation, 'God made them male and female. For this reason a man shall leave his father and mother and be joined to his wife, and the two shall become one flesh.' So they are no longer two, but one flesh. Therefore what God has joined together, let no one separate." (MARK 10:2–9)

It was Julie and Mike's rehearsal dinner, the evening before their marriage. The meal had been wonderful, the conversation jovial, the toasts had been warm and sincere. But then the mother of the groom wheeled a TV into the center of the room and announced a special surprise.

It was a videotape, displaying perhaps a hundred photos of the wedding couple, of both their families, of friends through the years. To a soundtrack of well-chosen popular tunes, the pictures reviewed Julie and Mike's lives, where they had come from, who they had grown with, what they were bringing to this moment of new beginning.

The final picture was a snapshot of the two of them. As that picture remained on the screen, a text slowly appeared. "Julie and Mike, we pray that your lives will be joy-filled, generous, and fruitful. We will be with you always. Love, The Moms!"

Human beings are "persons." By this we mean that we have an identity, are self-aware, and are capable both of taking in the world through understanding and of reaching out to the world through love. But human beings are not just any sort of persons. We are *embodied* persons. By this we mean that we are "alive" through and in our bodies, that our most human activities, knowing and loving, are mediated through our bodies and cannot occur apart from them. Indeed, destroy the body and the *person* dies.

(Of course, we believe that, in God's love, human persons continue to live after death. Exactly what this is like, however, we do not know. Some great thinkers have guessed that even after death we retain some "relation to embodiedness," whatever that might mean. In any case, our faith is that we are destined for the resurrection of our bodies so that, after death and for all time, we will again be embodied persons.)

Because we are embodied persons, the moral challenge of loving God and neighbor raises important questions about the use of our bodies. In this chapter we will consider three sets of these questions. In no way will we be able to share all the splendid wisdom of the Catholic tradition on these questions. The interested reader will need to explore the questions further in discussion and additional reading. But some overall perspectives can at least help us to engage the questions.

Since our bodies are the bridges across which we make contact with the world, they deserve respect.

Respect for one's own body involves coming to grips with its limits and its needs. Many of us, as young people, behaved as if our bodies had no limits. Staying up all night, surviving on "junk food," perhaps abusing alcohol or drugs. Most of us have learned the hard lesson that the body cannot be ignored. Sooner or later it reasserts itself and demands to be taken seriously.

At the same time, facing the reality of our bodies also involves facing the fact of death. In chapter 36 we talked about the central role in our morality played by the challenge to reverence the reality of life. At the same time, it remains true that no body lasts forever. Hence, if bodily survival is our goal, we all finally fail. This truth has led our tradition to give focused attention to issues of medical ethics or, as it is also called, the ethics of health care. And in particular, it has led to the formulation of a wise distinction between "ordinary" and "extraordinary" efforts at bodily care. On the one hand, respect for the body challenges us to treat the body well and not to abuse it. On the other hand, since none of us lives forever, the mere extension of life is not the highest value. So, while we are obliged to make use of "ordinary" means of care for the body, "extraordinary means" are considered optional in the tradition's teaching. As the *Catechism of the Catholic Church* expressed it, "discontinuing medical procedures that are burdensome, dangerous, extraordinary, or disproportionate to the expected outcome can be legitimate; it is the refusal of 'over-zealous' treatment. Here one does not will to cause death; one's inability to impede it is merely accepted" (no. 2278).

And how can we tell the difference between "ordinary" and "extraordinary?" As the just-quoted text suggests, the tradition defined extraordinary initiatives as those that are unduly painful, expensive, or inconvenient, or that do not offer promise of substantial benefit to the person as a whole. Obviously this definition is itself quite vague. It is simply a rule of thumb to be applied through prayerful and thoughtful reflection in community. But even if concrete questions are not answered by this distinction, we are offered a perspective, a balanced view that combines respect for body and acknowledgement that life on earth will end.

This bodily respect raises questions for us especially in times of serious illness. The myriad scientific advances of our time have produced many new questions in medical ethics. Which medical initiatives should be considered "ordinary" and therefore nothing more than signs of respect for the body? Which should be considered "extraordinary," perhaps because of the expense or pain involved or because they offer little hope of lasting benefit, and therefore optional? These questions plague us.

Even more troublesome is the need to answer these questions for others who may be too sick to do so themselves. And since even extraordinary efforts are permissible (just not obligatory), the attempt to decide what our parents or children or spouses or friends would want is often heartbreaking for those who must act.

No wonder we need a community to sort things out!

It is through our bodies that we make contact with the world — and most importantly with other persons. Through those two most characteristic human acts, knowledge and love, through comprehension and commitment, understanding and affirmation, we reach out with ecstasy and bring in with embrace. But even these acts occur only through — and never apart from — body. And in making this contact, our bodies make use of two media: words and gestures.* It is of the highest importance, then, that our words and gestures be truthful. For in the absence of that truth, how will we ever truly know or truly love as persons should?

In the last chapter we discussed some of the ordinary obligations of truth-telling. Here we need to consider the challenge to be truthful in our gestures, and most especially in that most intimate and important arena of "body-language" that we call sexuality.

Sometimes Catholics are accused of being "hung up" on sex. But our culture certainly doesn't reveal any shortage of difficulty in this area. The truth is that sexual urges are both wonderful and troublesome. And any tradition that is serious about helping us to love our neighbor with both care and wisdom will attempt to offer guidance in this area. For our purposes, we can summarize the Catholic tradition's guidance in four points.

First, sex is good. Not everyone believes this — and not every Catholic has always declared it clearly, but it is true. Our God is good. That good God has created us as embodied persons. Being embodied, we are gendered and genital. And so these realities, too, are good. If our sexuality is sometimes troublesome, the trouble is not that of a problem to be disposed of. Rather it is the trouble of a possibility to be acknowledged and celebrated and ultimately achieved. Consequently, because our bodiliness and our sexuality are good, our goal is integration, learning the "language of love" so that we are truthful in both word and deed.

And where can this language be truthful? The second item of wisdom from the Catholic tradition is this: that the wonderful goodness of sexual intimacies is true — and therefore fulfills its promise of true interpersonal intimacy — in a setting of abiding commitment. In order to "work," the sexual language needs a promised tomorrow. Our culture's name for that setting is, of course, marriage; and we will say more of marriage shortly. For now, though, one point must be made:

---

*The language used here: viewing human persons as embodied spirits, describing the most characteristic acts of persons as knowing and loving, and then naming the media as words and gestures, is taken from R. Westley, *A Theology of Presence* (Mystic, Conn.: Twenty-Third Publications, 1988). However, I take responsibility for the use of these terms and the development of the ideas here.

marriage is where genital sex belongs not because a rule says so, even less because God is some sort of "killjoy." Quite the contrary, it is so because only in the context of this trusting, abiding relationship can the promise of sex be achieved and we embodied persons find the intimacy we most profoundly seek.

But, and this is the third point, limiting genital expression to marriage and speaking that language well within marriage are not easy. To do so requires discipline. "Discipline" is not a word our culture likes to hear, but it is important. Discipline can be defined as the ability to delay gratification for a worthy reason and in service to a worthwhile goal. Whether the discipline involves studying to get an education, finishing a task to get a paycheck, keeping silent to prevent angry words from destroying a relationship, or foregoing genital behavior in situations where it would be false or destructive, discipline is unavoidable in mature living.

According to the *Catechism of the Catholic Church,* "chastity means the successful integration of sexuality within the person and thus the inner unity of man in his bodily and spiritual being" (no. 2337). Shaping bodily behavior so that it becomes the true language of persons, fully integrating the bodily and the spiritual: this is a project that takes a lifetime to achieve. And discipline is the tool that makes integration possible.

But discipline is not only a matter of abstinence. It offers a challenge to the sexually active too. For if single people report the struggle to control sexual urges in order to prevent bodily language that is false, married people report an equal struggle to develop a sexual language that fully expresses their depth of feeling and commitment. Paradoxically, one of discipline's challenges is to learn how to be truly naked with the person one loves, to empower the body to speak love with freedom and spontaneity, with care and playfulness. This task is also necessary if we are to achieve that integration of body and spirit that sexual maturity and personal holiness demand.

Finally, our Catholic tradition challenges us to take seriously the fact that sexual language is a life-giving language. Genital sexuality is not just machinery for procreation, of course. No, it is fundamentally a language of covenantal love. As the Second Vatican Council said, "This devoted love finds its unique expression and development in the behavior which is proper to marriage. The acts by which married couples are intimately and chastely united are honorable and respectable, and when they are carried out in a truly human way they express and encourage a mutual giving in which a couple gladly and gratefully enrich each other" (Pastoral Constitution on the Church in the Modern World, no. 49). But that love is, from its very inception, also a generative love, a love that goes beyond the two persons into a life-giving stance toward the world. And a preeminent example of that generativeness is procreation.

One of the great wonders of embodied personhood is the overlap, interconnection, perhaps we should say communion, between acts of sexual intimacy and acts of human procreation. As far as we can tell, this connection is true of no other bodily species. Obviously not every genital act involves procreation. Sometimes it is not possible, as in the case of older couples. Sometimes it is not right, as in the case of those who are not in a position to care for additional children. But no matter what the details of the individual circumstance, an essential component of truthful sexual language seems to be that it faces honestly the full range of that language's meaning, as both expressing love and involving human procreative potential and responsibility.

We have seen that the achievement of sexuality's human promise requires a promised tomorrow, and that the name for this setting is "marriage." Perhaps some further words about marriage as a moral challenge should be added here.

In one sense, this is the wrong place for the discussion. For marriage is far more than sex. Catholic teaching defines marriage as "a partnership of the whole of life" (*Code of Canon Law*, no. 1055). Marriage involves friendship, common living, the making of a home wherein faith and love and human values can be cultivated and transmitted, and the abiding project of engaging life's endless issues in a shared manner. Indeed, married couples speak with eloquence of the multifaceted nature of their lifestyle, in which explicit issues of sexuality are only one small component. But, since sexual urges play a significant role in the undertaking of marriage and since marriage becomes for the partners the primary locus for achieving the integration of body into person, perhaps this place will do for some additional comments on the moral challenges of marriage.

The core of Catholic teaching is, of course, that God wishes marriage to last forever. The words quoted by Jesus at the beginning of this chapter are noteworthy not only because he asserts the call to marital permanence. They are also significant because of the reason Jesus gives: namely, that divorce is "not how God intended it in the beginning." In quoting the Book of Genesis, Jesus is saying something terribly important: fidelity is not a Church rule or some latter-day religious regulation. It is the way God made human persons. This human world, as we have come to understand it with faith's help, is the sort of world where human persons achieve true and full integration of body into personhood when they remain faithful to the promised relationships they have undertaken. On the one hand, accepting the limits found in a particular relationship is a way of facing squarely the finitude of bodiliness that we discussed earlier. The embodied person cannot be everywhere or do everything; choices must be made. At the same time, discovering the endless challenge of growing in love teaches that spirit flowers not in fleeing body but in embracing it, finitude and all.

Of course, we can fail in this human challenge of faithful loving. All of us know examples of the tragedy of marital failure. It inevitably brings sadness to all involved. But our God is a God of forgiveness, not of retribution. And embodied existence must also be able to allow for starting over and learning. In our day, the Catholic community struggles to find the best way of manifesting compassion in the area of marital failure while continuing to hold clearly the challenge to seek marital fidelity.

This struggle to serve the institution of marriage — and thereby to serve married persons — is not new for the Church. History shows that members of the Catholic community have related to the reality of human marriage in many different ways over the centuries. In fact, the Church has increased its involvement only when secular authorities have abandoned their traditional roles. Perhaps there is only one constant in these varied involvements: pastoral concern for married persons. So it is not surprising that, in our day, too, the Church should struggle to express that concern. Those who join the Church benefit from this tradition of care — and accept a role in offering it yet again. In joining the Church, they join also the struggle to find the language — a sort of "ecclesial body language" — that will be as true as our personal body language should be.

A wise commentator claimed that human persons are the paradoxical joining of animal and angel. Life is simpler if one attempts to be only one of those, but it is not more satisfying. And in the end it is not really true. The challenge is to acknowledge both dimensions of the human and, over the years of life, with the abiding help of God and in a setting of communal sharing, to achieve the integration that is our fulfillment. Providing that setting and supporting that project is one of the central roles of Church.

Questions for Reflection and Discussion

1. Do you have personal experience with the moral dilemmas of modern medicine? What have you learned from the experience?

2. Have you ever had to make difficult medical decisions for others? Do you find the insights of the Catholic tradition helpful to that process?

3. For some people "morals" is synonymous with "sex." What do you think about sexual morality? Is too much made of it? Not enough? Are the questions that are usually asked the right questions? If not, what should the questions be?

4. Based on your experience, if you could tell the next generation one thing about sex, what would it be?

5. Has your religious faith-vision made a difference in the living of your human sexuality? If so, how?

6. Do you think marriage ought to last forever? Can anything be done to help people achieve that ideal? How do you think we should respond to the event of divorce?

7. How do you think the Church and its leaders can best serve marriage — and thereby married persons — in our day?

Faith in Action

Chapter 34 argued for the importance of joining communities of moral discernment. Try to find an opportunity for comfortable, candid conversation about the topics in this chapter. Ask those who are married to share their experience; and if you are married, try to put that experience into words. Or to put this another way, try to talk about what is truly important to you.

Prayer

God of Jesus Christ, what a wonder it is that you saved us
by sending your son to become embodied just like us,
showing the beauty of body and sharing the struggles of body.
Let the example of Jesus guide us in our own journeys of integration.
Amen.

39

Social Living

"Why do we fast, but you do not see? Why humble ourselves, but you do not notice?" [*the people ask.*]

[*And God responds:*] *"Look, you serve your own interest on your fast day, and oppress all your workers. Look, you fast only to quarrel and to fight and to strike with a wicked fist.... Will you call this a fast, a day acceptable to the Lord? Is not this the fast that I choose: to loose the bonds of injustice, to undo the thongs of the yoke, to let the oppressed go free, and to break every yoke? Is it not to share your bread with the hungry, and bring the homeless poor into your house, when you see the naked to cover them, and not to hide yourself from your own kin?... Then you shall call, and the Lord will answer; you shall cry for help, and he will say, Here I am."* (ISAIAH 58:3–4, 5–7, 9)

Mary Lou is in a bind. Seventeen years old, she's already seen a lot of life. She was repeatedly sexually abused by an uncle when she was fourteen. A baby, now two years old, was the result. After she had the baby, she never got back to school, completing only the tenth grade. She's on welfare, living in the projects, getting by with food stamps, Medicaid, and help from her mother.

Mary Lou is stubborn; she wants to make something of herself. She wants to get her baby out of the projects, into a safer setting. She wants to finish high school. She'd like to get a job. But now it seems like the enemy isn't her uncle; it's "the system."

If she works, she loses welfare. If she doesn't work, she can't afford even the minimal expenses connected to going to school. If she either works or goes to school, she'll need help with the baby, more help than her mother can provide. If she wants to try to solve all this some other way, she has to go downtown to meet a caseworker. But it's hard to make an appointment because she and her mother don't have a phone. And all this must be dealt with before sundown; with gang activity so uncontrolled, she dares not go outside after dark.

Mary Lou is growing short on hope.

In chapter 34 we discussed the important role that Catholic tradition has always ascribed to community. Community is not simply a "place," an "unreal location" where "real individuals" live and pursue their personal ends. Rather, community is the broth of life, the primeval "soup" out of which individuals come to exist, develop as persons, and flourish as human beings. "The social character of human beings indicates that the advancement of the human person and the growth of society are dependent on each other. For the origin, the subject and the purpose of all social institutions is and should be the human person, whose life of its nature absolutely needs to be lived in society" (Pastoral Constitution on the Church in the Modern World, no. 25).

Every human person comes into existence as a result of that most communal of acts, sexual intercourse. Every person grows in the community called family. And every person achieves maturity as a result of a personal commitment of generativity in which he or she decides to create community somewhere with some other person or persons. So important, then, so fundamental, is community, that the Judaeo-Christian tradition spoke of the "people of God" and claimed that it is only through and with one another, and never alone, that we find God and God finds us.

But there is a problem. In chapter 35 we noted that sin is not only actual, it is also original. That is, even when no one person seems to be at fault, the human world retains a capacity for harm, a potential for destructiveness. So true is this that we can speak of "structural sin," meaning the capacity of human systems and structures to do harm as well as good.

So, while community is the soil for human flourishing, community is also fragile. And while it has the potential for making us our best, it also has the potential, when it goes awry, for destroying us or making us into monsters.

So healthy, holy community must be cultivated. And that means that Christians, called to love the neighbor as the self, must be solicitous not only for persons but also for structures. This concern for structures is sometimes called "social justice." And the points made above explain why the Catholic Church clearly asserts that "action on behalf of justice and participation in the transformation of the world fully appear to us as a constitutive dimension of the preaching of the Gospel" ("Justice in the World," Statement of the Synod of Bishops, November 30, 1971, no. 6).

This moral perspective is sometimes difficult for Americans to accept, bred as we are to think in very individualistic terms. But it is part of the moral challenge, as understood in the Catholic tradition. So in this chapter we will discuss some of the issues considered by Catholics when they reflect on the morality of social living.

LIFE ISSUES. Everyone knows that love of neighbor starts with a basic respect for the life of the neighbor. It can hardly be a sign of my love for you that I kill you! The moral dilemma arises when there is a conflict of rights. And in a special way, our tradition has wrestled with the conundrum of how to express love in the face of another's aggressive, perhaps even life-threatening, actions.

One part of the tradition has always focused on Jesus' challenge to turn the other cheek (Matt. 5:39) and has concluded that a response of violence to violence can never be justified. Instead, these members of our community call for a lifestyle of pacifism. In no way a "passivism," this lifestyle actively struggles to bring about human relationships of peace and justice by steadfastly refusing to "play the game" of violence. In so doing, pacifists believe they are embracing Jesus' challenge to recreate the world with God's grace.

The Catholic tradition has always included people of this vision, but it has included others as well. Indeed, the more common view has affirmed the right to self-defense. This view argues that in a sinful world, people will, sad to say, sometimes try to inflict evil on their neighbor. The neighbor, of course, does not deserve the evil and is not obliged to accept it. Rather, the neighbor is justified in taking reasonable, proportionate steps to defend herself or himself.

It is interesting and important to note that our tradition has not said: "Since you are unjustly attacking me, you have lost your right to my care. So I can do with you what I will." No, the human dignity of persons is not based on their virtue or even on their good will. Even the evildoer cannot give away that intrinsic human value. So it is self-defense that is justified, not retaliatory aggression.

Society, too, has this right to self-defense; or at least, that is the conclusion drawn in this strand of our tradition. If self-defense is justified at all and if community truly plays a central role in human flourishing, then the community is also justified in defending itself. This line of thought led to arguments in favor of various anti-crime measures: penal systems, policies of deterrence wherein the evildoer is punished, not just resisted, in order to convince others not to act similarly, and, perhaps most controversially, capital punishment.

What is more, many of these same arguments have been raised in considering the case where the evildoer is not an individual but a group — a nation or other societal unit. The question here is, of course, about war. Some members of our tradition have asserted the pacifist position. Others have claimed the legitimacy of self-defense, formulating their argument in what is known as the "just war" principle. They urge that we start from a presumption that every war is wrong, since in every case it causes such terrible evils. But they also judge that in rare, narrow circumstances where, first, the goal is just (being self-defense) and, second, the activities are just (being proportionate to the aggression and protective of innocent bystanders), that exceptional war could be justified.

These pages are not the place to sort all the complex arguments about these matters. Our goal must simply be to achieve clarity on the key ideas: community, essential to human flourishing, needs protection; all human persons, saints and sinners alike, retain their core dignity no matter what their behavior; and responding to these two truths as disciples of Jesus is difficult. The challenge for us is to live our own lives out of these principles and to work with our neighbors to help them become enacted in public life. At the least, we must join the conversation about how they can be actualized in our moment of history.

RESOURCE ISSUES. We have seen (in chapter 37) that all persons have the right to own things. But at the same time, we saw the *social* rationale for this right: that only when ownership is clear can community develop. As the *Catechism of the Catholic Church* put it, "the right to private property...does not do away with the original gift of the earth to the whole of mankind. The universal destination of goods remains primordial, even if the promotion of the common good requires respect for the right to private property" (no. 2403). This same focus makes us realize that all persons also need access to wealth, since the opportunity for appropriate possessions is also a precondition for trusting community. But both personal attitudes and structural patterns can get in the way of this. Several issues have received extensive consideration in the Catholic tradition.

First, there is the abiding evil of discrimination. People are not utterly equal, of course. On the contrary, we are infinitely diverse as

a human family. But the differences that are considered in a particular situation should be those truly pertinent to the task or project
at hand. To take into consideration irrelevant differences is discrimination. No matter what the variable is (race, ethnic group, gender,
sexual orientation, socio-economic group, geographical location, age,
etc.), discrimination is an affront to the dignity of its victim.

Sometimes the discrimination is firmly lodged in individual hearts;
then we have bigotry. More often, perhaps, it is woven into the
structures so that, almost without any intention, it happens that
some people are "more equal than others." The obligation of social justice challenges us to identify and root out this structural
discrimination too.

An obvious locale for problems of discrimination is that of work
and wages. So the Catholic tradition has given this locale special attention, arguing that every human person has the right to a "just wage."
Several points are involved here.

First, people have a right to enter and participate in community. For
this to happen, they need money to live on. The usual way of acquiring
money is work. So human persons have a right to work. Consequently,
social systems should be such that all those willing to work are able
to do so. Second, since work is meant to generate the wherewithal to
join community, a person who works conscientiously at a full-time job
ought to be able to acquire thereby sufficient funds to be able to live
in a modest but dignified fashion. A "just wage," then, is the wage
sufficient to achieve that goal. And third, income above and beyond
the just wage ought to be somehow commensurate with contributions,
granted that there are many different forms of contribution. Income in
no way related to contribution is, after all, nothing but discrimination
in lively operation.

After the issue of discrimination, a second issue concerns ownership.
We have seen that private property exists to provide the clarity and
certainty that can facilitate the building of community. Private property, then, does not exist as a way of keep people apart, but rather
of bringing them together. It follows, then, that, paradoxically, private
property has a social function!

Over the last century the Catholic tradition has found it helpful to
highlight this truth by speaking less of ownership and more of stewardship. "Ownership," it was thought, gave too much the implication
that "what's mine is mine and you have no claims whatsoever upon
it." "Stewardship," on the other hand, suggests that "what's mine is
truly mine to control and use. But the use should be not only for my

benefit but also, ultimately, for *our* benefit. So in the very act of using my possessions, I must keep you in mind, as well."

In our time, faithful Christians struggle mightily to discern the implications of stewardship, trying to take into account the impact of our individual lifestyles upon access to basic necessities of so many others in the human family. We will need to keep exploring these questions in the Christian community.

We will also need to explore the ways in which the principles of stewardship are violated, and sisters and brothers in the human family harmed, not as a result of personal selfishness but rather of destructive structures. For such structures surely exist. Experience teaches that history is always written by the victors. Similarly, social structures are always constructed by the wealthy. It follows, then, that even with the best of will, such structures will tend to favor those who are well off at the expense of those who are poor. The result, if not resisted, is that the rich will get richer and the poor will get poorer.

The Catholic tradition has, however, tried to resist this tendency. And it has done so by calling for "a preferential option for the poor." Many arguments support the call for this option. Not the least is the bias toward the poor and suffering of the biblical stories of the Old and New Testament and the pattern of Jesus' life and teaching. Another argument, implied here, is the paradox that, if we are to love our neighbor well, we need to fight the tendency to overlook the poor by conscientiously looking out for the poor. The absence, then, of a conscious preferential option for the poor is not neutrality; it is a de facto preferential option for the rich! And this no Christian should tolerate.

CITIZENSHIP. The problem in addressing all these sorts of original sin and in defining the claims of social justice is that the culprit is the structure. And most of us feel that we have no way to truly affect the structure. This is a point well taken. At the very least, our circumstances are so diverse and our opportunities so varied that no book like this can begin to specify precisely how any one person should respond. But respond we must.

The Catholic tradition affirmed our obligation to work to change structures when it challenged us to be "citizens," in the fullest sense of the world. Far from being called to leave the world, the Christian is called to enter into the depths of the world, sharing the life of the world, and seeking to make a difference. Well, then, what does citizenship require? A few comments can contribute to an answer to these question.

First and most obviously, citizenship requires conscientious participation in public processes. Taking the time to vote, preparing well for that act, accepting the call to jury duty — actions such as these would be a minimum. Second, citizenship requires whatever further initiatives are possible in a particular situation. The dictum declares: "Think globally but act locally." Much can be done to affect structures by action at the local level. Participation in community organizations can make a real difference, while remaining relatively uncomplicated and undemanding.

And third, citizenship requires bringing our personal convictions to the public conversation. Because of our American reverence for pluralism, some people argue that moral convictions are "private" and don't belong in public discourse, particularly when those convictions are perceived as part of one's membership in a religious group such as the Catholic Church. But as we have repeatedly seen, Catholic moral teachings are not Church rules applying only to Catholic lives. They are honest efforts at wisdom about how to care for human persons everywhere. If I find that wisdom convincing, then my love for my neighbor requires precisely that I speak up, not remaining silent but rather sharing the gift that I have.

Of course, if I am not convinced by this wisdom, then I cannot speak, for it would never help to lie. But it will be with sadness that I will admit that I have no helpful wisdom to offer. And if I am aware of a polarization of views in the wider community, my love for the neighbor will challenge me to speak my views with moderation and respect. But it will not invite me to silence.

It is hard to figure out how to impact the structures that shape so much of our lives. But we must struggle — together — to do so. For that, in the end, is what it means to love your neighbor truly and wisely and well.

Questions for Reflection and Discussion

1. Do you have experiences that show the power of structures to hurt as well as help? What are these experiences and what have they taught you?

2. What do you think of those two strands of the Catholic tradition: "pacifism" and "self-defense / just war?" Which do you find more faithful to the life and message of Jesus? Which do you try to live?

3. Many people seem to think that criminals give up their human dignity and their right to our respect by their behavior. This chapter argues otherwise: that dignity is so intrinsic to human persons that even the person cannot give it away. What do you think about this?

4. What is your experience of discrimination? What do you think we can do about it?

5. What is your reaction to the Catholic vision of "stewardship" and of a "preferential option for the poor?" What is the connection of these ideas to your life?

6. How do you experience the two tasks: "Be a good Christian," and "Be a good citizen?" Are they synonymous? in tension? mutually exclusive? Can you give examples of how you deal with these two challenges?

7. Some people think that the American ethos is so individualistic that this Christian social vision cannot live among us. What do you think? And what might we do to help it live?

Faith in Action

Take the time to learn something about the community in which you live. Are there any community organizations you could support? Is there a meeting, even just one meeting, that you could attend? In some small but real way, could you make a difference?

Prayer

God of all people,
how tightly interconnected you have made us all,
linking us unavoidably to each other — and to you.
Heal your world, redeem your creation.
Let the saving action of Jesus, through us,
conquer the sin that holds us captive. Amen.

40

Being Church for the World

There are varieties of gifts, but the same Spirit; and there are va-
rieties of services, but the same Lord; and there are varieties of
activities, but it is the same God who activates all of them in
everyone. To each is given the manifestation of the Spirit for the
common good.... Now you are the body of Christ and individ-
ually members of it. And God has appointed in the church first
apostles, second prophets, third teachers; then deeds of power,
then gifts of healing, forms of assistance, forms of leadership,
various kinds of tongues. (1 CORINTHIANS 12:4–7, 27–28)

Robby Vincent could have gotten into trouble. If he was lucky it wouldn't have been serious trouble, but you never know. Still, things weren't going well at home, he was bored with school, his best friend had moved away. The burdens of adolescence were overwhelming him, and he could have gotten in trouble.

Luckily, Miguel and Stephanie were there. They weren't experts in teen-helping any more than they were experts in catechetics. After all, their own two children were only toddlers. But they had agreed to take a group in the parish high school religious education program. And the leaders of the program, knowing that religious commitment is based on relationships, had a novel approach: the group of teens remained with the same couple for the four years of high school, the leaders working on new content rather than the teens working on new relationships each year.

So when Robby hit the skids, early in junior year, Miguel and Stephanie were there. They weren't experts. But they gave a place to talk, a place to hang out. They offered a little advice and a lot of support. At a couple of brief, right moments, they prayed with him and for him. And somehow it worked.

That's why it meant so much when Robby invited Miguel and Stephanie to his college graduation. They went!

In the last several chapters, we have tried to discover how we should behave in the world, utilizing the wisdom of the Church. Now, as we

conclude these reflections on Christian moral living, we want to note
that it is *as* Church that we serve the world. For our service of the
world is not merely an activity, it is a vocation.

Throughout the pages of Scripture, stories abound of God's call to a
beloved people. From the call of Abraham to the call of Paul, a pattern
is revealed: "I will be their God, and they shall be my people" (Ezek.
37:27). God takes the initiative, extending an invitation that is both a
promise and a challenge. It is a promise, because linked to God's call
is the assurance of God's help. And it is a challenge, since the call of
God is not really optional; a positive response is the only doorway to
our own ultimate fulfillment.

For some centuries, Catholics were accustomed to speak of "call-
ings" or "vocations" as applied only to those seeking priesthood or
religious life. Recently, deeper reflection on the stories of Scripture has
reminded us that all the followers of Jesus are called, that each of us
has a vocation that comes straight from the hand of God. "Protected
by such great and wonderful means of salvation, all the faithful of
every state and condition are called by the Lord, each in their own
way, to that perfect holiness whereby the Father is perfect" (Vatican II,
Dogmatic Constitution on the Church, no. 11). It is ours, this call that
is promise and challenge, as surely as it is anyone's. Indeed, the Greek
word for "Church," *ekklēsia,* comes from the verb *kaleo,* which means
"to call." Church is, quite literally, the gathering of the called. We are
Church, and being Church is our vocation.

But what is the vocation of the Church? It is to serve and save the
world. Scholars tell us that the Church is the community of those who,
nourished by memory, embrace mission. And what is that mission?
To participate in the saving, healing, forgiving work of Jesus. That is
why the Church is sometimes called the "mystical body of Christ,"
following Paul's usage in 1 Corinthians. It is — really, *we* are — the
living presence of Christ reaching out in service to our brothers and
sisters in the human family. That is why we can say that, in seeking
to live our moral lives, we are acting not only as individuals but *as*
Church. And that is why, to be yet more precise, we can say that being
Church-for-the-world is our vocation.

This insight is one that Catholics spend their whole lives plumb-
ing. Understanding who we are, in the grace of Christ, and learning
to enact this true identity is a life-long project. From the moment
of our Baptism, when this vocation became ours, to the day of our

death, when our mission will be concluded, we never end the project of understanding and enacting this identity. And it is a project that, being community, we pursue not alone but together. Indeed, we could say that the purpose of the coming-together of Church is to ratify and reinforce this identity, allowing us to discover who we are by acting as who we are, together.

But it is not a simple thing for a community such as the Church to come together. Whether the common act is worship or whether it is a social or educational venture, there are human needs that must be met for it to succeed. There is need for leadership, for organization, for facilitation, for hospitality. In a word, there is need for ministry. "Ministry" is simply the word by which we denote the service we Christians provide to one another so that, together, we may be Christ in mission to the world. Ministries do not exist for themselves; they exist that mission may take place. But ministries are important, because only with the benefit of their contributions can that mission be successfully pursued.

One of the most wonderful rediscoveries that God gave the Church through the Second Vatican Council was the realization that all Christians are called to ministry, as diverse as these calls may be. "This very diversity of graces, ministries and works gathers the children of God into one, because 'all are inspired by one and the same Spirit' (1 Cor. 12:11)" (Dogmatic Constitution on the Church, no. 32). The true understanding of Church does not see it as a "thing," an organization or structure or program to which we relate as clients. We are not the recipients of the activity of the Church. Rather, the Church is a gathering of disciples in which we relate as members. Our interactions are mutual, sometimes receiving the care that comes from others, sometimes offering that care in return. Thus, Baptism, the dying and rising by which one is incorporated into the body of Christ, the Church, is at the same time one's initiation into ministry.

The fact of the matter is that this understanding of ministry is not shared by all the members of the Catholic community. In part because it is so newly rediscovered and in part because realizing that I am responsible for an active role is not always welcome news, many Catholics are still in the process of accepting this insight of Vatican II. At the same time, some members of the clergy, a group who in recent centuries have carried the burdens of ministry almost single-handedly but have, for that very reason, sometimes experienced Church leadership as a private possession, are now exhibiting inspiring goodwill and courage as they struggle to embrace and enact this new, but actually more traditional, vision. They are sharing ministry, realizing that ministry is the possession of all.

What shall be my ministry? Each one of us needs to answer this question, indeed, needs to answer it repeatedly through life. In the typical parish there is an astonishing range of ministries: liturgical, social, educational.

Some are relatively formal, even involving official designation by Church leaders. The most obvious examples of this are the ordination of deacons, priests, and bishops, as well as the formal installation of so-called lay ministries. Such formal ministries rightly call for special educational preparation. After all, the people of God deserve quality service; to give them anything less is a scandal of the first order.

Other ministries are less structured. Parents, during their child-rearing years, may choose to make a contribution as catechists in the religious education program. Retired folks may make themselves available to provide support in times of grief. Teenagers may organize and staff a soup kitchen. Gregarious parishioners may utilize their natural gifts for the sake of the community by serving as ministers of hospitality at Sunday Eucharist.

What is important is not the specific focus of the ministry. Even less important are the distinctions among the ministries. Rather, what is most important is the common thread of meaning that runs through them all: they are actions by members of the Church, serving other members of the Church, so that all, together, may serve the world in the Spirit of Jesus.

In chapter 34 we explored the experience of common reflection and mutual support that should characterize Church. It is important to bring back that theme here. For we have been seeing that ministries exist for the sake of the community. That means that "my ministry" is not something for me to elect on my own. Rather, it is something that the community should confirm and empower.

This communal discernment is not usually complex. It can be as simple as an invitation from one's fellow parishioners to undertake a work. Sometimes it is structured a bit more, as in the case where catechists are validated at the beginning of the school year with a special blessing at the conclusion of Sunday Eucharist. And occasionally, it is given beautiful liturgical formality, as when a bishop explicitly asks the congregation for a sign of its approval before proceeding with an ordination.

But no matter the shape of the communal discernment, it is important. For it incarnates the truth of our mutuality: I am authorized to give when you are willing to receive. And we together engage in this reciprocal action for the building up of the whole community, which that community should at some time and in some place affirm. We are not "Lone Rangers," doing our own thing or imposing our view on unwelcome neighbors. We are sisters and brothers, members of a community of disciples, interacting in fluid but intentional ways, out of a common vision and for a common purpose.

In the end, then, our moral lives are really spiritual lives. For one thing, they are expressions of our personal spiritualities. They manifest our faith in an everyday way. They are discovered with prayer, carried forward with sacrifice, given away with trust. For another thing, they are expressions of our personal gifts, of our unique and individual spirits called by God to life in and for the world.

But as St. Paul made clear in the text that began this chapter, our moral lives, our lives of mission and ministry, are spiritual lives for yet another reason: they are revelations of the one Spirit of God. They are the "manifestation of the Spirit for the common good."

Questions for Reflection and Discussion

1. How do you react to this chapter's claim that you have a "vocation"? Some people can even describe when they are called, or in what way. Do you have experiences like this?

2. What is your assessment of the Catholic Church's efforts to care for the world? What are the strong points in that effort? What deserves greater attention?

3. Do you find that most Church members have a sense of the mission of daily life? What could be done to encourage that sense?

4. Think of the activities that fill your everyday life. Can you see these activities as part of your mission? How so? What would make them more effective as mission?

5. Have you seen ministry in action? Name and describe the ministries from which you have benefited.

6. Have you exercised any ministries that were particularly satisfying for you? What dreams do you have for the future?

Faith in Action

What can you do to help? What are your gifts, your talents? Talk about this with those you trust. And try a little discernment with leaders in your local faith community.

Prayer

God of the Gathering, we believe that you have called us,
as you have called each of your beloved through the ages.
Help us to hear the call, to accept the mission,
and to make a gift of ministry.
Let your love for us be reflected
in our acts of love for all we meet. Amen.

Recommended Reading

Beguerie, Philippe, and Claude Duchesneau. *How to Understand the Sacraments*. New York: Crossroad, 1991.

Catechism of the Catholic Church. Washington, D.C.: United States Catholic Conference, Libreria Editrice Vaticana, 1994.

Hoffman, Elizabeth, ed. *The Liturgy Documents*. 3d ed. Chicago: Liturgy Training Publications, 1991.

McBrien, Richard P. *Catholicism*. Rev. ed. San Francisco: HarperSanFrancisco, 1994.

Marthaller, Bernard L., O.F.M. Conv. *The Creed*. Mystic, Conn.: Twenty-Third Publications, 1987.

O'Connell, Timothy E. *Principles for a Catholic Morality*. Rev. ed. San Francisco: HarperSanFrancisco, 1990.

O'Malley, William J., S.J. *Why Be Catholic?* New York: Crossroad, 1994.

Contributors

The Writers

WILLIAM J. O'MALLEY, S.J., has been a teacher for thirty-four years. He currently teaches theology and English at Fordham Preparatory Seminary in the Bronx, New York. He has published twenty-three books and nearly a hundred articles, five of them Catholic Press Award winners. His books include *Why Be Catholic?; Clever Foxes and Lucky Klutzes; Building Your Own Conscience (Batteries Not Included);* and *Yielding: Prayers for those in Need of Hope.*

MITCH AND KATHY FINLEY are widely recognized authorities on family life and the Church. Married since 1974, they are the parents of three sons. A popular speaker and teacher, Kathy is also an adjunct instructor in the Religious Studies Department of Gonzaga University, Spokane, Washington. She received a B.A. in Theology from Gonzaga University, an M.A. in Religious Education from Fordham University, and an M.A. in Counseling Psychology from Gonzaga University. Mitch is an award-winning writer and the author of several books, including *Everybody Has a Guardian Angel . . . and Other Lasting Lessons I Learned in Catholic Schools; Heavenly Helpers: St. Anthony and St. Jude;* and *The Gospel Truth: Living for Real in an Unreal World* (all published by Crossroad). Mitch received a B.A. in Religious Studies from Santa Clara University and an M.A. in Theology from Marquette University. Together Mitch and Kathy co-authored an award-winning book, *Christian Families in the Real World* (to be published soon in a revised edition titled *Building Christian Families*).

KATHLEEN HUGHES, R.S.C.J., a Religious of the Sacred Heart, holds a doctorate in Liturgical Studies from the University of Notre Dame. She is currently academic dean and professor of liturgy at the Catholic Theological Union at Chicago. She is past president of the North American Academy of Liturgy and serves on the advisory committees of the U.S. Bishops' Committee on the Liturgy and the International Commission on English in the Liturgy (ICEL). Among her publications are *Silent Voices, Sacred Lives: Women's Readings for the Liturgical Year* (a collaborative work) and *How Firm a Foundation: Voices of the Early Liturgical Movement.*

BARBARA E. QUINN, R.S.C.J., is a member of the Religious of the Sacred Heart. She is currently serving as a pastoral associate at St. Ig-

247

natius Parish in Chicago. She holds a master of divinity degree from Weston School of Theology in Cambridge, Massachusetts, and is presently a candidate in the Doctor of Ministry program at Catholic Theological Union in Chicago. Barbara has done extensive work with adults in the United States and abroad in theological education, formation, spirituality, retreats, and spiritual direction. She served as the founder and director of a program for leadership development for the laity in two different locations.

TIMOTHY E. O'CONNELL, PH.D., is professor of Christian ethics in the Institute of Pastoral Studies at Loyola University of Chicago, where he served as director from 1982 till 1994. He is the author of numerous articles and six books, including *Vatican II and Its Documents: An American Reappraisal* (editor). The revised edition of his *Principles for a Catholic Morality* was published in 1990.

The Editors

RAYMOND A. LUCKER, bishop of New Ulm, Minnesota, has been a pioneer in religious education, catechesis, and ministry. A theologian and prime mover in the nationwide development of the Confraternity of Christian Doctrine, he is the author of four books, including *My Experience: Reflection on Pastoring.*

PATRICK J. BRENNAN is pastor of Holy Family Parish Community, Inverness, Illinois. He is also director of the National Center for Evangelization and Parish Renewal. He teaches on the faculties of Loyola Institute of Pastoral Studies, the Catholic Theological Union, Mundelein Seminary, and Regis University, Denver. He is completing a doctorate in clinical psychology and is a practicing psychotherapist. He is the author of *Re-Imagining the Parish; Re-Imagining Evangelization;* and *Parishes That Excel,* all published by Crossroad.

MICHAEL LEACH is the publisher and executive vice president of the Crossroad Publishing Company. He has edited more than five hundred books, many of them Catholic Press Award winners, and authored three books of his own. He is a past president of both the Catholic Book Publishers Association and the ecumenical Religion Publishers Group.

Index